A SECOND LIFE

About the Author:

Christian Schoyen is a Life Architect and the founder of the belief system, *A Second Life*. For the last twelve years he has been the CEO of a successful international headhunting company that he founded, serving global Fortune 500 companies such as Coca Cola, Microsoft, and Johnson & Johnson.

Christian has committed his life to helping others grow and evolve to achieve their fullest potential. With his expertise in human behavior, he has been coaching thousands of people on how to improve their lives and careers—essentially to build better lives from the ground up. For more than two decades he has worked across the United States and Europe and has studied the patterns of people who have been successful in maximizing their opportunities as well as finding a balance between materiality and spirituality. With his vast knowledge in human development, he travels as a speaker throughout the United States to build the belief system, *A Second Life*.

Before launching his headhunting company in 1997, Christian worked for two world leading headhunting organizations: A.T. Kearney and Ward Howell International in Los Angeles and Chicago. Prior to entering the field of recruitment he founded a newspaper covering the job market for people seeking employment. He is the author of *Secrets of the Executive Search Experts*—the U.S. best-selling book for companies on how to recruit—as well as self-help books on "how to get the job." Christian also makes films about how belief systems affect peoples' lives.

Christian graduated with a business degree from Pacific Lutheran University, Tacoma, Washington. He conducted his studies in multi-cultural belief systems at California State University, Northridge, California, and is certified in motivational self-programming. Christian works out of Los Angeles and New York.

About the Co-author:

Christin Tellefsen is a headhunter and a life coach. She is the Managing Director of Executive Search Research–Scandinavia and a senior partner of the firm. She has more than fourteen years of experience conducting senior level, global headhunting assignments.

Prior to building up the company Executive Search Research–Scandinavia from 1997 and co-founding Executive Search Research USA in 2001 she had previously worked for the world's largest retained executive search firm: Korn Ferry International. Christin conducted her undergraduate studies in psychology at California Lutheran University and is the co-author of several books about recruitment. Christin also makes films about how belief systems affect peoples' lives. A leading Scandinavian business magazine has ranked Christin as one of the top five female headhunters.

In addition to being an expert on human behavior through recruitment and career coaching, Christin is also a level III Reconnection healer.

A SECOND LIFE

God is giving you a second chance

by CHRISTIAN SCHOYEN with CHRISTIN TELLEFSEN

If your life is messed up, it's not your fault

Gaia

Los Angeles New York London

A Second Life
God is giving you a second chance

Published by Gaia
www.asecondlife.com

ISBN: 978-0-578-02610-7

Library of Congress Cataloging-in-Publication Data

First Edition June 2009

Printed in the United States of America

The only intent of the authors is to offer information to help you improve your life. The choices you make are entirely up to you. The authors and the publisher assume no responsibility for the results of your actions.

Editor: Linda Laucella
Cover Designer: Ellen Shotton
Graphic Designer: Anne Andresen

Photo credits:
Serene lake view: Arnold Melleby
Joyful child with unlimited possibilities: Chang/iStock Photo
Disillusioned/defeated man: Bob Thomas/Stone/Getty Images
Triumphant adult/free at last: Viorika/iStock Photo
Cyborg: Papantoniou/iStock Photo
Christian, 18 years: Arnold Melleby
Polar meltdown: Arne Naevra/Scanpix/Norway
Tree of Life/dying: Hafemann/iStock Photos
Tree of Life/thriving: DNY59/iStock Photos

THE PROBLEM

If your life is messed up, it's not your fault

You have been brainwashed by society to fail. But you can still be saved. We can help you change everything and make your life good again.

You have been deceived and lied to. God gave you life to be cherished and enjoyed to the fullest. Instead of telling you the truth, society tricked you into making wrong decisions and turned you into a victim. Now your self-worth is low, your outlook is bleak, and you feel helpless.

You have been denied your free will. You are doing the best you can, but nothing seems to work out right. That's because your actions are based on negative brainwashing and belief systems that have been forced on you. You believe your thoughts, decisions, and actions are your own, but they are not. Your free will has been taken away from you.

You have been victimized, used, and manipulated. You have been brainwashed to be a robot that only pleases others, instead of being the true you. You have been manipulated to feel guilty and fearful when your thoughts and actions are not aligned with society's rules. Years of your life—perhaps your entire life—have been stolen from you while you played the dis-empowered puppet for someone else's gratification. You are not who you think you are.

You have been tricked into living a meaningless life. You have been indoctrinated to be self-centered, to believe your value as a human being is measured by what kind of job you have, what kind of house you live in or car you drive, how you dress, and who you marry. You are tangled up in financial slavery, tricked into not knowing what truly matters, lured onto the road to nowhere. Nobody told you this mentality based on external values would leave you with no worthwhile accomplishments when your time runs out, that your life will be wasted.

You have been brainwashed to believe you are powerless and alone. Your personal power is enormous, but you have become a slave to wrong information and fears. You are only a shadow of what you're capable of being. You know the truth: that people in authority care more about themselves than people like you. Your employer cares about you only as long as you create a profit. Your neighbors are too busy struggling to even acknowledge your problems. If you can't pay the rent, mortgage, or car payment, or your savings run out, you will be cornered. Medical care is so expensive that an illness in your family might be game over. You worry that before long there will be no money to buy food, pay your utility bills, or buy gas for your car to drive to work—if you still have a job . . . and a car. You have little hope that anyone will give you a helping hand. As you keep spiraling down, your self-esteem also goes down, further reducing your chances of getting control. You know you cannot count on anyone except yourself—**you are all alone.** As long as you remain a victim of society's brainwashing **you might not survive.**

But did you know the reason you feel miserable, like a helpless failure, is not your fault? God did not intend for you to come here and crawl on your knees your entire life. Your mental enslavement has caused you to make wrong decisions, feel guilty, and fearful. Nobody gave you the information you needed or warned you about being brainwashed with wrong belief systems. **You did not stand a chance.**

It is our intention and goal to provide the solution to your problems—a system you can follow to save yourself and regain control of your life. While doing so you will also reinforce the basic principles upon which this country was founded, as stated in the Constitution—that all men are created equal, with the right to life, liberty, and the pursuit of happiness—and help bring America back to the way it's meant to be: the greatest nation on earth.

By integrating the principles of *A Second Life* you will be able to break the chains of mental slavery that have held you back and crippled you. You will be prepared to face life's battles knowing surrender is never an option. By regaining control of your life, you will live an existence with inner peace and happiness; you will master all the five key areas of life; you will be One with yourself, living your life's purpose. You will be free at last. You will be empowered to use your unique God-given gifts and talents to be all that you can be, knowing how to **play the game of life and win—which is to achieve and live in Oneness!**

THE SOLUTION

Rebuilding Your Life Step by Step

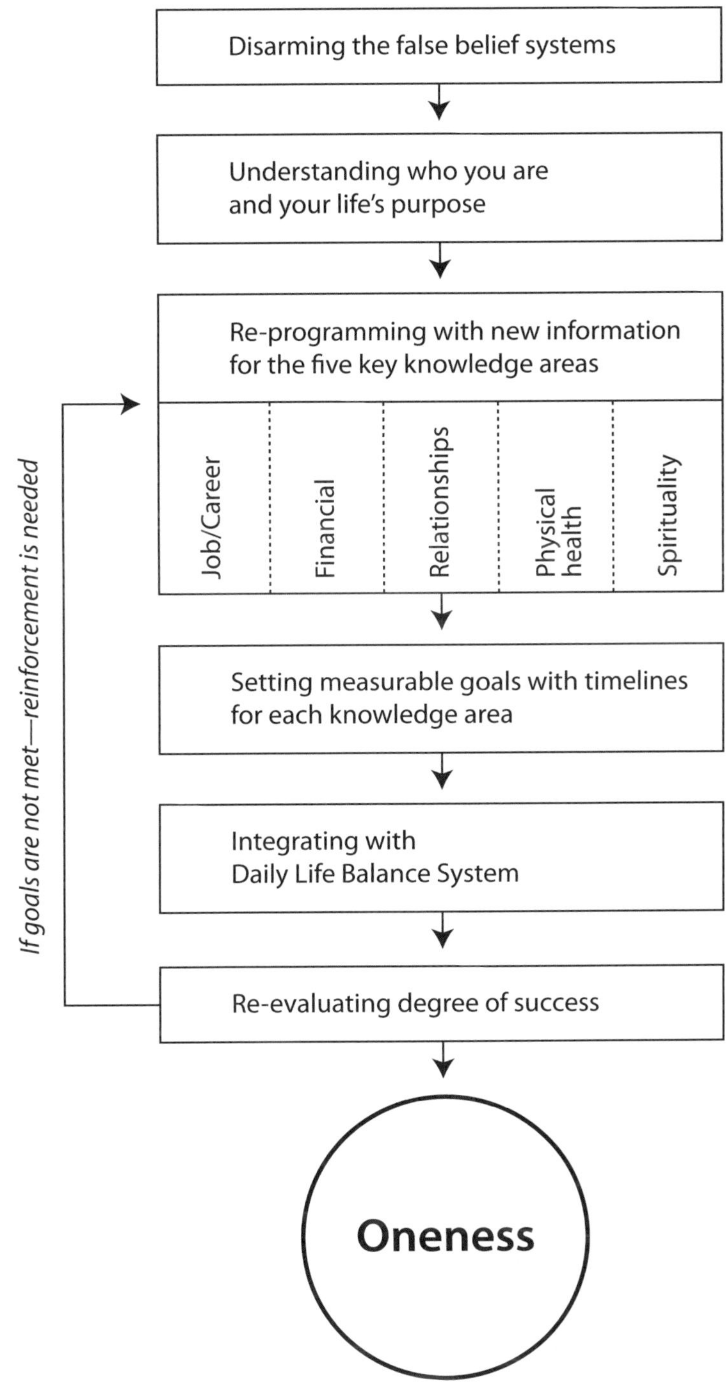

Your life reflects your state of mind.

Christian Schoyen

Table of Contents

THE FIVE KEY KNOWLEDGE AREAS OF LIFE TO BE MASTERED

Preface

I was first introduced to the belief system of *A Second Life* more than twelve years ago when I joined a recruitment company founded by Christian Schoyen. Christian had studied the life patterns of people throughout history who mastered the principles of the Vitruvian Man—living in Oneness by achieving the necessary balance between spirituality and materiality. As time evolved I became Christian's business partner in the recruitment company, where I was able to meet with thousands of people and assess the patterns of how they conducted their lives. Simultaneously, together with Christian, over the years I worked to improve and perfect the principles of A Second Life's belief system to make it complete.

Through integration of the belief system in my own life I have personally experienced a total transformation and have achieved the balance and the new life that enables me to live in Oneness. My spiritual awakening made me realize that everything I was ever told or taught by society was conditioning/brainwashing that had caused me to detach from the true me. After this awakening I re-programmed myself to be connected again with my true self and by mastering the five key knowledge areas have experienced both inner peace and a happy, purpose-driven life with anything being possible. By mastering the principles of *A Second Life* I have experienced being all that I can be while living as my true self.

It is a privilege to share with you through this book the road to a new, better existence—a life of unlimited potential that you too can achieve.

Christin Tellefsen
Co-author

Introduction

Narrated by Christian Schoyen

There once was a young boy who at the age of eight experienced a day that would change his life forever. It was a Sunday in the last part of May. He was awakened at eight o'clock in the morning by the loud noise of his uncle's lawnmower cutting the grass next door. A minute later, still lying in bed, he heard his mother knocking on the door and saying, "Get up now, otherwise you're going to sleep away your life. Remember, laziness is the root of all evil." Actually, the boy didn't mind getting out of bed because he planned to wear his American Indian costume that day. To him there was nothing more exciting than playing like he was a real Indian in the "wild west" stories he had read, running around wearing his feather headdress, carrying his bow and arrow, and shooting everything that moved.

Dressed in his Indian outfit, the boy sprinted the couple hundred yards over to his grandfather's house. Peeking inside, he saw his grandfather sitting at the kitchen table and playfully pointed his bow and arrow at him. "Get your hands up, or you're dead!" the boy said as he slowly moved toward his grandfather. But when close enough, his grandfather reached out, grabbed the boy, and tickled him. The boy giggled as he tried to wiggle away, but his grandfather got him in a bear hug. When the boy calmed down his grandfather lifted him up, placed him on his knee, and said with all seriousness that he had something very important to tell him about squirrels.

"Squirrels?!" the boy repeated.

"They're little devils that live in the trees," his grandfather said. "You must be very careful because they'll try to kill you if you look into their eyes, or even if you just get too close to them." The grandfather went on to explain that the squirrels kill their victims by going for their throats. "With their sharp teeth they bite into the jugular vein and then suck out so much blood that you end up dead."

The boy's eyes were wide with astonishment and fear.

"So watch out for the killer squirrels," the grandfather said seriously, but added with a smile, "And don't ever try to outrun those little devils because they'll always be faster than you."

A short time later the boy was still wearing his Indian outfit when his family was preparing to get in the car and drive to church. His mother looked at him and told him he needed to change into different clothing right away. "I don't want to be embarrassed by having my son look 'a little off' by not dressing like everybody else."

During the church service the minister preached about all the ways people were not living according to the word of God. In a sermon that seemed to go on forever he talked about all the sins people were committing that were ruining their chances of going to heaven—including giving the opinion that all gay people were going to burn in hell because of the lifestyle they were living.

That night the boy was too scared to sleep. He kept thinking about all the people he knew who were going to hell. First, of course, he was sure he would be one of them because he had taken apples from his grandfather's trees without asking permission. He also thought about Ken, the local hairdresser, who people in the village said was "the only gay person in town." And then there was his grandfather, who didn't go to church at all, and his uncle, who always cut his grass on Sunday, even though it was supposed to be God's day, and he never went to church either. The boy tried to close his eyes and sleep, but he kept seeing the little killer squirrels waiting for him in hell. I was that eight-year-old boy.

As the years went by I did my best to always steer clear of the killer squirrels. Then one day, when I was twenty-two years old, a friend and I were walking across campus to the library at the University of Oregon. Suddenly I spotted a large group of squirrels looking at me from a short distance away. My mouth got dry, my heart started beating very fast, and I walked as quickly as I could in the opposite direction. My friend, who struggled to keep up with me, said, "The library is over there. What's wrong?! Why do you look so scared?"

"We should not risk our lives going near the killer squirrels," I said.

Thinking I was joking, my friend could not stop laughing. Only then did I realize that my belief in killer squirrels was based on a practical joke made on me by my grandfather fourteen years earlier. Looking back, I remembered that my grandfather was always a jokester who meant no harm, and he probably forgot that he told me the squirrel story, but it had become my manifested reality.

Were there other "truths" I had been told but never questioned? Was everything I was told just a bunch of lies and indoctrinations that ended up becoming my truth and reality? Suddenly I questioned everything about my life: How I felt inside, what I was thinking, how I was acting, and where I was heading. Were they all a result of the things I had been told all of my life, which had become my belief systems—as opposed to what I truly felt and desired inside? I was shocked to realize that the common denominator in these belief systems running my life was that I was living my life to please other people and to seek their approval—not to satisfy myself and be all that I could be. Not only that, but many of my belief systems were based on fear, and all of them were negative.

Discussing these ideas with other people, I found out that I was no different than anybody else. To some extent everyone lives a life of lies, a life where they are not who they think they are because they're unknowingly programmed to have certain beliefs and then they live accordingly. Everyone suffers to some degree from mental slavery.

Like most people, I was living in a self-imposed prison, in a state of mental slavery—the worst kind there is—wasting my life, being controlled by unnecessary fears. The most frightening part was that I didn't even know the brainwashing had been going on throughout my entire life. I only knew that life was a struggle and I never felt completely fulfilled, no matter what I did. Just like me, most people don't even realize they are being brainwashed and controlled by their fears. We believe we have free will, but we don't.

When I thought about it a while, I realized that an element of my mental slavery was doing things to feed my ego—which was merely insecurity craving attention. I was not living each day in alignment with my true self, utilizing every possible gift I had been given by God in a fearless, purpose-driven life. So I wondered: What if I could free myself from the mental slavery of pleasing other people, and in the process kill my fears and ego? Could I live a life aligned with my passions and my heart? Would I then be free to be the person I really am inside?

Although at the time I wished someone could give me all the answers so my life would be exactly what I wanted, in retrospective I'm glad they didn't because then I wouldn't have had the chance to make mistakes in life from which I could learn and grow.

I knew I wanted to erase the negative brainwashing that had disempowered me, and I wanted my life to be all that it could be. But how could I get to that place? To disarm the negative belief systems, I first had to go head-to-head with fear. An important step was to fully understand what had limited me, which is described in the famous quote: When you're eighteen, you worry about what everybody is thinking of you; when you're forty; you don't give a darn what anybody thinks of you; when you're sixty, you realize nobody's been thinking about you at all.

That first wakeup call when I was twenty-two years old also led to a deeper insight. I realized that the "killer squirrels" story was about something much greater than our little furry friends in the trees. Instead of being told about the killer squirrels, what if I had been told that there is no God and afterlife, that people whose skin is a different color than mine are bad, that people who believe in a God with a different name than my God are worshippers of evil? What would my fears be then? Or what if an organized religion had "indoctrinated" me to live a life tainted by guilt, fear, and anxiety?

The way we feel about ourselves is so powerfully formed by what we're told and the beliefs of our society that it's time we rethink the messages we have received, are acting upon, and are conveying to others every day. When someone is told they are a loser or given the impression they are not loved by their parents or other important people in their life while growing up, how do they know that's not true? When mass media continually imposes stereotypes of how one should look, think, and act in order to fit in and be loved and accepted, why are we surprised when everyone tries to live up to those standards, no matter how misguided or superficial they are?

This is not just about everybody else. It's about you. It's personal. What if other people were programmed to have a negative view and fearful attitude about the career or profession that is in your heart, your religious beliefs, or your sexual orientation? What if you were trained to believe that displaying more "bling" in your cars, home, or clothes was an indication that you were more successful, and even happier? What would you value then? And would you be afraid the people you are trying to impress would learn the truth: that the image you convey does not match the way you feel inside?

If your life is out of control and you are struggling, it's because you have been victimized throughout life by destructive programming that has dis-empowered you, kept you from living your true desires as your true self, and separated you from God. You have become crippled and can never be free from the mental slavery until you accept the fact that you have lived your life based on lies, lies people have told you all of your life and trained you to believe.

During my awakening process I thought about how so many people are trained by the fear/reward concept often used on dogs, with their only reality being their own backyards where they are punished for not doing what they're told and rewarded for being obedient. Too many people have lost their ability to think for themselves. Their "backyards"—the geographical world in which they live or the potential within their heart—may not be as limiting as a green patch of grass behind a house that is a dog's reality, but the brainwashing of many human beings has the same affect by programming them to live a limiting existence based on fear and compliance. Fear-based belief systems can cripple and completely destroy someone's entire life—unless they break free. Nobody should live a life in unhappiness and out of control because of the negative and destructive belief systems and brainwashing that hold him or her prisoner. God gave each of us our life to be cherished, respected, and for each of us to sparkle as the true diamonds we all are inside.

Every person on this earth deserves love and happiness. We all carry the key inside to unlock the door, escape our mental prisons, and enter a purposeful life filled with love, inner peace, and happiness.

HOLISTIC AND INTEGRATED LIFE SUPPORT SYSTEM

This life manual will help you find the key to being in command of your own life by disarming the negative belief systems that have controlled you through fear. You will learn that there is no such thing as being in a situation that is too difficult to overcome or being at an age when it's too late. The timeline for your awakening and emergence into a new life is not about getting to a destination in weeks or months from now. Instead, it will happen as soon as you commit. Your destination in life is not around the corner when you have achieved a specific goal, as the ego tricks you to believe, but rather the journey itself. No one can tell you what journey will bring you love and happiness. Only you can discover that truth within yourself. This life manual provides a roadmap for you to follow in order to re-discover your true self. It will serve as your compass in life and the lighthouse that illuminates your life journey as you are awakened to evolve from merely going through life in survival mode to joyfully living your true purpose in life.

If you are so trapped mentally by negative energy that you feel out of control, lost, hopeless, or simply unmotivated and unsatisfied, you will find your own answers by embracing the information in this life manual with every cell of your body. Your limiting programming and brainwashing that has mentally enslaved you will be deleted, you will reconnect with your true self within, and become indestructibly "One" with yourself and God.

A Second Life is a belief system created for all of you living in the greatest nation in the world, the United States of America—which serves as a role model for the rest of the world. This belief system restores and reinstates the principles upon which the United States of America was founded: that every man and woman is created equal and has an unalienable right to life, liberty and the pursuit of happiness. No longer will you be held down or held back, living a life of limited potential because you were indoctrinated and brainwashed by society to fail. You will learn how to reconnect with your true self, your passions, and your purpose. Your life will evolve to such a high level that anything is possible and can be achieved with courage and action.

For most people, life is like a roller coaster ride on rusty unstable rails. It sometimes takes you nowhere, and at other times it takes you to the very top or to rock bottom. Although ups and downs are just part of life, not being able to control your journey causes uncertainty, fear, and a feeling of helplessness inside. One of the main purposes of this life manual is to teach you how to gain control of your life by becoming a warrior who not only welcomes your daily battles but also knows that you will rise to victory every time you stand face-to-face with life's challenges.

Your life is a game masterminded by God, presenting you with many challenges that he wants to you win. The battles you fight serve a purpose: for you to evolve and become who you truly are, instead of living life in denial, pleasing everyone but yourself. Victory can be achieved only when you know how the game of life works. Winning at the game of life is when you become your true self. *A Second Life* will teach you how to win.

The first thing you must know is that you have been manipulated and brainwashed throughout your life with negative and destructive belief systems. Much of what you think and believe is a result of dark energies controlling you, stopping you from fully enjoying life. The wrong information you were indoctrinated to believe has led you to make wrong decisions in the key areas of life. Without knowing it or consenting to it, you have been programmed to live your entire life playing a role to please others. In reality you are not living your own life. It has been stolen from you. Your every thought and action is being controlled by false belief systems. Although most people believe they are living as free individuals and making their own choices, in actuality the opposite is true. They are living a false reality that has been created by what they have been told and trained to accept. There is no prison worse than this mental slavery.

To better explain the concepts and ideas of *A Second Life's* belief system, the metaphor is used of the human race being a modern advanced robot with the hard drive (mind) connected to Soul, which connects to the Server (God). Your original programming, which is the true you, was overwritten throughout your life by society's indoctrination, turning you into a robot—a predictable machine—controlled by the system. As a result you have created and are living a distorted reality that limits your true potential. But a new, better world is waiting to be discovered.

Once you delete society's programming, re-program yourself, and activate your true self, there will be no turning back. Every day can play out in your favor when you free yourself from the mental slavery of your brainwashing. By dis-empowering the negative programming running your life and activating God within you will become the creator of your own life, thus creating your own destiny and be free at last. By living an existence in Oneness you will never again be searching for what's missing inside. Instead, you get to be who you truly are. The person you were in your old life will no longer exist; you will be a better, happier, more fulfilled YOU. You will feel complete, guided toward living a fulfilling, joyful, and purpose-driven rest of your life here on earth—as well as making America an even greater place through your contribution, creating heaven on earth.

This life manual applies the best of proven life methods, merging those originating in ancient times and throughout human history with the findings from extensive human behavior studies of thousands of successful people in current time. All the best knowledge has been integrated into this simplified holistic multi-level support and belief system. As you follow this guide to enter your new life existence, which is the life God intended you to live, you will be presented with real life case studies to show you how the belief system of *A Second Life* will impact you. Although it's not an easy task to learn how to live well, once mastered, the rewards are limitless. Life is a journey during which we are meant to learn, grow, and enjoy.

There are many thoughts and ideas about how to live the true way of life, but few that provide a holistic support system for your daily challenges while also fulfilling your spiritual needs. Most people live their entire lives as trial by error, with the unfortunate result being that many endure a life not fully lived. But by simplifying life and breaking it down as a defined and understandable process, we have the best possible opportunity to live a harmonious life with our purpose fulfilled while we are here on earth. The ultimate goal is to unlock the strength inside so that we can live to the fullest in every capacity, as God intended us to do. Then, one day when looking back, we will have no regrets, but only gratitude in our hearts, knowing that we utilized all the gifts and resources we were given, in the right way.

By integrating the principles and knowledge of *A Second Life* with its re-programming and activation, you will greatly improve your own existence, fulfill your life purpose according to your original DNA blueprint, and become a role model to others.

FIVE KEY AREAS OF LIFE

As people we are complex. Our life circumstances change from year to year, sometimes even on a monthly, daily, or hourly basis. But we all feel incomplete and out of balance if all five key areas in our lives are not somehow covered or fully developed. In *A Second Life* there is a process to ensure that the five interchangeable key areas of your life are covered and developed in the best possible ways and in the right order.

Each person functions differently. Someone may be financially well off, but lack spirituality. Another person may be spiritually fulfilled, but have no career or job success. Others sacrifice relationships with loved ones and themselves in order to acquire money. Many ignore the basic requirements to maintain good physical and emotional health. Everyone feels a void when a key area of life is not sufficiently developed. In order to achieve inner peace, happiness, and become one with God and your true self, you must fulfill every aspect of your life, and in the proper order of importance.

To enter a new existence and *A Second Life,* a holistic life support system needs to be mastered to maximize the five key areas of life:

- Job/Career
- Financial
- Physical Health/Wellness
- Relationships (with yourself and others)
- Spirituality

When all five key areas of life are mastered you will achieve the balance that is required to feel truly fulfilled.

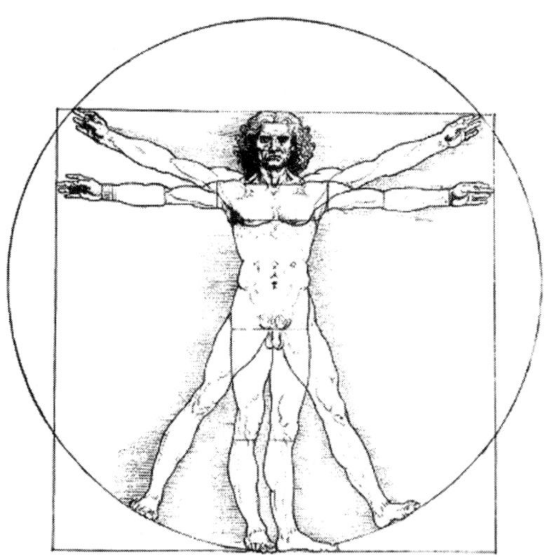

Vitruvian Man

The life balance principles in *A Second Life* are greatly influenced by Maslow's Hierarchy of Needs, God's Hierarchy of Needs, and Leonardi da Vinci's Vitruvian Man. The image of Leonardo da Vinci's Vitruvian Man, which has fascinated me all my life, is a universal symbol for love, relationships, success, health, and indivisible wholeness balanced with spirituality—ideas that have existed and been honored throughout time as the basis for excellence in human existence. Maslow's Hierarchy of Needs is a well-respected, decades-old psychological theory that defines the needs that motivate humans. Often portrayed as a pyramid, the most basic needs for survival are at the bottom. Next level up are the needs for feeling safe, then the needs for feeling loved/belonging, next level up is self confidence and esteem, and finally at the top are the needs to be met in order to feel complete and fulfilled.

The backbone of *A Second Life*, as well as the main purpose of your life, is to achieve Oneness. But in the earth school you first need to learn to survive before you can learn to evolve. Once you have mastered the foundation of life, which is survival, you will be able to graduate to the next level, which is personal growth, spirituality and living a higher purpose. Then your life will be based on God's Hierarchy of Needs, which is when you have evolved to the next evolutionary stage that separates human beings from wild animals.

The only reason many people spend almost their entire existence from cradle to death in their current life on just getting by, surviving, and not evolving to the next level is entirely because society's brainwashing has crippled them. By learning and integrating the knowledge and system of *A Second Life* you will finally be able to gain control of your life and current situation and be prepared for future challenges. This multi-dimensional life support system operates on several levels, enabling you to learn how to control your feelings and thoughts by eliminating fears of the unknown and integrating happiness.

Through *A Second Life's* way of thinking and its Seven Commandments, your life's purpose will be revealed and your life will be greatly simplified as you learn to live according to the higher purpose you came here to enjoy in an existence with inner peace, happiness, and unconditional love as an evolved human being who is here to make a difference.

One of the most important keys is to accept who we truly are and not who others tell us to be. We are not here to live a life to please others. We are here to serve God, who is within each one of us. He wants us to be happy and live without fear and limitations. By being God's divine unique creations we are destined to be whatever we desire in this lifetime. Without the fear-driven roles we have been trained to play in order to please others we are free to live a life aligned with our heart and passions. When we are activated to Oneness there are no more voids to fill. There is only limitless unconditional love for all of God's creations—ourselves, humankind, as well as the animal kingdom and our planet. There is no judgment toward ourselves or others. We know in our hearts that our purpose is to contribute to making the world a better place. Ego gratification will not longer exist as a motivation to do anything; our actions are driven by passion and love. We see God in everything, including ourselves. We forgive everyone who caused us pain, knowing they were also running on negative programming. We know that the past and future do not exist, that all we have is NOW—which is taking place right this moment. We no longer have anything to prove to anyone else. We go to sleep each night smiling with the assurance that if this is our last day on earth we have finally returned home, as Oneness is all there is.

Living life with pure intentions, driven by unconditional love, created from a reality of who we really are will feel like a familiar "truth" we once experienced, but then lost touch with and have been seeking all our lives. Once awakened, you will feel as if you have been asleep during your entire life. Once you experience your awakening to enlightenment, you will know that all of your life you have been living in a world where lies became the truth, but you can finally see the lies as what they truly are because you are connected with the truth within yourself. In your awakening, others no longer have the power to control you or keep you down or make your life a struggle. In Oneness you are free to be one with your true self, God, and the Universe. God has always been patiently waiting for you to return home again so that you can live the life you were destined to live.

The teachings from those who were successful in the past and walked the earth before us, as well as those currently living that have mastered the balance between spirituality and materiality, offer us a unique opportunity to learn from their example. They show us how to live in the best possible way, with love, integrity, purpose, and inner peace and happiness. It's far easier to learn from each other than risk spending a lifetime of trial and error on our own.

All that's required for you to enter and enjoy *A Second Life* is an open mind and the dedication to undertake the work presented in this guide. Your life will be transformed and you will be one step closer to "Heaven on Earth," which is something each one of us is also able to create for ourselves by committing to living in Oneness.

MY BACKGROUND FOR TEACHING YOU THE PRINCIPLES OF *A SECOND LIFE*

The principles of *A Second Life* were discovered through a study I conducted over two decades of the patterns of thousands of peoples who have successfully maximized their opportunities in life while achieving a balance between materialism and spirituality. The findings of my study, which included people presently living as well as those who lived thousands of years ago, showed a clear road and path to a life beyond most people's "created" realities to a new, better world. The knowledge I acquired dramatically transformed my life to a life in Oneness through my commitment to *A Second Life*, as it has the lives of the vast number of people I have mentored and counseled during the last fourteen years. During my journey toward gaining control of life, I discovered through my own re-programming and activation a world far beyond the reality created by the false belief systems that previously controlled my thoughts and actions.

Once I began to live as One with my true self, I could see many lessons that I still needed to learn:

- Detaching helped me view a situation from a different perspective.
- I was conditioned by others to believe what was important in life.
- Many of my values were not my own ideas, but merely beliefs imposed upon me.

My newfound freedom opened a door to a life without fears, filled with unlimited happiness in Oneness with my true self and God, where the only truth was that within myself. It was as if I woke up from a deep sleep.

Through my own awakening I discovered that my life purpose is to share with as many people as possible the knowledge I gained during my experiences. After all, why shouldn't everyone know that they have the choice to re-program and activate themselves in order to live a new and better reality, where they can claim control of their own lives and live the happiness and fulfillment they all deserve? I know without a doubt that once awakened anyone can become the creator of their own life and finally be free to live their life as God intended.

Like everyone else, I have experienced both hardships and victories in this lifetime—which includes everything from being homeless and sleeping on other people's couches to becoming a self-made multi-millionaire by building a business from the ground up with no starting capital. Currently I maintain this successful corporate international headhunting company I founded that serves global Fortune 500 companies such as Microsoft, Coca Cola, and Johnson & Johnson. In my own awakening, I realized that the things I once considered to be of great importance—such as acquiring several homes in the world's major cities, buying the most high-end cars, and living a tri-coastal life—was only gratification to the ego if I looked at life as something more than a game.

Life must be lived as play.
Plato

By living as One with God I believe everyone can achieve great materialistic success, but that it should never be viewed as anything more than an adventure or challenge for yourself, to see what you are capable of, as everything that you obtain in this lifetime will be taken away from you on your final day. In my awakening I came to realize that everything that I have accumulated through my hard work was actually on loan from God for as long as I was around. By integrating of *A Second Life's* principles into my life, I learned to find the balance between spirituality and materiality and achieve inner peace.

Based on my extensive knowledge of human behavior from recruiting more than three thousand people for jobs and coaching thousands more in career development and life planning, I was able to write the U.S. best-selling book *The Secrets of the Executive Search Experts*—which has been declared "the bible" on recruitment for corporations and headhunting companies. I have also authored several self-help books on "how to get the job" and share my knowledge during speaking engagements.

During the first part of my life—before I awakened to a life in Oneness—external gratification, as well as showing others how successful I could be, drove me to push so hard. As I awakened and become one with God, my drive become even stronger, but my reasoning and motivation for excelling, as well my values, changed. I also realized that my fears and previous need to prove myself vanished. Even though I still enjoyed pushing boundaries by setting and reaching goals that aligned with my heart, it become more of a personal challenge than comparing myself with others. I learned that true happiness was found within. My biggest accomplishments became not what I was able to acquire financially, but how I used my God-given gifts based on my expertise in human behavior and teachings of *A Second Life* to help people change their own lives.

My greatest reward in life has been the opportunity to serve God, not what my ego desires, by sharing my knowledge and findings of *A Second Life* while teaching people to become empowered to live truly meaningful and fulfilling lives. It is an honor to see people learn how to re-program and activate the new existence that is their birthright—where they are One with God and become creators of their own lives by freeing themselves of the negative programming that has kept them mental prisoners. My mission is to change the world by awakening as many people as possible from their dreamlike "flat-liner" lives, as I once awakened myself from mine.

A Second Life

A Belief System for Human Survival and Growth

A Second Life's Belief System

The belief of *A Second Life* is that there is only one God/Creator/Source (which will be referred simply as God). Human existence evolves in three stages from birth to eternal life. There are three basic beliefs about life as it should be, and Seven Commandments, which are *A Second Life's* operating system. These universal truths apply to everyday life for all people living in the twenty-first century who want to improve their lives while making America an even better place.

EVOLUTION OF HUMAN EXISTENCE FROM BIRTH TO ETERNAL LIFE

The evolution of life existence is defined in three stages: a First Life, a Second Life, and a Third Life. Most people remain in their First Life during their entire existence. But by following this life manual you will evolve to *A Second Life*, which will open the doorway to your new and better existence—as well as prepare you for a Third Life, which is eternal life.

A First Life is a life distorted by society's false belief systems, which have caused you to develop a false self, disconnected from your true self and God. Such a life lived with fears results in only a fraction of your potential and true talent being used. It is life lived in a void, based merely on an ego-driven existence, with the objective being just to get by, supported by the belief that instant external gratifications will satisfy the emptiness felt inside. This is a life without higher purpose. A life *not* lived according to God's blueprint. A wasted life.

A Second Life is a life lived *according to* God's blueprint, with spirituality and materiality in balance while here on earth. It is a life where your God-given talents are developed and you serve others with those gifts. Such a fearless life is filled with inner peace, happiness, integrity, gratitude, and love, which manifest as Oneness with God and your true self. This is a life fully lived with no regrets, so that on the day when your final life review takes place before entering a Third Life you will look back on an unselfish life filled with unconditional love and compassion for all of God's creations, our fellow brothers and sisters, the animal kingdom, and our planet.

A Third Life: Eternal life.

THE THREE BASIC BELIEFS IN *A SECOND LIFE*

You were born as a unique uncut diamond created by God as a perfect divine creation.

Who you are is best explained by Michelangelo's response when asked by an ardent admirer, "How do you create your beautiful sculptures?"

"The beauty is already there, my friend," Michelangelo said. "I do not create beauty; God creates beauty. I merely chip away the surrounding marble so as to reveal the beauty. The beauty is already within. It's already perfectly in place."

Each of us has within us the potential to be all that we can be. You are so unique that God created only one of you. No other person on this planet has the exact same DNA as you. Your task now is to perfect the diamond you were born as, to discover and reveal your full glimmer and spark.

Society created a false and disconnected YOU by its indoctrination.

For a lifetime you have been indoctrinated by beliefs of others. Your current circumstances in life are based on how you think, feel, and act—all of which are a result of layer upon layer of negative and destructive belief systems that have indoctrinated you from birth to current day. At this moment you are a sum total of the

thoughts and values of your family, friends, your community, your country, your race, sexuality, gender, experiences, events, and the media you have been exposed to and absorbed. These destructive belief systems have been operating like a virus infecting your hard drive. They have created a false you. They have blocked you from God and your true potential and stopped you from being you who truly are, your true self.

Only by re-programming your subconscious mind can you re-boot, re-activating your connection to God and the true YOU.

You change your life by changing the way you think. The gateway to your new life is through you inner world, your subconscious mind, which affects how you think and act. It needs to be cleaned as well as altered. By being re-booted and re-programmed

with new positive thinking in accordance with *A Second Life's* Seven Commandments (the operating system), knowledge, and beliefs, your unconditioned self will be re-discovered. With your new belief system integrated in your subconscious, your old life and reality will be erased. Through cleansing of your "hard drive," access to your main server/God will be reopened and you will re-activated. Once this re-programming and activation is achieved, you will be able to live according to God's blueprint and utilize all resources and gifts given to you. Then you can be all that you can be, with a new, better, purpose-driven life, which you control.

A SECOND LIFE'S OPERATING SYSTEM

Through *A Second Life's* system for human survival and personal growth, your life will be changed forever. Your existing indoctrination that has infiltrated your original programming will be eliminated, your connection with God will be restored, and your new and better life that is in alignment with your true self will be activated. It's an exciting new world you are about to enter.

A Second Life's Seven Commandments provide an operating system that is the foundation upon which every aspect of your life will function at optimal levels and in balance.

A Second Life's *Seven Commandments:*

- Take full responsibility for your life
- Unlock your life's purpose
- Utilize God's gifts given to you
- Live in excellence with integrity
- Extend love to yourself and others
- Show gratitude
- Be of service to others and leave a legacy

Commandment #1: Take Full Responsibility for Your Life

Even though it's not your fault that you've been living life as a robot, now that you realize what has happened, from this moment forward everything will change. You can no longer deny or avoid the truth.

You will increasingly notice the discomfort you feel when your actions and reactions are based on indoctrination and not your true nature. Doubts that you have had about how and where your life has taken you will more strongly surface. Questions about your motives and priorities will begin to nag at you. Soon you'll feel certain that such questions need to be answered. If you choose to deny, ignore, or avoid the truth, your discomfort will lead to disillusionment.

Clearly it's time to take stock, conduct a life review in order to assess what is really going on, and determine where you go from here. After doing so, you must accept responsibility for your life from this moment forward. As you review how you got to be who you are and where you are right now, placing blame on others is not useful. Instead, operate on the assumption that anyone who has had a negative influence on your programming did not intend for it to have a harmful effect or result. They too were programmed and indoctrinated. Their actions toward you were based only on what they know to be truth. And although it was a false truth, usually it was not intended to cause you damage or harm.

Instead, wholly accept that this is a new day—which it is—and view any challenges you face as opportunities to learn and grow. These are the signs you'll need to follow in order to enter your new life, *A Second Life*, and take full responsibility from now on for re-creating your life as it was intended to be. As you do so, know that you are not alone. During your journey out of the darkness of your false reality into the light of your purposeful life you are being guided and supported by God.

Commandment #2: Unlock Your Life's Purpose

Choose now to no longer live as your false self. While using *A Second Life's* system and procedures to clear away the programming that has created your false self, your life's purpose will be revealed to you. It may not appear suddenly, all at once in a vision or a revelation, but slowly through small moments, with subtle signals. This is a process. In order to fully embrace this opportunity, you need to be open, alert, and present. Become conscious of your actions and reactions. Notice what feels automatic or uninspired. Use the tools you are learning in this life manual to stop yourself from continuing to operate on automatic pilot. Take over the controls of your own life.

Commandment #3: Utilize God's Gifts Given to You

Your path will be revealed to you in many ways, but certain clues will convince you that you are finding your God-given gifts: They will be easy, natural, inspirational. Once you begin to discover your gifts, developing them will be a joy. By using *A Second Life's* procedures and techniques, you will devise a plan that will result in your living a life full of passion, purpose, and fulfillment.

Commandment #4: Live in Excellence with Integrity

When each day of your life is filled with passion, purpose, and fulfillment, only the best will be acceptable to you. There will be no second best, no runner-up. But you will not be competing with others. Knowing who you truly are and understanding your true gifts and talents will inspire you to act on them to the fullest degree—not to impress others but to satisfy yourself, to honor your connection to God. Your standard will be to always live in excellence with integrity.

Commandment #5: Extend Love to Yourself and Others

Only by loving and valuing yourself can you truly love and value others. They, in turn, will recognize and honor your good will and love will return to you.

Commandment #6: Show Gratitude

The positive feelings and reaffirming interactions you have every day will make the world a wondrous, abundant place to live. For this you will feel grateful. Gratitude can be expressed in many ways: with words of thanks, by deeds of kindness, through gentle touches and understanding listening. The gratitude you feel and show through your thoughts, words, and actions will reinforce everything good that you have chosen to be part of your new life.

Commandment #7: Be of Service to Others and Leave a Legacy

There will always be people you encounter along the way in this journey that is *A Second Life* who are not as fortunate as you. Perhaps they do not understand the robotic patterns of their lives that have led to their misfortune. Perhaps they have met a challenge too great for them to overcome. Some have simply lost their way. Others will be living in the delusion that they are better than you, smarter than you, richer than you. Whatever is going on with them is not your responsibility to fix. However, by using your God-given gifts you can ease their way and show them things they might otherwise not see. By setting a good example, you give them a glimpse of how fulfilling a purposeful life can be.

Although you *are* obligated to give back to society in some way by being of service to others, the manner in which you do so needs to resonate with your true self. Only then will you be giving back genuinely and from your heart—and your sincerity will be recognized and appreciated by those you are helping.

Some people have a strong desire to do volunteer work—even if they can only commit to a few hours a week. Others choose to pursue careers in public service or social services, knowing they will likely be sacrificing monetary gain in order to help others. But those are not the only ways you can leave a legacy.

Your interactions with other people on a daily basis can have a more significant impact than you might realize. When you see that someone needs assistance, lend a helping hand. Convey a friendly attitude, smile or passing comment during casual interactions with others. Take a few moments to thoughtfully reach out to someone who seems lonely, isolated, or needs a friend. Your words and deeds—whether directly or indirectly—are an example to everyone you interact with or encounter during the course of your day, and provide opportunities for you to show others the value that can be derived from living a life of integrity and God-gifted purpose. Kindness, thoughtfulness, and consideration, at the very least, as well as love, are contagious. By generously spreading goodwill, your example can also become your legacy.

1 Coding to Oneness: Achievement Levels to Living *A Second Life*

Level 1
Disarming the False Belief Systems Running You

YOU = A ROBOT

One day recently I went to a Starbucks near my home at around 7:30 in the morning. After buying my coffee, instead of leaving, for some reason I decided to sit down and observe people.

A man in his late forties in a pinstriped suit walked in with a newspaper in one hand, ordered a coffee, and quickly left. A physically fit blond young woman wearing sweatpants briskly strode past on the sidewalk outside with three small dogs, leashes in hand, while on the other side of the street an overweight lady in her mid-thirties stood on the corner smoking a cigarette. Soon a fifty-year-old construction worker came in to get his "morning Joe." As he left, he held open the door for a red-haired woman in her forties who rushed past him. They didn't speak to each other, or even make eye contact. A few minutes later a casually dressed couple came in together. They stood several feet away from each other, one looked up at the menu on the wall, the other ordered from the barista behind the counter, who appeared to be bored and unenthusiastic while efficiently serving customers. As I watched all of these people I noticed that none of them seemed the least bit interested in each other or interacted with anyone around them. They were all so wrapped up in what they were doing that they looked like robots walking around in a trance.

Out of curiosity I went back to that Starbucks at the same time the next day, then two days later, to observe again. The exact same people reappeared on those days, behaving in the same ways I'd seen before. It felt almost as if I were watching a movie over and over, with every day repeating itself—similar to the movie "Groundhog Day," only without anyone learning how they could live their lives any better. If not for my own conscious decision to step out of the scene, I would have been a participant in the "7:30 A.M. at Starbucks" movie.

How many people are so conditioned that they go through the routines of their days like predictable machines or programmed robots, as though everything in their world is fixed? The reality is that most people live as though they have no other choice.

As an experiment, position yourself near an area where there are a lot of people and stand back and just observe. What do you see? Now imagine you are watching a movie, a science fiction movie, and the people you're watching are actually cyborgs—human beings that have both natural and artificial operating systems. Watch the way they move. Notice the way they interact with each other—or don't. Do you see passion and purpose in what they're doing, or any kind of awareness in them that something new and worthwhile could enter their world? Or do they look like they're just going through the motions?

Now imagine that someone else is observing you. What conclusions would they reach? You = a robot?

YOU = A ROBOT?

For anyone who is in denial, consider this: The human brain has been compared to a computer. At birth each human being is connected to God (the main server) through their brain (hard drive). From that moment on, input is received from outside sources—parents, siblings, family members, society, television, radio, music, educators, books, friends, loved ones . . . on and on it goes. Each of these influences is like a software program being downloaded onto people's hard drives, changing their original operating system and almost always disconnecting them from God and their true selves.

Slowly it happens without anyone's agreement or knowledge, gradually we are separated from our original programming and unlimited potential. Instead of using our God-given gifts in passionate pursuits that will bring us personal joy and fulfillment while we are also being of service to others and society as a whole, we operate more and more in obedient compliance to the software that is the will of society. Worse yet, during the process, most people are exposed to negative influences (viruses) that have an even more dramatic effect on their original operating system, leading them even further astray.

It's not your fault that you've been programmed by all the influences in your life from birth until this moment and are essentially now living as a robot. After all, like a computer with new software, once certain information is downloaded into your brain, a given sequence of actions automatically occurs.

Most of us are trained as children by a reward and punishment system, not unlike that used with the family dog. It creates in us a yearning for the rewards given for being "good" and a fear of punishment or rejection if we do not comply with the desires of our authority figures. Soon we adopt their belief systems, which in our minds become the laws or rules we accept as truths by which we must live in order to survive. Everything in life is framed by these particular belief systems—our actions, our opinions, our judgments, our very sense of self. Still, there remains somewhere within us the spark of our true nature that cannot be extinguished. But when that spark cannot ignite our true passions, we feel uninspired, unfulfilled, anxious, depressed, or out of control. We lose the clear connection between God and our true selves and go through the motions each day with limited potential, like robots. Eventually we are not even aware of all the ways our lives could be different and are unable to even see what we are missing.

If you've ever seen someone crossing an intersection or a street looking down at their handheld electronic device texting instead of looking for oncoming traffic, haven't you wondered if they are concerned about their own safety or have any regard for their value in the world? Could a person who is always talking on his or her cell phone while in public be missing an opportunity to meet another person who could potentially be the love of his or her life simply because they've shut off all avenues of connection with strangers around them? What about the routines that people establish, which, admittedly, ease them through each tedious day, but also result in a complete loss of passion or even appreciation for the beautiful moments, events, or encounters available to them if they would only notice?

Come to a full stop right now and look around. What do you see? How would your world look to someone who has just entered it for the very first time? What have you been overlooking, ignoring, denying, not appreciating, not doing?

Answer these questions honestly:

- How do you embark on each day—with excitement and enthusiasm or with a sense of disinterest or dread, a feeling of just wanting to get through it?
- Do you work at a job only for the money you're paid or because you truly feel a passion for what you do?
- Are you financially secure?
- Are you physically healthy?
- How do you interact with coworkers on the job or greet your loved ones when you return home from work at the end of the day?
- Do you engage in leisure activities that are rewarding for you, your loved ones, and, perhaps, society as a whole?
- Do you feel a genuine connection to a higher power and know without question that you are always being guided along the right path during a journey that is worthwhile and fulfilling?
- In what ways do you operate in your life that show you truly know and love yourself, you are connected to God, and you are making a contribution to mankind as a whole?

If you are unable to answer these questions or are distressed by the answers you have given, don't despair. There is a way back.

GETTING INSIDE YOUR SUBCONSCIOUS MIND TO CLEAR AWAY YOUR FALSE SELF

Every person operates from two minds: the conscious mind and the subconscious mind. Whenever you are aware of what you are doing or want to do it's your conscious mind at work. The subconscious mind is where all your beliefs and memories are stored, which generate your emotions and unconscious actions. The subconscious mind is already programmed and set for 85 percent of us before we reach adulthood. And society's indoctrination—which is held in the subconscious mind—continues even when we are adults. Clearing away that false programming (indoctrination) is paramount in order to begin living a different, more purposeful life.

Meditation, prayer, and self-programming are the most effective tools you can use to erase your negative programming and re-boot, opening a clear channel between yourself and God. These tools also provide ongoing assistance to you for maintaining your focus as you move forward living *A Second Life.*

Meditation

Meditation is a mental discipline that has been practiced for over 5,000 years by people who want to get beyond their conditioned "thinking mind" and enter a deeply relaxed state of awareness. Your goal is to calm the mind and focus your attention in the present moment for ten to thirty minutes twice a day—once in the morning and once in the evening. By doing so you will get a better vision of how your life would best be used by connecting with your true self and God inside. It also helps clear your indoctrination by society and re-store your original programming in your mind.

There are various meditation techniques, but all are grouped into two categories: concentrative meditation and mindfulness meditation.

For concentrative meditation, sit quietly in a location away from distractions and focus your attention on your breathing, an image, a sound, or words (mantra). As you allow your mind to be directed *only* to your focus (breath, image, sound, words), all conscious thoughts will drift away. By doing so you allow messages from your true self within or a higher power (God) to be revealed to you.

Quiet your mind. Allow it to become a blank canvas on which the artist within you can paint magnificent pictures of the better life you have been given as a blessed gift.

For mindfulness meditation, sit quietly in a location away from distractions and simply witness whatever goes through your mind. Do not react or become involved with thoughts, memories, worries, or images and soon you will understand that they no longer have any power over you.

Quiet your mind. Allow the indoctrination of your programmed life to fade away, being replaced with your magnificent new life being lived in alignment with your God-given gifts.

Meditation is a healing tool from God for mind, body, and soul. While it helps you achieve clarity of purpose and stay mentally balanced, clears your indoctrination by society and re-stores your original programming, it is also a component of maintaining good mental and physical health, and assists in faster healing of physical ailments.

As you embark on your new purposeful life, your awareness will increase, becoming a form of meditation every moment of every day, making you more conscious of everything you do, enabling you to be the best you can be.

Prayer

People of all major religions commonly and routinely use prayer to communicate with a higher power—God or however they refer to it. Through prayers, people worship, request guidance or assistance, confess sins, make amends, or express thoughts and emotions. There is often a sense of hope associated with prayer.

The belief of *A Second Life* is that daytime is for battle; nighttime is for resting. Therefore, praying twice a day provides a feeling of support and connection to God that sustains and reinforces daily life.

In the morning pray for strength. This is my daily morning prayer: *I am more than my physical body.* (This reminds you that you are very powerful as a person.) *Make me an indestructible warrior who can win any battle that comes my way. Help me become one with my true self, you God, and the universe. Make me strong. Make me exist in the past, present, and future and all realities at once.*

In the evening, instead of asking for God's help, express gratitude for what you've already received. Do this, not just with words, but with your full heart. Affirm that your success is a certainty. The difference between man and God is that man only believes and God *knows.* Now, as you are aware that you are one with God, this means that you no longer just believe, you also *know.* Thank God for all you have been given. Acknowledge that you accept God's gifts. My evening prayer is: *Thank you for this amazing, amazing journey that is life.*

Self-Programming

Throughout your life your subconscious mind has been constantly receiving messages and holding onto those messages. This is "society's programming." The subconscious mind does not know the difference between what is real and what you believe. But anything—indeed, everything—you have accepted as "truth" can be changed. Self-programming is a systematic procedure to input messages *you choose and control* into your subconscious mind. By doing so you can delete society's programming and replace your limiting beliefs, thoughts, and behaviors in your subconscious mind with positive beliefs and thoughts that result in positive behaviors.

Self-programming can be done in many ways, but the easiest and most effective ways are with self-talk or by visualization. Self-talk is exactly that: talking to yourself while in a focused state of mind. Visualization is creating a new picture for your life in your mind while in a focused state of mind.

Before you begin, have a game plan in mind. It could be specific if you're focusing on one area or aspect of your life, or general for your life as a whole.

During the self-talk, if possible play music that lifts your spirits in the background to heighten your senses and make your adrenalin rush through your body. When specific music is playing often during your self-talk, the intensity will become greater. Later, when doing the self-talk or even just listening to the music, it will trigger the power within you to be released, reinforcing your re-programming. The music and intensity for your self-talk should be high energy during the morning and daytime and more serene at night.

You will begin by relaxing your conscious mind so that it stops thinking, much like you do in bed at night just before you fall asleep. Willingly shut off feedback from your other senses that can distract you. With your thinking mind turned off, your subconscious mind, which is an obedient servant, will follow the instructions it is given. Your subconscious mind will then respond to those instructions, manifesting your new way of thinking and behaving in your new awakened life. Repetition and reinforcement are needed to keep your new way of thinking on track until all of your old indoctrinated false programming has been replaced with your new belief system of *A Second Life.*

Here is a basic procedure to follow for either self-talk or visualization self-programming:

- Go to a location where you can sit or lie down comfortably without being disturbed.
- Set a timer for ten minutes.
- As you settle in, find a focal point to stare at. Any object that's pleasing but does not stimulate your mind will do. I like to use a lit candle.
- Allow your mind to stop thinking. Just stare at your focal point (candle flame) and take several long, deep breaths.
- As you slowly do a countdown—either from one to ten or from ten to one—feel your body relaxing. Feel your body getting warmer and warmer. Feel your body getting heavier and heavier.

- Allow your body to become deeply relaxed.
- Your body and mind feel at peace, at rest.
- From now until the timer gently brings you out of your deeply relaxed state, you will concentrate on feeling rested, relaxed. You are calm and comfortable as you stare at your focal point. Your body is quiet, your hands are warm and heavy—they feel slightly tingly.
- As you give yourself permission to feel the relaxation throughout your entire body, your eyes will slowly close.
- If you are using self-talk, begin to repeat the message—either targeting a specific area of your life or generally—you want to program into your subconscious mind. (The self-talk messages I input during self-programming are usually general: *Make me one with God. Make nothing stop me. Make me strong and indestructible. Nothing can stop me because I am one with God. Nothing will ever touch me. I will always win. Make me strong to overcome any battle and strong in mind and never give up on my goals. There will never be any surrender. As long as I have a breath in my body I will keep fighting, and even after I will still be fighting.*
- If you are using visualization, visualize a picture of yourself as the true you living a life of purpose in alignment with your God-given gifts. Allow the picture of your old self to fade away in the photograph of your memories. That person no longer exists. The only purpose that image now holds is to prove to you that it was a fruitless existence you were living as a robot programmed to believe a false truth.
- Visualize every step of your journey to reach a specific goal or the ultimate outcome in your new life. (By doing so you remove any fear attached to the unknown. In my mind I picture that it has already happened.)
- When your timer rings, open your eyes, slowly count backwards from three to one, until you are present, alert, and aware of your surroundings.
- Get up, move around, and go about doing what you need to do feeling a new awareness of how your life is changing in positive ways every moment.

As you embark on the journey that is your new life and while you continue on your path to success, you can self-talk or visualize whatever you need during these sessions to re-program your subconscious mind. Your self-talk and visualizations can be tailored to the areas of your life you are developing more fully or they can provide support when you face challenges.

Many people find it helpful to create a manifestation board to reinforce their self-talk and visualizations. They draw or paint pictures of their new life or cut pictures out of magazines, paste them on poster board, or post them on a bulletin board. Display these pictures of your new life in a place where you see them all the time so that you are constantly reminded of your goals. When you look at the pictures, place yourself *in* them, so that you are a part of the picture. You want to see your new life clearly, and feel yourself achieving your goals. Eventually it becomes your being. It becomes something you can almost touch. And then it is manifesting.

Level 2
Understanding Who You Truly Are and Your Life's Purpose

DISCOVERING YOUR LIFE PURPOSE

God has given you unique talents and gifts that no one else has so that you can make a very special contribution to the world. You are drawn to do those things because they ignite your passion, connecting you to your true self and God within. That passion is the clue to figuring out your life purpose (DNA blueprint), which is programmed into you at birth. Unfortunately, for most of us, our original program has been overwritten during our lives with the software of society's expectations. But you can look beneath society's programming to discover the plan God has mapped out for you. Anything you do that comes from that place while building your new life can only lead to success.

> *Do you want to know who you are? Don't ask. Act!*
> *Action will delineate and define you.*
>
> Thomas Jefferson

To discover your unique gifts and talents, make a list of the things you are good at and are fulfilling to do. Think of the things you do naturally in the course of your day, the things you have done throughout your life that seem effortless and are satisfying. (During your Life Review in the next chapter you may discover other things that do not immediately occur to you at this time, which you can then add to your list.) These are not things that society's standards require you to do, but rather things that come from within you. They are the things—both large and small—that you love the most, the things that inspire you, motivate you, excite you, bring you joy; the things you have a desire to do even if you don't have to. Your passions = your life purpose.

Passion is so powerful that it can change your life. If you listen to what resonates inside you, what your heart yearns to do, this is your inner voice, your DNA blueprint that when followed will guide you on the journey that is your new purposeful life, being all that God intended for you to be.

> *The greater danger for most of us lies not in setting our aim too high and falling short, but in setting our aim too low and achieving our mark.*
>
> Michelangelo

Life Review

If you want to know where you're going, you have to know where you're starting from and how you got to where you are right now. You must learn to distinguish between society's programming and your original DNA blueprint. Only by learning to clearly see the difference can you move forward on your true life path.

During this self-examining process it's important to look at the big picture of your life and your entire lifespan to ensure that you clearly realize the urgency of beginning your new life, *A Second Life,* right now. At the time of your birth you were awarded a specific amount of time for this journey called life, and the months have been counting down to the time when it will all end. Right now, as the countdown continues, you need to decide how to best use your remaining time before it's all gone. It's up to you to choose whether you will use it in a manner that is worthwhile and fulfilling, or if it will be wasted and pass you by.

The following chart is set at seventy-eight years, which is the average lifespan of people in the United States. If you smoke, drink, don't eat properly, have an unhealthy lifestyle, or a family history of illness, then you need to take off some years—leaving you with even less time. This also goes the other way around, meaning if you have a family history of living beyond the U.S. average and/or live a healthy lifestyle, then add years to the scale.

Place yourself on the following Life Assessment Table to see where you are—meaning how many years of "your time" you have left.

Life Assessment Table

Your current age: ______ = Time Used

Years left (subtract your current age from 78): ______

	Birth to Teens		Young Adult		Middle Adult		Late Adult		Retirement to Death	
Years Lived	**0**	18	19	30	31	49	50	65	66	**78**
Years Left	**78**	60	59	48	47	29	28	13	12	**0**

After calculating your time (years) used and those that you have left to live, next place yourself in the appropriate category below to see and understand where you have been and where you are right now.

Age 0–18 years: From birth to young adult you unknowingly get programmed, which sets precedence for how life will play out for you. During these years you are supposed to become independent and carve out what you "believe" is a life of your own. The challenges you encounter = opportunities for your growth.

There are three levels of adulthood: young adult (19–30 years), middle adult (31–40 years), and late adult (50–65), but basically the entire time is spent in the active work world. Your thoughts and actions based on your programming and experiences determine how you feel about the way you're using life's minutes: a) gratitude for all the choices you've made, b) dissatisfaction, or c) numbness/a feeling of emptiness.

From retirement to physical death (65–78 years) you slow down your activities, and many people catch up on the little things they were too busy to do earlier in life. Having more free time, you have the opportunity to reflect on your life and how you've lived it. Your inner voice will let you know if it was all that you wanted it to be—which determines if your gift of this life was utilized to the fullest according to God's wish or it was not all that it could have been, and thus, wasted.

The fear of death follows from the fear of life.
A man who lives fully is prepared to die at any time.

Mark Twain

Reviewing Your Past

With this perspective on how much of the time you were allotted for this life that you have lived so far and how much time you have remaining, review how you have used your time. As you review your life so far, first think about the larger picture and then allow the smaller scenes of your life to provide your answers. Ask yourself the following questions:

- What have you accomplished in your life?
- Why have you done the things you've done?
- Why did you do them the way you did?
- Were the choices you made based on your true desires or on what was expected of you?
- Who have you been trying to please?
- What do you most regret?
- What are you most proud of?
- In what ways have you grown as a person during your life?
- What ideals or people have been your role models?
- Do you feel you've made a positive contribution to the lives of others—not just loved ones, but strangers as well—and your country?
- How have you served God?
- How have you honored your true self?

Every experience you have had provides an opportunity for you to learn. Looking back at your life right now, you will immediately see that fear has been your biggest obstacle, and it continues to this day: fear of disappointing others, fear of not living up to society's standards, fear of being unloved and alone, fear of failure, joblessness, homelessness, starvation, ill health, suffering, even fear of death. The truth is, by living with that kind of fear, you have been dying a slow death each day, disconnected from God because you are not fulfilling your life purpose. You have been living in this way because you are a victim of society's ultimate power over you: you are society's robot. Only by realizing this is true and accepting it can you change everything.

As you begin to move forward into living your purposeful life, ask yourself: What do you have to lose? Your answer should be: Nothing! When you learn to detach from society's expectations of the outcome you will be motivated instead by what you need to do in order to fulfill your own, unique life purpose, a higher purpose.

Understand without a doubt the reality that only two things truly matter in your life: pleasing God and honoring your true self! Although analyzing every step you have made in your life that brought you to this point helps you gain perspective and helps you see what you could have done differently, in actuality it does not matter now. None of that matters now. What does matter is that you change your beliefs about who you are and the way things should be, that you look at your life and the circumstances you find yourself in differently. Now you can begin to erase the negative indoctrinated programming that has overwritten your original blueprint and held you back. By creating a new vision of your life you can reconnect with your original DNA blueprint, develop a game plan, and begin to transform your life. Through effort and hard work you can become all that you were meant to be.

In order to clearly see your vision of how your life is played out it is recommended that you now write your own obituary. A clear view of how you want to be remembered will help you create an unconscious game plan for how to make this vision a reality—which will happen as soon as you are clear about what you want. While writing your obituary, know that you can do anything you set your mind to do once you are free from your old programming. You are one with God inside and you are here to serve him—not what your ego desires—by utilizing all of your gifts given. Your potential is unlimited.

Once your obituary is written you will recognize what truly matters in your life. You will notice that the qualities and accomplishments you desire for yourself and your life can be exhibited or developed right now, this moment.

Only a life lived for others is a life worthwhile.

Albert Einstein

With the new perspective you have gained, how will you live your life from this moment forward? Answer these questions based on your aspirations to be living your magnificent new, purposeful life, *A Second Life* in alignment with your God-given gifts.

Beginning This Moment

- What are you accomplishing in your life?
- Why are you doing the things you are doing?
- Why are you doing them the way you are doing them?
- Are you making choices based on your true desires or on what is expected of you?

- Are pleased with the way you are conducting your life?
- How are you improving each day?
- What are you most proud of?
- In what ways are you growing as a person?
- What ideals or people are your role models?
- Do you feel you are making a positive contribution to the lives of others—not just loved ones, but strangers as well—and your country?
- How are you serving God?
- How are you honoring your true self?

Level 3
Maximizing Your Daily Existence to Survive, Grow, and Win in the Game of Life

Even though it's not your fault that you've been living as a robot most of your life, now that you are aware of it, all of that has changed—you can never forget that someone else has been controlling your life. Until this moment your life has been a reflection of your indoctrinated false beliefs, your robotic thoughts and actions. If you are wildly successful and completely fulfilled in every way, then you don't need to be reading this guide. But if you are living with doubt, disappointment, disillusionment, even despair and misery, then you have not been living on God's track, but off track.

Now it's time for you to take control of your life. In order to do so you must accept full responsibility for what you do from this moment forward. You, and only you, are accountable to God for everything in your life from now on.

The key is that you embrace this new belief system and conduct your life in ways that are a reflection of your true self. Then you will be motivated to work hard to create your own life—*A Second Life* in alignment with your God-given gifts—a life filled with joy, happiness, and unlimited success.

Success is not based on luck. No one is handed it. You can't sit around and wait for it to happen on its own. It takes proactive planning, work, and tenacity. To be successful you must be actively creating your life, not passively letting life happen to you. You must set goals for yourself and stay focused in order to achieve them. Your results will be the direct outcomes of your thoughts, feelings, and consistent behaviors. They are the ultimate reflection of the true YOU.

I find that the harder I work, the more luck I seem to have.

Thomas Jefferson

THE DAILY LIFE BALANCE SYSTEM

In order to maximize your existence you will be integrating *A Second Life's* Daily Life Balance System to ensure that all bases are covered both short and long term in life. The system is structured on the premise that in order to live a balanced life every important aspect of life must be covered on a daily basis.

The goal is to live today as though it's the last day of your life, but at the same time as though you are going to live forever. To achieve this requires you to have a good plan that you will always stick to. Living life to the fullest means living in the moment, but also setting goals for the future that provide a clear plan for reaching your milestones. Without a plan, discipline, the right information, prioritizing the time given to you by God in the best possible way, and hard work you will never get anywhere in life. Nothing happens by chance, and when you are aligned with God you can achieve anything you set your mind to do.

Life's journey is very similar to going on a road trip. You can choose to head out with no roadmap whatsoever and see where it takes you. This can be very exciting for people who have a strong sense of adventure and the ability to enjoy exactly where they are at any moment. But you can also end up in places where you would never choose to be, and where you are required to do things you don't want to do in order to survive. The other option is to follow a map with milestones and goals to reach, knowing ahead of time what you want to experience along the way, and where you would like your journey to end.

Another way to view your life is like it's a business and you are the president of the company. First of all you need a good business plan. Only with a clear agenda and a very process-driven mentality can you be successful.

A harsh reality of life is that very little happens overnight. My own experience is that everything that I have achieved and all that I have become are the results of hard work, good planning, and processes. This does not mean that you are not going to enjoy the present moment, which is all you have right now. But the key to creating the best possible balanced life is following a solid, proven, methodical program—which provides a good support system—that makes sure all areas of your life are covered at all times.

Mastering *A Second Life's* Daily Life Balance System provides that support. The basic belief is that for each day you need to give attention to and seek to balance these integral areas of your life:

- Physical: exercise, correct nutrition, adequate sleep/rest
- Life Maintenance: work to pay bills to exist and maintain your lifestyle, as well as save for the future
- Spirituality: meditation/prayer for motivation, inner peace and clarity, as well as to connect and stay connected with your true self and God through Oneness
- Future Growth: seeds planted for the future so that you can grow
- Leisure Activities: time spent doing things that are fun, not related to work or out of responsibility

The amount of time spent on each area of your life will differ depending on your present situation. But it's important that every area get adequate attention and coverage every day, no matter what. Your goal is to strive for a balance.

Survival, of course, is mandatory; then personal attainment can be achieved thereafter. This means that Life Maintenance will take up most of the time for most people. During some days and weeks your job will require so much of your time and energy that it will affect the other four areas of your life, but you still need to give them enough attention, even if it's less time than would be ideal—you can never skip one area entirely. The challenge after you have applied yourself during a full day of work is to use your inner strength to devote some time to cover the other four areas. But by going the extra mile you will always know that you are doing your best to live in the here and now while still planting seeds for an even better future. When an area hasn't gotten enough attention, as soon as possible after such days you will need to make up for it by applying yourself even harder on that area.

By covering each of these areas daily, you are living life with a good balance, enjoying the present while also going somewhere positive in life.

Live as if you were to die tomorrow. Learn as if you were to live forever.

Mohandas Gandhi

Think creatively about how you can fit everything in somehow. Rather than engaging in an entire half hour of exercise you'd ideally do, ten minutes can be enough from time to time. Keeping up with some type of healthful physical activity is key because it's tied so closely to your mental state of mind. If your job/career requires you to work overtime, thereby taking up the evening hours you'd planned to spend with your family, when you do get home make a point of sitting down with your loved ones for fifteen minutes of uninterrupted conversation about what happened during their day. Be realistic about eliminating things from your calendar that you truly don't have time to do without depriving a more important area of your life. Don't put yourself in a position where you are socially trapped if you can't comfortably participate and enjoy the activities. Sometimes you'll need to make difficult choices, but always choose what's best for your new purposeful life.

Always stay disciplined and remember that you are the creator of your own life and your reality is a result of your thoughts and actions. Weakness has no place in your life, only commitment and discipline. Living *A Second Life* means there is no defeat, because you are the creator of your own life now and in the future.

This Daily Life Balance System works best when you plan each day. Make a habit of writing a "to do" list and ranking the items according to their priority. As each task is completed, cross it off your list. By day's end try your best to have all items completed. If something does not get done, then add it to the list for the following day. Combine this technique with positive visualization. At night, right before going to sleep, close your eyes and see a movie in your mind of the next day already happening and what you are going to do. Approaching every aspect of your life with a positive attitude and filled with gratitude reinforces always doing the best you can.

In this life's journey God gave each of us a certain number of years, months, days, hours, and minutes to use as we please. We can choose to spend our time exerting minimal effort or we can choose to do our very best at all times. Always doing your best shows respect for the greatest gift of all, LIFE.

The key to being all that you can be in life is to stay disciplined, tap into your reserve energy, make the right choices with your time, and maximize each minute you apply to the Daily Life Balance System. It's important to emphasize that this system requires an ability to wisely use your time. While doing so you are overriding the old belief systems that held you back and building a strong foundation for your entirely new life. With persistence and hard work you will see progress made more and more each day, each week, and each month. Eventually your old routines will be totally erased. Your old life will become so distant that it is no longer part of your existence.

The more energy you devote to the methods and knowledge presented in *A Second Life's* belief system, the more successful you will be.

ALIGNING YOUR LIFE WITH YOUR GOD-GIVEN GIFTS

Your God-given gifts = your passions. Your passions serve as your motivation. They propel you forward in life, carrying you successfully toward your destination of fulfillment. But first you must tend to basic needs for physical survival and maintenance.

The respected psychological theory, Maslow's Hierarchy of Needs—which defines the needs that motivate humans—is portrayed as a five-level pyramid.

Figure 1: Maslow's Hierarchy of Needs

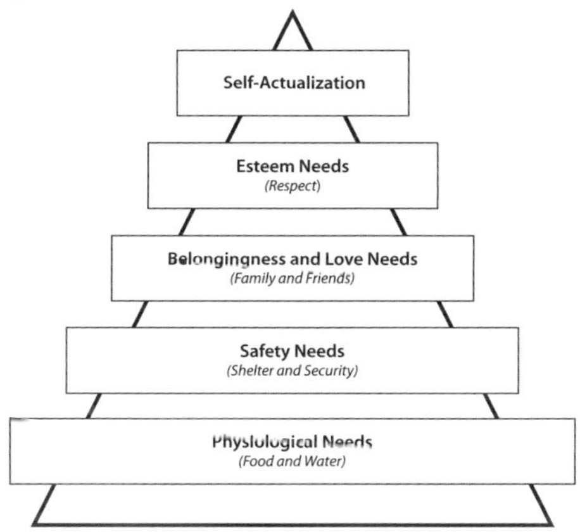

The four lower levels are grouped together as needs associated with physical comfort and security. The most basic needs for survival are at the bottom. Next level up are the needs for feeling safe, then come the needs for feeling loved/belonging, and next level up is self-confidence and esteem. Finally, the top level is associated with the needs to be met in order to feel complete and fulfilled (self-realization).

Abraham Maslow published a paper with this theory in 1943 after studying people of exemplary achievement, such as Albert Einstein, Jane Addams, Eleanor Roosevelt, and Frederick Douglass—rather than studying mentally ill or neurotic people—and successful college students. Maslow found that people were motivated to progress up the ladder of the pyramid starting from the bottom. Only when their basic needs at the bottom four levels of the pyramid were met did people become motivated to seek self-realization—fulfillment of their needs to be all that they could be.

The goal of *A Second Life* is to spend as much time as possible on activities at the top of the pyramid—universal love and self-realization—and as little as possible on the survival elements at the bottom. Once you have mastered and become proficient at survival—which you will be taught in *A Second Life's* Five Key Knowledge Areas of Life to be Mastered—the door for you to enjoy life to the fullest, as well as live with a purpose by having the time and means to be of service to others. Too many people spend their entire lifetimes struggling just to survive and never get to experience the joy associated with living at the top of the pyramid.

A Second Life believes that the model you strive to live in this lifetime is called God's Hierarchy of Needs—which is the reverse of Maslow's pyramid in terms of time spent and what is important in life.

Figure 2: God's Hierarchy of Needs

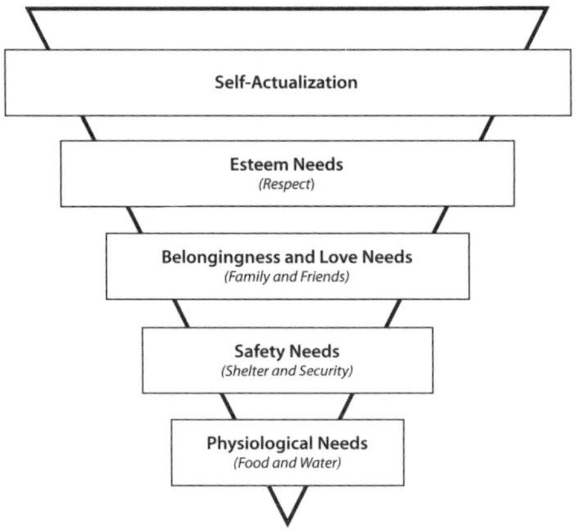

The key to graduating to fully living according to God's Hierarchy of Needs is mastering survival in the earth school. Those who spend a lifetime in an existence of just getting by will always be trapped in a reality controlled by the ego and the dark forces, living a life not unlike that of a wild animal. God created the human race to be so much more, but as long as the negative belief systems are controlling people, the evil side stops human beings from evolving to the next level toward their full potential. Once freed from the chains of mental slavery all people have the opportunity to rise, as every person is God's divine creation and can do anything he or she sets their mind to do. When people are released from the slavery that has trapped others for thousands of years and their freedom is secured, they can live according to God's Hierarchy of Needs and be able to experience Heaven on Earth as they became activated to Oneness.

The unexamined life is not worth living.

Plato

HOW TO PRIORITIZE AND USE YOUR MINUTES

The only guarantee there is in life is this: You have only so many minutes remaining before your physical death, when you cross over to A Third Life. Not only that, but the level you've evolved to on earth—in regard to living a life in Oneness—determines where you start out in the next life.

Understand clearly, it's not about whether you have spent a lifetime studying some scriptures; instead, it's all about how you have utilized your God-given gifts and your allotted time. It will never be about how many people you converted to believe the same religious doctrines as you, because God merely wants you to be a role model who inspires through *how* you live life. So don't waste your minutes by letting the ego/dark forces control you. If that is how you are living, your life is a self-created hell on earth and your next life will be the same, because how you go is the way your next life will be. This is what it means to evolve in earth school, to overcome and learn from the challenges that God is giving you in order for you to grow and evolve, to become One with God's kingdom inside, which is all love and no ego, so that in your next life you'll be in a better place.

Therefore, it's important to learn to use your given time wisely. Effective time management enables you to live with focus and purpose according to God, love, and self-realization, using your talents and gifts to give back to society, making America and the world a better place. Always think of how you prioritize and use your minutes, and remember: time spent is something you can never get back.

Time Management Assessment Exercise

Every thirty minutes write down what you have done during the previous thirty-minute time frame. Do this for an entire twelve-hour period of time (not to include regular bedtime sleeping hours) on two different types of days—one for a workday, one for a non-workday.

Start from the minute you get out of bed in the morning. Include all the things you do, no matter how mundane they may seem, everyone you interact with, everything you eat and drink. For the workday, include travel time to work, what you do during your work hours, everyone you interact with. For the non-workday include your downtime activities, such as reading, watching TV, using the computer, exercising, playing sports, etc.; your family activities and responsibilities; and giving attention to your spiritual development. Keep your notes short so you don't spend too much time keeping track of how you use your time. Be honest. This quiz will not be seen or graded by anyone else, but is a tool to help you learn how to live *A Second Life*.

After doing this on two different days, look over your lists. What do you see? Is there balance in the way you use the minutes in your life? Are your days filled with worthwhile endeavors and activities? Or is too much of your time wasted? (By the way, those minutes are gone forever; you'll never get them back!) Are you so absorbed in frantic distractions that you can't stay focused on the important things in your life? Are you living like a robot or making conscious choices?

If you find you're always putting things off till tomorrow, wake up! Tomorrow may never come. Take control of how you use your precious minutes today. Create new habits and routines.

Time Usage Re-alignment Tips

- Adjust your priorities based on the Daily Life Balance System. Become conscious each day of how much time you are devoting to each area of your life:
  - Physical health/wellness (exercise, nutrition, sleep)
  - Maintenance for survival (job to create income for existence)
  - Seeds planted for the future (expanding knowledge, further developing existing skills, and developing a future business idea)
  - Meditation/prayer (motivational, inner peace and clarity)
  - Relaxation/social interaction (enjoying the present)
- Understand what your time is worth. Successful executives have learned to outsource. If someone can do something better than you, hire them to do it for you while you do something more important. If you can't afford to hire someone, barter.
- Create a co-op lifestyle. A co-op is a business model in which a group of people invests in a commercial enterprise. Not only do the investors buy goods at the co-op, they also receive a share of the profits. The co-op model can be transformed to fit various types of needs and activities: carpooling, job sharing, childcare trading/sharing (commonly called "play dates"), even grocery shopping. Seek out like-minded people with similar needs and arrange to cooperatively support one another. In addition to better using your time, you'll be establishing and maintaining worthwhile relationships with others.
- Keep a list of your own ideas for re-alignment of your time usage.

A GROWTH PLAN FOR YOUR TALENTS

Without enjoying the present—which is all that we have—we miss out on everything that life has to offer. But if we don't plant seeds for the future while also developing our God-given gifts we will never be all that we can be. Only when all areas of your life are fully developed and work together can you become a fully formed person whose life has genuine substance and meaning in the eyes of God. Your life purpose is not fulfilled just by having job/career success, financial gain, finding a husband or wife, or creating a family. You also need to achieve excellent physical and mental health and sincere relationships (with yourself and with others), all built upon a spiritual foundation that honors God by giving back to the world.

If you honestly look at your life from God's perspective what do you see? Are you fully developing and using your talents or are you allowing some of those gifts to go unused? Each and every talent you have was given to you for a reason. They *all* play a valuable part in your existence as unique expressions of who you truly are.

Giving your attention and focus to only one area of your life hooks you into that area like an addiction. It becomes all you think about. It becomes all you "need." You are driven to it and it alone, believing that it has more importance than anything else. Yet somewhere deep inside you know this feels wrong. You know that life is not about just one thing. You feel the lack, the something missing. Such singular focus sends your life into an endless loop of repeating the same things day after day after day. Round and round you go. And although you may feel as though you're making progress, what you're actually doing is creating bigger and bigger circles. And as you know, traveling endlessly around in a circle does not get you further along the road during the journey to your destination. This is no way to fulfill your potential. Excelling at one thing is not success. It is a deception created by your indoctrination to achieve a false goal.

Think of the tension you feel when too much of your time is consumed by one area of your life and others are being ignored. There is a nagging within you, a tugging at your soul. Just as the human body cannot be healthy with only one source of food, the human soul needs all of its potential to be nourished in order to feel satisfied and fulfilled. Finding balance by giving appropriate attention to every area of your life lifts the burden. It eliminates the persistent tension you feel when an area is lacking.

Now, imagine the sense of freedom you will feel when no area of your life is tugging and nagging at you due to lack of attention and unsatisfied need. When you can smoothly transition your attention from one area of your life to another and another, a flow is created with your God-given gifts being used to their greatest extent.

You have more energy because you won't be drained and exhausted by one thing. And you'll actually be better at everything you do. Creating and achieving wholeness is the only true path to fulfillment.

Ideal Life Time Usage

Now view your life as the ideal life it can be. Write down the ways you can better use your God-given gifts and talents toward fulfillment of the Daily Life Balance areas of your life:

- Physical health/wellness (exercise, nutrition, sleep)
- Maintenance for survival (job to create income for existence)
- Seeds planted for the future (expanding knowledge, further developing existing skills, and developing a future business idea)
- Meditation/prayer (motivational, inner peace and clarity)
- Relaxation/social interaction (enjoying the present)

God has given you specific talents (passions) for a reason. If you don't use them to be all that you can be, you are disappointing yourself, as well as God.

UTILIZING YOUR TALENTS FOR A HIGHER PURPOSE

The goal of following *A Second Life's* belief system is to achieve balance between materiality and spirituality in order to gain full control of your life. This is done by living each day as though it's the last day of your life, but also as though life will last forever.

There's nothing wrong with wanting to use your talents to earn a lot of money and feel financially secure. But the opportunities to do so are given to you by God, and your obligation is to use *all* of your riches—whether they are money, knowledge, skills, or your beliefs—to contribute to making the world a better place.

You are never alone on your journey to fulfillment. Of course God is always behind you 100 percent, but you can also learn a lesson from the people who have assisted you along the way. Perhaps it was a teacher or a minister—as in my life—or maybe a friend, loved one, or even a stranger who believed in you and encouraged you when you were unsure of yourself or had lost your way. Think of those people. What do you remember most about them? Do you recall how much money they had or their material possessions? Or are you grateful for the way they made you feel, the boost they gave you when you needed it? As you honor the gifts of assistance you have been given by others, consider how you would want someone else to remember you.

Think for a few moments about how your talents show up as being for a higher purpose—or not—in the five key areas of your life: job/career, financial, physical health/wellness, relationships (with yourself and others), spirituality. Answer these questions:

- How do you conduct your business?
- What is the true value of financial success?
- What kind of message does your physical health and well-being send to others?
- Do your relationships reflect the love you feel for yourself and God?
- In what ways do you acknowledge that without God you would not exist, that the world and everything in it would not exist?

Now, reflect on how your talents could better be used for a higher purpose in each of the five key areas of your life. Do you see the opportunities in everything you do?

- Job/career
- Financial
- Physical health/wellness
- Relationships (with yourself and others)
- Spirituality

ALWAYS REMEMBER: *You and your life make no sense without a higher purpose.*

One of the most inspirational stories I've heard is the life of Abraham Lincoln, the sixteenth president of the United States. Not only was he able to overcome many roadblocks he encountered during his life, he also committed his existence to serve the greater good—and changed history during his presidency.

Abraham Lincoln was born on February 12, 1809, in rural Kentucky. He received little formal education as a child—briefly attending a one-room school in Kentucky when he was five and again at six, and after his family moved to the backwoods of Indiana he attended school for a short time when he was ten and again at twelve. By age fifteen he went to school during the fall and winter, but worked in the fields of his neighbors' farms the rest of the year to help support his family. He also borrowed books to read whenever he could do so.

Even though Abe didn't have traditional schooling, life presented him with many lessons to be learned from his experiences, and many challenges to be overcome. At the age of seven he shot his first wild turkey, but suffered such great remorse that he never hunted game again. When he was eight he was kicked in the head by a horse and nearly died. Later that year his mother died. When his father soon remarried, young Abe was blessed to get a stepmother he developed a close relationship with and three step-siblings. But not long afterward his married sister Sarah died during childbirth.

When Abe was nineteen he and a friend decided to earn money by taking a flatboat of farm produce cargo down the river from Indiana to New Orleans. During the trip they were attacked by seven black men, but then—as though God was showing him the other side of the story—while he was in New Orleans Abe witnessed a slave auction for the first time. From this time forward Abraham Lincoln's life illustrates his willingness to make the most of what life offered him, his dedication to hard work, his perseverance, his desire to make a difference in the world and make his country a better, fairer place for all of its citizens.

His family moved again when he was twenty-one, this time making an arduous 200-mile journey to live on uncleared land along the Sangamon River near Decatur, Illinois. It was there that Abe made his first political speech—in favor of improving navigation on the river. The next year he made another flatboat trip carrying cargo to New Orleans. His father moved again, but instead of going with him Abe settled in New Salem, Illinois, where he worked as a clerk in a nearby village store and was allowed to sleep in the back room. During this time Abe taught himself basic math, read Shakespeare and Robert Burns, and participated in a local debating society.

He first ran for political office at age twenty-three, as a candidate for the Illinois General Assembly, but he lost the election. Further disappointment arose when the store he worked in went out of business. Undeterred, Abe and a business partner, William Berry, purchased another store, but it failed as well, leaving Abe badly in debt. That is when his public service career began. He was appointed postmaster of New Salem and deputy county surveyor later that year. The next year he ran for the Illinois General Assembly again; this time he won. He also began studying law. As it seemed to always happen in Lincoln's life, after a time of good fortune came challenges. His former business partner in the store died, increasing Lincoln's debt, and then the young woman he was engaged to marry died.

Lincoln's life took a positive turn as his stature in the Illinois General Assembly grew. He was reelected and became a party leader, and he also received his law license. Although he began courting a woman named Mary Owens, in late 1836 he suffered an episode of severe depression. In 1837 his leadership contributed to the Illinois state capital moving from Vandalia to Springfield. Abe moved there and became a partner in a law firm. He proposed to Mary Owens, but she turned him down and their courtship ended.

As his law practice flourished during the next couple of years—and he was also re-elected to the Illinois Assembly—he traveled through central and eastern Illinois practicing law. During this time he met Mary Todd at a dance. They became engaged, but he broke up with her the next year and suffered another period of depression. Continuing to work, he formed a new law partnership. During a summer trip by steamboat to Kentucky he saw twelve slaves chained together.

Not seeking reelection to the Assembly in 1842, he continued with his law practice, resumed his courtship with Mary Todd, and they married. Their first child was born a year later. Abe ran for a U.S. congressional seat and lost. He dissolved his law partnership, set up practice alone, and campaigned for Henry Clay in the presidential election. By 1847 Abe and Mary had another son, Abe was elected to the U.S. House of Representatives, and they had moved to Washington, D.C., where he made a name for himself as a vocal and active participant in government and politics.

Again leaving politics in 1849, he returned to Springfield to practice law and was granted a patent for a flotation device that would assist a boat's passage through shallow water—to this day he is the only U.S. President ever granted a patent. Unfortunately, in 1850 one of his sons died, even as his flourishing law practice in fourteen counties of Illinois gained him the reputation of being "Honest Abe." During the next six years a third son was born to Abe and Mary, but a month later Abe's father died. The couple was blessed with another son, Abe reentered politics, helped to organize a new Republican party in Illinois, and was nominated by that party to be their vice presidential candidate, which gained him national attention. Although his party did not win that national election, Abe's political activities and impressive legal casework increased his reputation and public popularity. By 1860 he was engaged in high-profile political debates and gave an impassioned speech on slavery in New Haven, Connecticut, in which he said, "This nation cannot exist with half of its men free and half enslaved ..." He was subsequently nominated to be his party's presidential candidate and went on to win that election, becoming the sixteenth president of the United States.

Abraham Lincoln's presidency would be a pivotal time in the history of the United States. Not long after he was sworn into office, the Civil War began; it would a bloody and long war, continuing for most of his term in office, but would end with many of the injustices that he saw existing in his country being righted, particularly the abolishment of slavery in the United States.

Lincoln's legacy shows that with dreams, actions, and persistence anything is possible in this lifetime. What he had was a strong faith in God, dedication to serving a higher purpose, and a strong work ethic, all qualities that enabled him to learn from his life challenges, overcome them, and evolve as a person. Despite everything he accomplished in life, he didn't take himself too seriously, but had a strong sense of self-irony. It was not uncommon all of his life for people to make fun of his lanky build and stature—he was 6'4" tall, which was a rare height in those days—and his facial features were hardly considered handsome. Rather than be offended and become defensive when disparaging comments were made about his looks, he often replied, "If I had another face, don't you think I'd be wearing it?"

Abraham Lincoln is an example of a person who lived his life with purpose and being One with God, thereby not allowing *anything* to prevent him from succeeding in the game of life.

I know God will not give me anything I can't handle.
I just wish He didn't trust me so much.

Mother Teresa

Level 4
Activation to Oneness: Re-programming Yourself by Your Daily Actions

As you re-established your connection with your true self and God, opening the door to your new life, you must take an important step: Walk through that door to activate yourself in a life of Oneness. Begin the magnificent journey toward inner peace, purpose, prosperity, and fulfillment in service to others by re-programming yourself by your actions every day.

Figure 3: Activation to Oneness

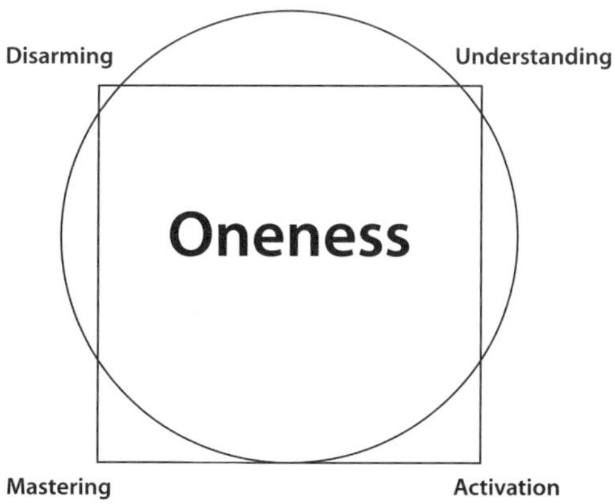

Disarming the false belief systems running you

Understanding the true you and your life's purpose

Mastering the five life pillars required to survive and grow in the game of life

Activation to Oneness by erasing your old life and being re-programmed to the true you

BE ALL YOU CAN BE—BUT NOT ALL AT ONCE

Everyone wants to believe that change happens overnight, like the sun shining after a storm. But even as you begin a bright new day, keep in mind the greater goal: creating and living a brilliant new life. Planning is required to map your magnificent journey. Fortitude and persistence are needed to stay the course. Progress will then be made step-by-step.

Past negative, self-defeating patterns in your thoughts, reactions, and actions, as well as feelings of fear and disappointment, may still surface and try to hold you back. Learn to recognize them as the invaders that they are. They are part of your robotic programming, viruses that have limited your potential to be all that you can be. Decide right now that they will no longer have any power over you. Instead, consciously choose to live the unlimited potential of your true self that is your gift from God.

Tracking Yourself

Each day make a mental or written note of problems or difficulties that appear in your life because of your automatic behavior. Doing so will train your mind to recognize the pitfalls that have prevented you from traveling on a smooth road and the roadblocks that have prevented your success. See those roadblocks as opportunities to learn. As you become more and more alert each day, you will quickly understand that there really is no need to make a fuss or overreact, that if you wait a few minutes or even a few hours a problem usually fades away. Use the tools you have learned to connect with your subconscious mind—meditation, prayer, and self-programming—to center your thoughts on your calm, self-directed true self. Soon you will see that anything that seems urgent and troubling will turn out to be a blessing in disguise. You will know that God is always with you, keeping you safe.

Also make mental or written notes each day of your successes, whether they are small or huge. Each success activates the next new step, reinforcing the changes you are making. Before long your daily lists of successes will be far greater than your difficulties, confirming that your own re-programming of your true self has gained a foothold. Your life is being transformed more and more each day.

CORRECT KNOWLEDGE + ACTION + DISCIPLINE = POWER AND ENLIGHTENMENT

Simply reading this life manual is not enough. You must also put your energy into integrating the principles explained and work hard to follow through on what you're learning. Otherwise this knowledge is useless to you. There are not shortcuts to success—none! You must commit to it, put in the hours, work for it, and stick with it.

Learning, accepting, and acting on the correct information conveyed in this life manual will result in your living a life with unlimited potential, free of struggle, disillusionment, and disappointment. Your rewards will be the personal strength and knowledge to master life and be in control. But this is only valid if the information you are learning is integrated through your actions, hard work, and perseverance.

Most tasks in life, no matter what they are, need an intensive commitment. If you possess information that will help you advance in life, you must integrate that knowledge with determination and discipline. By never giving up and always, no matter what, always sticking to the correct life knowledge in this guide, the reward is unlimited personal power and enlightenment through oneness with God. By embarking on *A Second Life's* belief system with action and discipline, you will gradually evolve, becoming a person who gets to use all of the resources God has provided specifically for you. This puts you on the path to inner happiness and a life lived with no regrets. You will live a new existence free of the mental slavery that has held you back and kept you down. You will be free of society's false belief systems. But you must never waver in your actions, dedication, and discipline to your new way of life; otherwise you will slide back to your old life that kept you down. Once you connect with your true self in *A Second Life* you need to always know inside that you shall never surrender. And why would you? Now you are free. Now you are a role model and inspiration for others who will follow your path.

NURTURING ENVIRONMENT = GROWTH

A positive, life plan focused environment is important to reinforce the steps you take to create your new life and keep you on track as you continue to perfect it.

What kind of environment do you exist within? How do you influence it? How does it influence you? Does it reinforce and support the magnificent changes you are working so hard to enact and maintain or does it keep you stuck in the old programming that has limited your life and potential? The effects our interactions with other people in our environments have on our lives were recently proven during a scientific study.

Scientists from Harvard University and the University of California San Diego reported in a British medical journal article published in December of 2008 that happiness is contagious! (These are the same researchers whose previous study found that obesity spreads like a virus within networks of people, as does smoking.) The long term study, which included a social network of 12,067 volunteers who were linked to each other through 53,228 ties, has shown that the more happy people you know, the more likely you are to be happy as well. Look around at your social network, your family members, friends, and neighbors. What do you see? What kind of influence do they have on you? And what kind of influence do you have on them?

Your emotional state of mind affects everything you do. It can be seen in the ways you live your daily life, the actions you take, in the choices you make. Now that it has been proven scientifically that it also affects everyone around you, you have an even greater responsibility to be a positive force in life, not drag it down. In order to do so you must not only continue to develop your own true self and work to be the best you can be, you must also recognize when negative influences of people around you are infiltrating, poisoning, or undermining your hard work to achieve an elevated and enlightened new life. When you are a strong, powerful bright force of good, living a life of purpose in alignment with God, you are also having a positive influence on other people.

By being conscious of your actions, your motivations and your God-given purpose every day, in small ways and on a large scale, you reinforce your intentions to continue on your path living *A Second Life.* In this way you create a nurturing environment around you at all times that supports your growth, and in the process your good intentions spread to others. By taking good care of yourself, you also take good care of others.

THERE IS NO LIFE WITHOUT HUMOR

Although dedication to your new life goals is serious business, no human being is perfect. Everyone stumbles and bumbles along the way, but there's no need to be embarrassed or feel defeated. Keep everything in perspective. After all, life isn't brain surgery—unless, of course, you actually are a brain surgeon—and no one, including yourself, is going to die if you make a mistake. Learn to laugh at yourself. Lighten up! As you embark on this journey that is your new life you may sometimes look like a toddler rushing forward on unsteady legs. Delight in the joy of finding your footing; smile with pride when successfully navigating an obstacle. And when you stumble, laugh out loud, then pick yourself up and start out again.

Laughter is God's medicine. It shakes up your body, releasing pent-up stress, fear, and anger. It creates feel-good chemicals in your brain. It heals your wounds and feeds your soul. Generously share God's medicine with others. By bringing a smile or a laugh to others you will make the world a happier, more positive place for everyone you encounter, as well as yourself.

> *Happiness is when what you think, what you say,*
> *and what you do are in harmony.*
>
> Mohandas Gandhi

ACTING AS IF IT HAS HAPPENED = SUCCESS

You are what you believe you are. Even though there may be moments of doubt, live with certainty. Your positive purpose-aligned thoughts, actions, and reactions reinforce the changes you are living. Always behave as though you have achieved the success you are seeking. Live now as though you have achieved all of your goals. Live with a clear understanding that although living *A Second Life* is not about the illusion of success by acquiring material goods, there's nothing wrong with enjoying and appreciating the material rewards of your hard work. If you can afford to buy the "things" that bring beauty and pleasure into your new life, do so with delight. Keeping your appearance at a top level and living in a clean, comfortable home that is a reflection of the benefits of living with purpose *can* reinforce the hard work you do to maintain your new life. Also, paradoxically, by society's standards your material success is a living example that may inspire others to join you on your journey to make the world a better place. And certainly, acquiring financial security enables you to donate money and, just as importantly, spend time helping others. But keep a strong, purposeful perspective. Always maintain the balance between materiality and spirituality that is the true measure of success.

Shift your consciousness. You are a living, breathing, powerful, enlightened, purposeful person who recognizes the gifts given to you by God, gratefully accepts those gifts, and shares them with others. Every moment of every day live in that place. Exterior events have no affect on your truth, your intentions, or your motivation to be all that you can be. Negativity is of no consequence to you. It cannot affect you. You are confident enough in yourself and your beliefs to be flexible, embracing the unexpected and finding the benefits within it. You live from yourself, not in reaction to society.

ALWAYS REMEMBER: *Unlimited potential = Believing that it has already happened.*

2

The Five Key Knowledge Areas of Life to Be Mastered

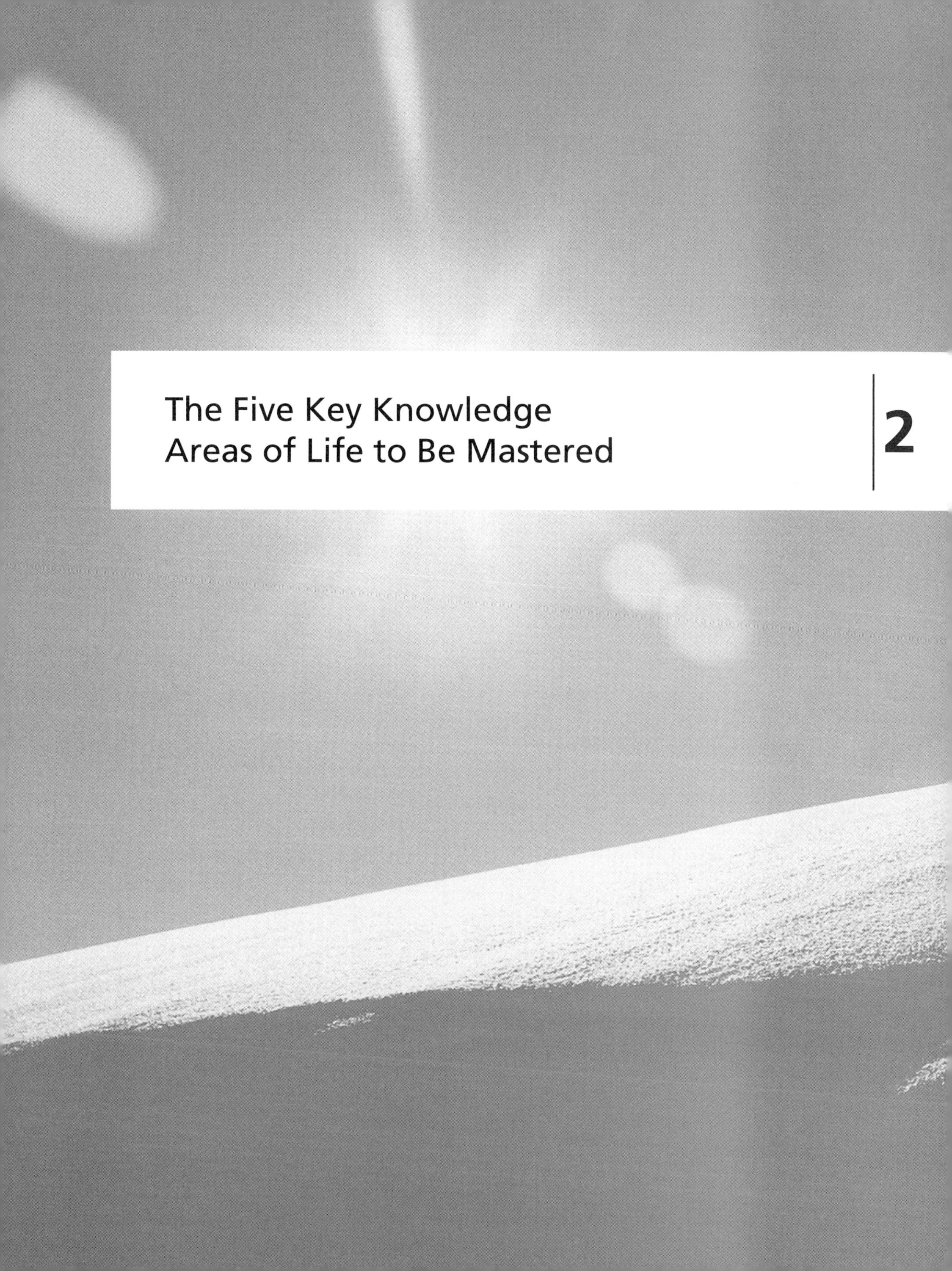

The Five Key Knowledge Areas of Life to Be Mastered

Achieving balance in the key five areas of life isn't always easy, particularly when we have been indoctrinated to believe that the dictates of society's rules are more important than honoring our God-given gifts.

Certainly the ups and downs of life present us with challenges. But many of our challenges are a result of the wrong thinking indoctrination we have been programmed to believe. We believe happiness is just around the corner if only we do this thing or that thing, that happiness will be found and the respect of others gained by achieving society's goals, that earning enough money will automatically eliminate all of our other problems. We have been programmed to believe that any sacrifices of our physical health, relationships, and spiritual well-being made while we seek career success are worth it. But most people are disappointed to realize after securing their respectable dream job that it does not result in the happiness they worked so hard to achieve. They realize that they were chasing goals that actually prevented them from living in the NOW—which is all there is.

The ideal is that each of us is a sum total of *all* that God has given:

- Our **job/career** provides us the **financial** resources to support ourselves and loved ones materially while giving back to society.
- Our **physical health** is the vehicle that houses the soul and carries us through our everyday endeavors.
- Our **relationships** with ourselves and others are a reflection of our values, principles, and beliefs.
- Our **spirituality** provides the consciousness of living in Oneness by being of service to others in our everyday lives while fulfilling our own life purpose using our God-given gifts.

Mastering each of these five key areas of life in ways that enable you to live a balanced life in alignment with all of your God-given gifts is necessary in order to successfully live *A Second Life* being the best that you can be.

Although it *is* possible to improve all areas of your life at once, often it is most effective to give more focused attention to one area at a time—while still being attentive to the other four. Which area of your life do you give the most attention to improving first? In the table below, circle a number for each area of your life, indicating how you rate it today on a scale of 1 to 10—with one = needs immediate attention and 10 = the best it can be.

Five Key Areas of Life Status Evaluation (10 = the best it can be)

Job/Career	1	2	3	4	5	6	7	8	9	10
Financial	1	2	3	4	5	6	7	8	9	10
Physical Health/Wellness	1	2	3	4	5	6	7	8	9	10
Relationships (with yourself and others)	1	2	3	4	5	6	7	8	9	10
Spirituality	1	2	3	4	5	6	7	8	9	10

1 Job/Career

You have job/career difficulties because you've been indoctrinated and brainwashed by society. This chapter will show you how to break free from the chains of society's mental slavery so you can regain control of your job/career situation.

Job/Career Contents

Introduction

Society's Rule: What you do for a living defines who you are.

The Truth: Society's rule is unfortunately true for most people living in the western world in the twenty-first century. But such a mentality—defining what are respectable occupations—corrupts our society by placing people in a box where they are judged by external circumstances. This belief system creates an illusion that respectability is tied to what you do, rather than what you stand for and who you are as a person. Not only is this way of thinking an insult to God—a denial of the individual precious gifts and talents God has given each and every human being—it's a recipe for disillusionment and defeat. After all, how can you live a fully realized life based on your God-given gifts and talents if you accept the idea that society's opinion of the work you do is more important than the true desires and passions burning within you?

Has conducting your life based on society's expectations resulted in your happiness or feeling of success? Do you look forward to going to work each day and approach each task with enthusiasm? If not, you are not alone. Far too many people are working for the buck or down on their luck out of work entirely, because they are not able to find the courage to do what they really want to be doing.

Any disappointment or disillusionment you feel about your current job/career situation is not necessarily the result of lack of trying or desire, but more likely because you are striving to live up to the standards of society. Society's standards encourage us to judge the value of people's jobs/careers by the amount of money they earn or their status/title, instead of whether it feeds their souls and enables them to serve others through their talents.

Now is the time to change all of that. By doing the work necessary to erase your indoctrinated programming and activate a new way of thinking, you will feel grateful for your *true* talents and gifts and find new ways to apply them in your job/career. When we no longer cling to society's rules we become more tolerant and respectful of one another and live in the present moments of NOW, enjoying each day for exactly what it is. Then everyone is free to pursue their own individual happiness, knowing that they are able to be the best that they can be *because* they are using their God-given gifts and talents for a higher purpose.

How can you set yourself free and embark on your true path? Break away from the indoctrination and brainwashing of society's rules. Begin today by changing your way of thinking. Take the first steps on the journey that is your new, self-fulfilled life in alignment with God. Follow this step-by-step approach to decide on a plan for your new job/career and set out on your new fulfilling life.

TEN STEP ACTION PLAN FOR MASTERING YOUR JOB/CAREER

As you follow each of these steps, do so with the understanding that getting a job, keeping the job you have, or improving your career situation must be approached with dedication, perseverance, and determination. This is not just about getting a paycheck; it's about developing this part of your life in alignment with your God-given talents. It's about making God proud by being the best you can be. Only then will you approach the work you do with passion and enthusiasm and be able to keep it in balance with the other four key areas of your new life.

Step One: Assess your current job/career situation

While assessing your job/career situation you must be completely honest with yourself; otherwise you're wasting your time and won't get positive results. Answer these questions:

- Do you have a job?
- Do you want to be more successful in the job you currently have?
- Did you lose your job?
- Do you fear losing your job?
- Why are things not working out both now and in the past? ("I don't know" is not an acceptable answer! If *you* can't figure it out, who will?)

Step Two: Assess yourself as an employee/potential employee

Would you hire or promote yourself? Why/why not?

Look at yourself from the perspective of an employer who may consider hiring you, or your current employer who may promote you, when so many other people are competing in a tough job market.

The first question you should ask yourself is if you would hire or promote yourself, and why/why not. This test will help you determine where you stand today, and also give you important information about what you need to change about yourself. Bottom line: if you would not hire or promote yourself, why should someone else do it? Answer these questions as objectively as possible:

1) Are you a person who radiates positive energy that people want to be around due to your 24/7 upbeat attitude/personality?
2) Are you a high energy, hard worker who always wants to exceed expectations by doing your very best no matter what your assignment?
3) Are you a person who always takes the initiative, rather than having to be asked to do things?
4) Are you independent and self-driven, meaning once you get going you don't need much input from your superior?
5) Are you always looking out for your boss or company's best interests rather than your own?
6) Outside of official work hours do you find ways to learn more in order to excel at your work, such as by reading, taking higher education classes, and seminars, etc.?
7) Are you always dressed and groomed professionally so that if clients dropped by you would be a good role model for the company?
8) Are you always loyal and dependable to your company?

If you answered "yes" to all of the questions above, you should not hesitate to hire yourself. On the other hand, if you answered "no" to any of the questions, you need to examine yourself further and change your thinking and behavior as soon as possible. The truth is, during over 3,000 recruitments I have conducted as a headhunter, not once has a client said, "Find me a lazy, rude, dishonest, repulsive, unstable job candidate with no drive and initiative." If someone wants to strongly stand out in the job market they better answer yes to all of the eight questions above. By being all that you can be you will always be needed and wanted in the job market.

What are your unique skill sets and talents?

When you are looking for a job, first of all it's important for you to be "hire-able." Before you can honestly tell a potential employer that you're the best person for the job they're seeking to fill—or convey such confidence during a job interview—you must know the skills and talents you would bring to the job. If you want to be more successful in your current job, you must understand how your unique skill sets and talents could be put to better use.

Make a list of all of your skills and talents, including everything you have learned to do through your education, training, or work experience, as well as things you naturally do well. How could those talents be used in a job or career?

What can you do to improve your chances or opportunities?

To spark the interest of any company/business, you need a written one-page presentation of yourself (your bio/résumé) that shows you are a good bet. The past usually sets the standard for the future. Still, it's never too late to change if you're not happy with your life and what you've accomplished up to this point. I believe we all have it in us to greatly improve and radically change our lives at any point we choose. This being said, the way the corporate world works is that when you apply for a job your bio, which is your life story, sets a prediction for the future and how well, or not well, you will do in a new job. Being a great talker isn't enough if your talk does not match your bio. In fact, it's easy for a professional who might be interviewing you to quickly perceive "fluff," meaning lots of smoke and no action.

Your bio/résumé: A bio/résumé usually doesn't lie and it seldom undersells—it's intended to do the opposite. It needs to be short and precise, with everything summarized on one page. It should nail in chronological order in bullet-point format each job you have had, including this information:

- the name of the company
- your job position or title
- the time period you worked there
- a short description of the company (size, products/services, etc.)
- your key work tasks
- the name of your supervisor

A separate section should include your education, where you went to school, dates you attended, GPAs, and degrees earned.

If your bio/résumé does not at least get you an interview, then you're on thin ice and either need to take out what could be viewed as negatives or consider adding side projects that are relevant to the type of job you are seeking. Red flags on a bio/résumé are gaps between jobs or attending school—which show lack of incentive or laziness—

and too many jobs in a short time period—which show instability—and no progression of accomplishments in your work history. Positive additions to a bio/résumé include side interests that make you seem vibrant and can easily trigger conversations between standard questions during a job interview, creating a more personal interaction. But don't overdo. Too many outside interests can imply that they are more important than your job, which is a strong negative.

A strong bio/résumé sums up your life and how it has been used so far. I always like to ask people if they are happy with their accomplishments. If they are it means he/she is living according to a set plan versus someone who lives on chance with no direction. Your bio/résumé should also reflect anything unique about you that required sacrifice, such as night or weekend classes or schooling or independent projects that advanced your skill set in your chosen career field. Better still is when a person's outside activities and background show that they devote time to helping others without getting paid. But again, do not overdo. These extra activities strongly help you stand out, but only if they do not give the impression they will take away from or interfere with your job by putting a burden on your time or energy. The main objective when hiring someone to do a job is that he/she can and will do the best possible job and make the greatest possible impact on the company. Very few companies tolerate employees who neglect their duties for whatever reasons, even by doing goodwill extracurricular activities.

Your bio/résumé may need to be tweaked to specifically reflect the skills, experiences, and knowledge you have that make you ideally suited for a particular job you are seeking. But don't allow yourself to be caught up in endlessly rewriting your bio/résumé. That type of procrastination is often the result of fear of rejection. Don't allow it into your consciousness. Just forge ahead with your best efforts. A little extra time tailoring your bio/résumé could make the difference by getting you an interview.

Also, never forget that your bio/résumé is just part of your presentation. Your interview is another part (which will be discussed shortly). When someone expresses an interest in hiring you, they will check your references from previous employers. Never list your references on your bio/résumé, but instead use a notation saying references will be provided upon request. You don't want your references to receive too many phone calls from people inquiring about you, or else they may become weary of responding and their glowing recommendations could become less enthusiastic.

Perhaps you now understand that everything you have done in your life, every choice you have made, will contribute to the opportunities and choices made available to you in the future. If you feel you have already fallen short, don't be discouraged—no one is perfect. Although you can't change the past, you can begin today to live with integrity in alignment with your God-given gifts, building a future with unlimited potential for happiness and fulfillment.

Step Three: Decide your job/career future in specific terms

Create a future bio/résumé for the following time frames: twelve months from now, three years from now, and five years from now.

When you want something in life, it's important to set a clear goal in order to achieve it. First, set a realistic target, but allow yourself to dream. Set a high goal that requires you to really stretch in order to reach it—this could mean you need to acquire a certain skill set or knowledge. Then ask yourself *why* you want to reach this goal? Is it because you want to test yourself to see how far you can go? Or is it because you feel that the new knowledge or position will give you a certain feeling of accomplishment? Maybe it's because you feel you can better serve a higher purpose by being able to help more people with your gifts or help them in a better way. The reasons can be many, but it's important that you know *why*, because your reasons are the key to your passions (motivation).

Second, in order to stay motivated you need to set milestones: small goals with steps to take in order to reach each one of them. My own personal experience is that I would not have reached any of my goals in life if I had not set a clear path to follow. Everything I have achieved in my life—and has been achieved in the lives of the candidates I have recruited—resulted from planning and hard work. Little in life falls into someone's lap unexpectedly. Life planning and time management are needed for each of the five key areas of life, including job/career. Planning does not mean you stop living for today and start believing that everything in the future will be so much greater. The only reason to make plans is to ensure that you get the most of this life. Remember to shoot for the stars, but never forego the principles of life balance, which are required in order to live *A Second Life*.

Step Four: Decide on a job/career action plan and timelines according to your future bio/résumé

Once you have set clear goals for your job/career you need to decide on an effective plan of action to achieve what you want. Use the tools you have learned in Coding to Oneness, Level 1, of this guide—meditation, prayer, and self-programming—to assist you in setting your goals.

- Will you stay in your current job?
- If you have no job:
  a) Are you willing to accept a temporary job while you pursue your dream job or work toward getting it?
  b) Do you plan to wait it out until you get the "right job"? If so:
    - Decide on a timeline. How long will it take to achieve your goal?
    - Define your approach. How will you get the job you want? How much time are you willing to allocate for your job search?

Many people believe it's better to spend an extensive period of time looking for a job where they can utilize their talents and get on a career track, rather than accepting a temporary mediocre job that may not advance their career or a job that would be considered a "second grade job" according to society's standards. This is a belief system based on ego and indoctrination that limits job opportunities and growth. When you really need a job, this type of thinking will defeat you. If jobs in your chosen field are scarce, it's far better for your state of mind, as well as your financial situation, to find the best job you can for the time being and do the best work you can at that job—until you can get back on your career track.

Step Five: Decide how important a job/career is to you

Evaluate what is important in regard to job/career versus other activities in your life by listing them in order of importance. Then ask yourself how much you are willing to sacrifice in order to get where you want to go in your job/career. And ask yourself why.

Years ago when there was no welfare, as there is today, or money from parents coming your way—with which you could "buy time"—getting a job as opposed to having a career was more geared toward the following order: 1) Survival—any job that could pay your bills would do. 2) A career—a job where you could utilize your talents and fully grow was a luxury.

Survival mode is no longer predominant in the current belief system. Today people are programmed to a great extent to believe that everything will work itself out, that finding "the right job" is better than accepting a job defined by society as "degrading." This, again, makes people feel like they are judged by what they do for a living instead of who they are. Maslow's Hierarchy of Needs was a key driving force in the past. And today, despite society's standards, Maslow's principle—that clearly indicate our first need in life is survival—still holds true. Then comes personal growth and fulfillment.

Those who don't work don't deserve food

If someone is healthy with a working mind there is no reason whatsoever that they cannot be an active contributor to our society. If someone is able to make a contribution, they should do so in some capacity. If their situation does not allow for a career track job, then a temporary job will have to do. If it's difficult to obtain a temporary job, then some sort of project can be embarked upon. This could be anything ranging from helping people in the community to an internship to obtain more knowledge and experience that would enable them to have a better chance in the job market. The key is to be active in one way or another.

Work builds character

There was a time when teens and young adults had to work for things while growing up. They had duties and responsibilities at home and got jobs during their time off from school in the summer. As a result, they learned discipline, developed character, and understood survival mode. Now, unfortunately, there is a completely different mindset.

Recruiters and employers always look at what people have done in the past as an indication of their futures because they know that character development does not happen over night, but comes with experience and molding. They look for a person who knows what work means because such people are usually more disciplined—a trait they developed by working for things in life rather than getting handouts. Discipline is an extremely important attribute to have in order to succeed in the workforce. Nobody wants to hire a person who does not have the discipline to arrive at work on time in the morning and stay until the job is done.

The hiring process is always about reducing risks—meaning a company would rather hire someone who has a steady job history with good references, rather than someone who has been "hanging out," or frequently changing jobs. Future employers do not like to hear too many explanations of "why this and that" did not work out in the past.

Step Six: Determine how you can contribute to making the world a better place by using your God-given gifts/talents in the workplace

In his inaugural address in 1961, President John F. Kennedy implored citizens of the United States: "Ask not what your country can do for you, but what you can do for your country." This motivation can easily be transferred to the corporate world—and all of life, in fact. We have been indoctrinated to wait for a clear sign about what benefits we will receive from our employer before doing something that is outside of our job description. The mentality is often: How will you reward me if I do such and such? The opposite way of thinking is to first think about what you can do for your company. Every employer likes this attitude because it clearly shows a team spirit; that you are not a person driven purely by the ego, but by something greater than yourself.

This approach and attitude, of course, needs to leave room and time for you to still have a balance between work and off time (time to recharge). But in order to grow and advance in your career, you need to put something in before you'll get something back. It's not possible to have it both ways. Your goal is not to feed your ego by always questioning what the company, your colleagues or others can do for you. True fulfillment comes by finding ways you can be of service to others.

Make God proud—Be all that you can be

By doing so you not only make yourself proud, but also please God. Each of us has been given the greatest gift of all—life. We need to treasure life by giving it our all.

God didn't say: I'm giving you all the potential in the world. Now go use it for your own personal gain and to feed your ego. Forget about everyone else. Don't even think about the other guy. Just get the most you can for yourself.

> *Life's most urgent question is: What are you doing for others?*
>
> Martin Luther King, Jr.

Each of us has been provided with unique gifts and talents that are endlessly beyond anything we can grasp—resources we need to tap into and develop as much as possible. By doing so you will be able to find ways to give back to others and serve a higher purpose with your talents, which is the true meaning of life.

The reality is that many people feel just "keeping it together" sometimes seems like a huge challenge. They barely have enough time or energy to get through the daily duties required just to maintain their existence. Clearly, how we use our time makes all the difference. When it comes to our jobs or careers there will always be choices to make about how we use our passions or invest our time. These choices are based on how we view our jobs/careers in perspective to our entire lives. Is your job/career a part of *all* that your life should be? Or does it define *everything* that you are?

No matter what job/career situation you are in, always make God proud. Do your very best and, most especially, be grateful that you are healthy, able to work, and that you have a job at all. By being grateful you show respect to the greatest gift of all—

life—knowing deep inside that you are doing your best to be all that you can be in life. As a recruiter I never pay much attention to what people do for a living, but rather how much effort and commitment they put into their work and themselves, which is demonstrated by how they carry themselves. Respect comes through these things, not by what you do. People who possess these positive traits are the ones who make me feel good when I meet them; they enlighten my day. As a recruiter these are also the people that I am always looking to recruit, because I know they have what it takes to truly succeed in life. These are the people who, no matter where you find them currently, will succeed because nothing can stop them when they are living according to how God wants them to live.

> *If a man is called a street sweeper, he should sweep streets as Michelangelo painted,*
> *or Beethoven composed music, or Shakespeare wrote poetry.*
> *He should sweep streets so well that all the hosts of heaven and earth will pause to say,*
> *Here lived a great street sweeper who did his job well.*
>
> Martin Luther King, Jr.

Step Seven: Learn the realities of the corporate world

How does the corporate world work and operate in regard to the mentality, procedures, and what it takes to succeed and excel? What's the difference between a "rising star" and a "warm body filling a chair"?

Knowledge is power. In many occupations, what you know, as well as what you are continually learning, will to a great extent determine your worth. A person who has acquired the right knowledge and skill set stands out and competes on a different level than others in the job market. Securing or keeping your job/career isn't enough. You must always continue to learn in order to grow that aspect of your life, which contributes to your being a fully realized whole person.

Many people say they don't have the time after work hours of their primary job to study on their own, attend school, or commit to a part-time job to expand their base of knowledge or skills. The truth is, most people do have the time, but they've decided to spend it on non-productive activities, such as watching television. Life is about priorities and how you use your minutes on earth. You can invest them by learning, growing, and evolving or you can choose to waste them. A recent survey showed that an average American has watched fifteen years of television by the time they reach the age of sixty—which is fifteen years wasted! Looking back on your life from the vantage point of your twilight years, what activities enriched your life more?

Educate yourself. Instead of watching television or wasting your valuable minutes in other non-constructive ways, take advantage of them by reading about your chosen career, attending classes, networking with others in your field, or brainstorming with other smart people or with yourself while taking a walk or getting some healthy outdoor exercise. Your opportunities to learn and grow are as limitless as your potential.

Learning and growing = utilizing our God-given gifts to the fullest—which is why he blessed us with our mind and body. By wasting time we are disgracing God's gifts. Our duty is to live a balanced, whole life by being all that we can be, which we do by constantly learning throughout life in order that we never stop growing and discovering our full potential.

Reality check: The company needs you only as long as you are making money for them. They are not your friends

Although you most certainly will develop friendships, and perhaps strong personal ties with your coworkers, always remember that we live in a capitalistic world where profit needs to be generated in order for a company to survive and evolve. When this is not accomplished there will be no security for you in your job.

The reason someone has hired you for a job is because you are the machinery for creating profit and sustaining it. You are needed only as long as this is taking place. Unless you can create an added value, you are a liability—which means you are at risk of losing your job because you are not needed. So always remember that the only reason you were hired and remain on the job is because directly or indirectly you can create profit. The more you are able to the create and contribute to the profits of the company by being a high performer and role model, the more likely you are to have job security.

Despite the fact that the company—your employer—is not your family or your friend, that doesn't mean that you should be lax in making a contribution to creating a pleasant environment; but it does means to never be blind to the truth, no matter how cozy it seems around you. If you don't perform or your company is doing poorly, you will be eliminated. Even if your superiors like you, remember that they have bosses they are accountable to, who has a boss, etc., etc., etc. Every employee is just a replaceable element in a greater system, which has dominance over everything else in order to survive and thrive. It's not personal. This is the market mechanism that determines who and what has the right to exist through natural growth and sustainability, and who and what does not.

Keeping this in mind, never forget that you don't owe anything to anyone. If you leave for a better job somewhere else, you will be replaced by someone who can do the job at least as well as you can, perhaps even better; otherwise the company will not survive and/or thrive. But if you are given an opportunity to grow and evolve to the next level in the company/corporation where you're currently employed, take advantage of the opportunity with God's blessing.

Don't be naïve—Your job insurance policy

Wherever you're working, always know that your purpose is to serve a function for a company/corporation that needs to make a profit. It's Economics 101. Their benefits (profits) for having you there must exceed what it costs them to keep you—although in some job situations it's more difficult to calculate your personal cost/benefits ratio because you function as part of team and your contribution can't be separated from the team as a whole.

When things are pointing upward in the economy and your employer's business is doing well, you'll have a job as long as your supervisor and coworkers are happy with you and your performance. But when things turn downward in the economy or people around you are not satisfied with you or your work, you are on thin ice. In a good economy, people who don't perform as well are more likely to get away with it than they are during an economic downturn. Not being a worker of excellence in a bad economy means you'll be the first to go. Your insurance policy is to not be naïve. Despite how cozy and friendly your job environment may seem, the company you are working for is there to create profit and you are there to make it happen. Therefore, they will rapidly eliminate your position if your services are no longer needed. The sooner you realize this the better.

In addition to always working hard and smart, to safeguard your position, keep any dissatisfaction you feel with your current job—such as coworker incompatibilities or your need for higher pay or advancement—to yourself unless you believe the problems you're having can be solved. If they can, make an appointment with your supervisor/boss specifically for the purpose of discussing your current position and your potential for future growth and advancement. During such a meeting, any problems you face and have been unable to resolve on your own can be an item on the agenda, but they should never be the expressed purpose for the meeting—otherwise your supervisor/boss will be put in a defensive position instead of in a problem-solving position and you may be viewed as a troublemaker.

Many people who are dissatisfied with their jobs or have problems that can't be solved begin looking for a new job. Good move. But then they feel a strong need to confide to their boss that they are job searching. What they don't realize is that by doing so they have broken the main rule, which is trust. The boss is not family and the fact that an employee already has a foot out the door says loud and clear that something is not working properly. Or the boss may suspect that the reason they've been told is a ploy to elicit a salary increase or a promotion. Put frankly, this is a bad way to operate and is equal to blackmail because any salary raise or promotion offered under such circumstances has not been achieved in a fair manner. Either of the two situations described is grounds for dismissal at the first crossroad.

Looking at the long term, you never want to burn bridges. If you're looking for a new job, do so discreetly; never let anyone else at your current company know. Secondly, if your present employer/boss knows you're out there looking—and doesn't fire you—it means he or she will be contacted for a reference check by anyone considering hiring you—something that's close to impossible if you run the process off the radar. Think about it. Would you want the company you're hoping to leave be a main source of information for a potential new employer?

During my long career as a high-level headhunter and life coach, I am almost always working with those who believe they owe it to their bosses to tell him/her that they are in the process of looking for a different job. Or they say they can't leave their present company because they "owe them so much." Loyalty is a worthy attribute, but it's a mistake to believe the company/corporation where you work would have the same consideration for you if it were in their best interest to replace you or eliminate your job. My answer to anyone who expresses such a sentiment is: Your highest authorities in life are God and your country, next is you and your family, then comes the company/corporation that employs you.

When your challenges at your current job are not insurmountable and your own problem solving, combined with the efforts of coworkers and your supervisor/boss seem to be improving the situation, it may be best to stay where you are. But even then—or when you actually feel happy and fulfilled with your work—still know that your company is not your family. Be prepared at all times, just in case something happens and one day you find out you won't be working there anymore. This means, always have your résumé ready, and never be naïve—you can't afford to be.

Step Eight: Execute your job/career action plan to get where you want to go by getting a new job or making your job all that it can be

Getting a new job

Where do you find a job? There are various places to look for a job. The *easiest* place to look is where the chances of succeeding are the *lowest.* So don't take the easy way out.

Getting a job must *always* be viewed as a job itself. It requires a game plan, a methodical process with a sequence of events you follow.

First, understanding the job market helps you understand your odds. What types of job searches lead to most people successfully finding a job? The statistics shows that a majority of all jobs—up to 90 percent—are never advertised and that only a small portion of the job market is covered through the classifieds in newspapers and on the Internet. An even smaller amount of jobs are obtained through recruiters.

As with everything else in life, the harder and smarter you work, the better your results will be. So it's best to spend most of your time on approaches that will give you the most positive results. When looking for a job, allocate *almost your entire time* to taking a direct approach. This doesn't mean you should ignore other approaches that are statistically less fruitful. Prioritize according to importance. While conducting your targeted direct job search, still check the classified ads and check in with your network for opportunities, but keep the time spent on these activities to a minimum every day as you need most of your energy and focus to go toward being proactive and approaching your target companies directly.

How to best approach a job opportunity: Be proactive

Although being approached by a headhunter is the best thing that could happen to you, unfortunately the chances of this happening are usually slim because only a fraction of the jobs are being channeled through this source.

Your next best maneuver is to be proactive. First, identify the potential companies where you would like to work. But, of course, be realistic. It's important to understand what you can bring to the table. If you have no knowledge or skills in the field of computer technology, the chances of your scoring a high-paying job with great benefits at Microsoft or Google as a programmer or technician are slim to none. So don't waste your time or theirs.

Ask yourself: What unique skill set or knowledge do I have that the company I am approaching needs? Getting a job is similar to sales: it's a numbers game. The product you are selling is yourself. Just like in sales, the more potential buyers you have who need the services you are selling, the better your chances of success. Few prospects and bad buyers—those who don't need your services, for example, Google, if you're a medical technician not a computer tech—means your chances of getting anywhere are slim. On the other hand, if you are realistic about how your skills and knowledge (reflected on your bio/résumé) could be of benefit to certain companies, you have just as good a chance as anyone else to get your foot in the door there.

Another consideration is geography. Are you willing to move to another place or do you prefer to stay local? Although commuting might be an option, most employers and headhunters know that even if a candidate claims he/she will have no problem driving two hours each way, the reality has proven to be that after several months commuting takes it toll.

Now that you've identified the type of companies that can use your skills and knowledge and you've decided on a geographical area, what do you do next? You are going to contact the companies by telephone, a personal visit, or email—but always know that you are not alone in doing so. There are lots of other people doing the exact same thing. This is where a good bio/résumé comes into play. The time you have put into polishing and tailoring your bio/résumé could make the difference. But again, don't let polishing/tailoring your bio/résumé become an excuse for not moving forward. Just like with anything else, the more you do it the easier it will be. Just keeping doing it!

In good times when there are fewer applicants for available jobs, companies and recruiters pay more attention to unsolicited bio/résumés. But when times are tough, with fewer jobs available, it's an entirely different story. Then the best chance you have when approaching companies directly is to make sure you stand out—without, of course, being "a stalker." Develop and keep a proactive mindset. Even though some people will think you're too aggressive, this isn't relevant if out of a hundred companies you approach, you get noticed by all of them—who now know you exist—and ten invite you in for an interview.

When I was starting out, I looked for jobs in both Europe and the United States and tried every approach I could think of. I sent applications in response to ads in the classifieds and tried to use my network. Neither did much for me. But when I used my direct approach, compiling my list and hitting the pavement, I always succeeded. All of my own job opportunities resulted from this proactive approach.

Here's a game plan: Use a system I call mapping, a systematic method to be as efficient as possible.

- Make a list in a table format (preferably on the computer) with four columns.
- In the first column put the name of each company (best that they're in alphabetical order—easy to do on a computer), their address, and main telephone number.
- In column two put the name of your contact person, their direct dial phone number, and email address.

- The third column is for you to note the dates when you take each action step.
- Column four is where you will write notes of status and next steps.

Again, don't put too much time into creating your list. If you get hung up on doing so, consider whether it's a form of procrastination. The point here is not to spend all of your time creating the list, but to use your time *finding a job!*

Before you start mailing/emailing your résumé, create the best possible prospect list you can. This should take no longer than a couple of days. You can use the Internet for identifying the companies (as well as their addresses and main phone numbers), but *do not* use it for determining the key people you are going to directly contact. The most accurate and quickest way to get that information is always by calling. Yes, you guessed it. You *will not* be contacting the human resources department, but finding out the name of the person in each company who is in charge of the department that could benefit from hiring you based on your skills. Call the main phone number of each company and ask who has such responsibility. As examples, if you are in sales, ask for the name of the person who heads up the sales department. Or, if you are in accounting, ask for the name of the person in charge of the accounting department.

Keep in mind that the higher you go in the organization the more authority that person has to make a hiring decision. The lower you go, the more reluctant those people will be to make a decision—a wrong hiring decision, particularly at lower levels of the hierarchy of a company, might mean that person is putting their own job at jeopardy (you don't need another person out there competing with you for a job).

Although many companies like to have job seekers filtered through their HR (human resources) departments, my personal experience is that if you have to deal with HR—as opposed to approaching the head of an appropriate (for you) department of the company—you're more likely to have your bio/résumé end up in a filing cabinet. And, by the way, when you get a personalized letter stating: "Thanks for your letter. We are impressed with your background, but have no current needs that match your qualifications. We will get back to you when an opening arises," this most likely means you will never hear from them again. This is, quite frankly, because the people sending these types of letters to you and other job applicants have more than enough on their plates and are just doing their best to stay on top of their current responsibilities. Usually they do not have time to keep track of all the people applying for jobs.

Also know that although the HR department may be "filtering" job applicants, many aren't authorized to do the hiring. The people who actually do that are department heads or managers in areas of the business where you want to work. Hiring is part of their responsibilities. Someone who runs a business area or is an upper-level manager of a department wants to recruit the very best people for his or her team to ensure that his department maintains a high level of performance.

Once you've completed your list, it's time to systematically get your résumé out there. Email it first, then call, then follow up again, and keep doing it until closure takes place. My own practice to make sure my bio/résumé hit its target was to use all the means available to me: phone, fax and email just to make sure. This way the people you are contacting can never say, "I am sorry, I did not get your résumé/letter/message." Just as if you are working in sales, you have not closed the deal until you get a job—and even then you are not safe until you physically start working, because sometimes job offers are rescinded after they are offered.

Remember, getting a job is a numbers game. The bigger and better your approach, the greater your chances are of winning. A job search process is no different than a sales approach. The key rule is that the chances of someone knocking on your door with an opportunity of a lifetime is close to zero. This means you have to do the work and use the techniques that work the best—which from my experience is the proactive direct approach. As I said before, if some of the companies you contact think you're too aggressive, don't worry about it. Other companies will assume that if you are a go-getter when it comes to getting the job, then you will use that same enthusiasm, follow-through, and energy once you start working for them. Remember: The harder you hit it the better your chances of success.

It may be temping to take the easy way out, by sending off some emails based on classified ads, posting your résumé online, or sending blind résumés to a lot of different companies. But that's identical to thinking that going to the gym and putting in five minutes of work will get you the body of your dreams, or that by buying a lottery ticket at 7-Eleven you'll become financially independent. It just does not work like that. It's better to understand right from the start that you always spend 95 percent of your time where you believe you have a 95 percent chance to succeed, and only 5 percent of your time where there is only a 5 percent chance of success. There are no shortcuts to nailing that dream job. By giving it your best and rolling up your sleeves you can get what you want—the job you deserve—and also know that you always put forth your best effort and that's all that you can do. That is living according to how God wants you to live!

The job interview process is like the dating game

Although a good bio/résumé is key to getting your foot in the door, in reality it doesn't show a potential employer who you really are as a person or what it would be like to have you around the office every day—your personality and attitude. That will come through during your job interview.

When you are invited to a job interview it means your chances of getting the job are great. After all, why would they waste their valuable time talking to you unless they believe there is a good chance you might be the right candidate for the job? My experience is that if you've succeeded in getting all the way to a face-to-face meeting with your potential new employer, then your skills meet their requirements and the rest is really up to you. Nine out of ten people can shift the outcome of an interview toward acceptance, rather than rejection, if they really understand what it means to be invited to a job interview. Someone who gets the opportunity to meet with a future employer usually either nails it or messes it up in the first few minutes. When prospective employees with great qualifications still mess it up it's usually because they don't have what I like to call the right "human touch." They do not know how to properly walk, talk, and behave around others—and someone else did.

This can easily be changed by turning it around, looking at it from the perspective of the person conducting the interview. Before a job interview, visualize yourself in the shoes of the interviewer. What impressions do you need to get from someone seeking a job? What questions are you most likely to ask and what answers do you want to hear? Beyond that, what posture do you want to see, what kind of speech pattern do you want to hear, and what kind of handshake do you want to feel?

Unfortunately 99 percent of people do not spend time imagining they are in the interviewer's position, which causes them to *not* nail it during their job interviews. As a recruiter I do feel bad when this happens. I see people who fail despite having the potential and the right background, because they are not able to nail that one meeting that could dramatically change their life for the better. (Lack of preparation can be reflected, not just in the job market, but also in all areas of life.)

When it comes to preparing for a job interview it's of great importance to practice, practice, and practice even more. First imagine yourself in the role of the interviewer. Then become who you are, the job seeker, and practice how you will show your potential new employer that you're the right person (*i.e.*, personality and attitude) for the job. Practice until it all sticks and becomes an integrated part of you.

Another golden rule of a job interview is that it's a two-way street—meaning you are there to sell yourself to the company and the company is trying to sell itself to you. It's all about structure with a natural flow. One key is to find common ground—so you don't sound like a programmed robot. Do some research to learn about the person who will be interviewing you by Googling him or her—but tell the person where you learned about him or her, otherwise you'll sound like a stalker. Glance around the interviewer's office to find items that indicate you have common interests: memorabilia, photographs, artwork, books, etc. Make nice comments. Stay positive, upbeat, high-energy, polite, and courteous. Bottom line, be prepared and know the questions and answers before you arrive, be likeable, and nail it by being the person you know they would love to hire—that's you!

Learn the answers and questions before the interview

When you practice before a meeting with a potential employer and you are going through potential questions and answers it's important to understand that these questions are usually very universal. Always know that the purpose of the meeting is to get to know you better than your one-page bio/résumé can present, have you elaborate on your skill set, and figure out if you are a high flyer, go-getter, or just a "warm body" who will make no additional contribution outside of minimal expectations.

Many job candidates get easily tricked or just don't know that if a conversation appears casual it does not mean they don't need to stay on point and cover the key information needed. Many times I have seen job seekers be thrown off-balance when a potential employer asks a question about a hobby or nonwork-related activity in the middle of the conversation. They start talking about such things and are unable to get back to the real topic at hand: the work done by the company and how they can make a valuable contribution. The sad reality is that when you're invited for an interview, that's your only chance to get that job. It's the same story as when a salesperson spends weeks setting up a meeting to present the company's product or services, and then messes up the one window of opportunity. It's totally unacceptable to screw up the conversation.

In the final analysis, preparation is what will determine if you are in or out, so every minute spent getting ready is worth it.

Many companies prefer a less casual, more structured interview process. They start by asking a job candidate to tell more about himself/herself—occasionally breaking into the conversation with questions—then switch during the second half of the interview to talking about the job and their company. Other times it might be in the reverse order, but what never changes are the key pieces of information that need to be covered.

One of the flaws I often see is when job candidates are asked to tell more about themselves and they do so too quickly, in only five minutes. This makes the interviewer question what kind of life this person has if they can describe it in such a short time.

And when job candidates focus completely on their skill sets and say nothing about who they are as people they can lose their potential new employer before they're halfway through.

Every company considers it a great test to see how effectively a job candidate is able to communicate when presenting himself/herself. During the late 1990s, several seminars cropped up to help people get a job—at least that's what it seemed, as I meet a number of people who would talk about themselves in the third person. This approach and method killed anyone's chance in less than two minutes. These job candidates would insist on using a Powerpoint presentation while referring to themselves in this way: "What Tom wants and needs are . . ." When I heard this I always knew what Tom needed . . . and that was to leave.

Another interesting attitude and approach I have seen is when someone—meaning a job candidate—enters the room in a cocky manner, sits down with his/her arms crossed and starts the conversation by just saying, "Sell me." When this has happened I have told these people politely that there is a mismatch, because I know for certain they should not be involved in any job process.

These are examples of what is to be avoided in a first meeting. What's key is to practice not only questions and answers, but also the format and structure of possible job interview situations—meaning how to get to the point and sell yourself convincingly and quickly.

Being prepared and knowing how to get to the point fast relates to all walks of life. And you can do so only when you know what you want.

There's a common technique for quickly summarizing yourself, called the elevator pitch, which is an excellent practice tool. You need to know how to sell yourself in the time it takes between when the elevator door opens until it closes. This means: who you are, what you want, and what is special about you or the service you can provide. By nailing this, you are prepared to meet any future job opportunity anywhere you happen to be, which may not necessarily be in an office. It could be a random opportunity in a social setting, such as at a seminar, social event, in a store, on a street corner, etc. The purpose is to create so much interest that you will be invited to a more in-depth meeting at a later time. The elevator pitch is also the backbone of your presentation in a face-to-face sitdown meeting. But in this case, the time frame I like to go by is anywhere from one to five minutes. It could be more, but the main thing is to be flexible according to your potential future employer's time. If he/she has only one to five minutes, then you better make sure to cover everything necessary in that time frame. The key is to always nail what is important.

Questions most commonly asked during a job interview

Here are the eight universal questions usually asked during a job interview, followed by how to effectively answer them:

1. Please tell me/us about yourself.

Answering Question #1: Focus on hard facts and what the employer needs to find out, which is, first of all, can you do the job they're interviewing you for. Talk about specific job experiences in your background that will speak on your behalf or strengthen your chances as a job candidate. Companies prefer, for the most part, to hire people who have done the same job or something similar elsewhere and have been successful at it. This is because the risk factor that someone will screw up is then very limited. So it's of very great importance in your answer or presentation to match up your experience with what the potential employer wants.

In addition, personal information about who you are is important. Everyone likes people who start out by saying where they are originally from and a little about their personal situation before they start hitting the hard facts. Then go on to where you went to school and run through the work history. Big time gaps in work history are not good; neither is jumping from job to job if you don't have a good explanation for why.

2. What are your strong/weak points?

Answering Question #2: Many job candidates feel very comfortable when asked about their strong sides, but have a difficult time with stating weak points. If little is revealed, the trick used by many companies is to then ask, "What would your current boss say about your weak sides?" And, in almost all situations, a company that's considering hiring you will do an extensive reference check and may ask your former bosses this question.

When you are not able to answer the question about your weak points, it may be construed that you are not good at assessing yourself, when in actuality you may be hesitant because you're afraid if you are too honest you might not get the job. The truth is, everyone has flaws. As a recruiter I don't mind flaws as long as they don't affect the job in question.

Some examples of the best way to answer is by saying things such as, "I speak only English and wish I had taken time to learn another language," or "I can get too eager because I get so deep into my jobs," or "I wish I was better at public speaking in front of large groups." You may notice that these types of answers convey weaknesses that can be overcome, which is very important. The key is that your weaknesses wouldn't affect your job performance.

Bottom line, by being open you come across as a person with nothing to hide.

3. Tell me about your previous managers that you reported to.

Answering Question #3: A key principle is that you never talk badly about your superiors or previous superiors. First of all, there's nothing for you to gain by doing so. Even if on a personal note you feel your previous superiors were totally incompetent, saying so will only backfire and reflect badly on you. Secondly, it's a matter of showing respect. And by giving respect to others, you gain respect yourself.

Also, as a warning, I have seen companies and recruiters get so "buddy-buddy" with a job candidate during an interview that he/she drops his/her guard and speaks the total truth about a previous boss, which later in another setting boomerangs at the candidate in a negative way. To be safe, no matter what, just don't do it.

God gave us three powerful tools: the ability to think, the ability to speak, and the ability to act. These three tools can be used to create a life of your dreams, but when not used properly, they can stand in the way of your dreams. When you are tempted to speak badly of others, understand that once those words are said, you can never take them back.

4. Where do you see yourself in the years to come?

Answering Question #4: This is also a trick question. When you have nothing to say you come across as having no aspirations whatsoever and if you speak too clearly about big plans it looks like you're going to leave the job when a better position or opportunity comes along.

The correct answer is: "My main interest is this job. I want to excel at and do my very best. That's my objective and main focus. As far as the future, I would like to believe that I will become better and better at what I do. If this means that I will naturally grow into another position with this company, time will tell. But again, my goal is this job and being the best that I can in this capacity."

5. What do you know about us?

Answering Question #5: The way you answer this questions indicates whether you are prepared. It's very important to know as much as possible about the company where you are applying for a job. By being able to tell them what you know, they see that you are serious enough to have done some homework before arriving for your interview.

Also, by learning as much as possible about the company, you will be able to ask the right questions and engage in an intelligent conversation about the company during your interview.

The key information to learn is the size, structure, products, services, history, the market, locations, etc., as well as details of the job you're applying for. Also know about any important events relating to the company and market it operates in that have taken place and been covered in the media. This shows that you follow the news and stay up-to-date on what is going on in the world. Plus, you'll come across as being very smart and truly interested in the company if you can figure out what competitors the company has and how the company's products/services are different (better!) than the rest of market.

6. Why do you think you are a good match for this position?
Answering Question #6: This is your window of opportunity to put all the hard facts on the table, convey the ways in which you are a very good match and why you are so unique. Remember, just saying that you are a hard worker and a very pleasant person is a given. You need to come up with facts about what you can bring to the table that others cannot. You will be able to be specific if you have thoughtfully assessed yourself, your skills, and experience while approaching your job search. The things you say that stand out could determine whether you get the job or someone else does. Think of facts related to your skill set, your experience, a network you may have developed, or strong job-related interests that will bear fruit in the near future.

7. What is your current salary?
Answering Question #7: Talking about salary can be challenging. If the new job is for a more prestigious company and the new job tasks are more challenging, then the candidate usually says at the start of the process that the job is more important than the pay if the company is offering less. But when a job offer comes through, the candidate will usually change the story, saying something like, "But I know what I am making today and this is less." Most companies know this will happen and thereby pay attention to the salary question to make sure they are not wasting time on the wrong candidate. The reality is that everyone, including the job candidate, knows that when they made a lot more money in the past and are willing to accept a big drop in pay for this new job, they are likely to grab the next position that comes along with higher pay and jump ship. This is to a great extent understandable when someone has a number of

years of experience under their belt and a certain lifestyle, expenses, and status quo to maintain.

But people need to look at the long term and understand that their own best interests should be driven to the greatest extent by seeking knowledge more than immediate gratification because the payoff down the road will be tremendously higher than just working for the paycheck and the ego. A hunger for more and more money is such a strong driving force that many people even go into fields/jobs/careers that don't provide them with much fulfillment besides making money.

When starting out in recruitment I was content to make not much money because I was hungry for knowledge more than anything else. I decided that for a period of time I would rather work for less money to benefit from learning as much as possible while being part of great, positive environments. I believed that eventually the rewards would be tremendous if I pulled through and sacrificed for some years. And obviously that proved to be true.

Money should be important and you should always try to ensure that you are paid market rate and what your efforts are worth. But you should never turn down great opportunities because of greed for a short-term paycheck when the long-term payoff is usually greater when you are driven by a quest for knowledge in areas where your passions can thrive.

When asked about salary the trick is to first get the company to reveal a number. Your best approach is to just say, "If you feel I am a good fit for this company and this position, I am sure we will come to terms," or "The main thing is whether I fit the requirements of what you are looking for, and if that's so then I would be very happy to receive an offer from you first because I am very interested in this opportunity." (Say this even if you are not.) By saying this you keep the focus on getting the job while not disqualifying yourself because of salary demands. You can negotiate a salary once you know that you truly have their interest—by getting an offer, not before. If they know that in your current job you earn much more than the new position would pay, that's a different story. Then you have to decide whether taking a pay cut is worth it to you, because they're probably not going to meet or exceed your current salary.

If you know from the start of the process that the salary range of a potential new job is below what you currently earn, you need to do some soul searching to decide if you still want the job. Simply ask yourself: Will this job take me further down the road to where I want to be in my career? If so, be prepared to answer their salary question truthfully by saying, "My pay today is 'X' amount of dollars and I know what my expenses are. I am not sure what your pay range is for this position, but I want to emphasize that at this point in my life I seek to learn more and expand my skill set. This is more important to me than anything else, even if it means taking a pay cut."

On the other hand, if you have no other choice but to accept a salary cut—whether it's due to a bad economy, the chance that your current job may be eliminated, or because you are unhappy and unfulfilled in your current job—ask yourself if this may be a chance to go in a better direction in life, where you will be experiencing new values and beliefs that can help you grow and evolve. If you believe this is correct, truthfully say to the hiring company that you are venturing into new territory where you genuinely want to try something new and different, and that the position in question is therefore of great interest to you.

Being honest—with yourself and your potential new employer—is the key here. Turn around and imagine that you are a company that is hiring. You don't want to go through the entire hiring process and then shortly afterward see your new employee jump ship. Being honest with yourself, as well as your potential new employers, will never backfire on you.

8. What do you do outside of work, or what nonwork-related interests do you have?

Answering Question #8: Companies ask a job candidate this question because most really do want to hire stable people with good, balanced lives.

Incorrect answers are: "I like to hang out at the bars," or "I have no interests except for watching television." Nobody wants to hire a bar hopper or someone who spends all of their spare time glued to the television. On the other hand, having too many outside interests can give the impression that they are likely to affect the quality of your work in a very negative way. I have seen numerous occasions where people say that maintaining their social life with friends is important to them—meaning their weekly outings with friends will always be more important than deadlines at work. A negative impression can also be given when people say they engage in a lot of sports activities as either a participant or a fan, because it can mean that adjusting their schedule to attend or view a sporting event can interfere with or be more important than any activity at the company.

For the correct answers, the key is to show there is balance in your life. Safe activities to talk about are: going to the gym, spending quality time with family, and going to church, the movies, or the theater, etc. Having a unique interest, such as astronomy or something else mainstream (meaning not bizarre), will always be a positive.

And because most companies want employees who have stable lives, being married or having a boyfriend/girlfriend is a great plus.

How to walk, talk, dress, and look for a job interview

First impressions can get you in the door, but you also want to stay. Even before a word is spoken, you are judged by what you look like. This is human nature. The mind and "gut feel" works so fast that within a few minutes a decision has already been made.

If recruiters and potential employers could get away it, only a five-minute first meeting would be necessary—to them the remaining time too often is wasted on what is considered a wrong person, but to be polite and courteous they engage in a lengthy conversation. Most recruiters, including myself, have made up their minds that the person is wrong just by seeing them enter the hallway—before they've had a chance to say one single world. The information explained in this section can help you avoid being one of those people by understanding how recruiters and potential employers think. Keep in mind that recruiters and potential employers very often like to recruit people like themselves and, of course they want employees who will be good representatives for their company.

In my younger days even I messed this up more than once by either saying the totally wrong things or dressing in such a bad way that I am now surprised that I did such a thing. When I was twenty-one I went to the office of a leading U.S. consulting firm to apply for a part-time job wearing an off-white linen suit and a pink shirt. This was in the late eighties and the outfit was a great going out socially outfit at the time, but it was a disaster for the corporate world. I lost the job before I even got to say a word. I never once repeated that mistake because I realized what I had done. And, after all, the best way to learn is by trial and error. And looking back now, I could not have agreed more with the people who rejected me for the job.

When going for a job interview you'd better dress the part so that won't be a reason for them to reject you. How do you know what to wear? Look at the environment where you are applying for a job and dress accordingly. If you have to, do reconnaissance. Park or stand near the building where the company is located and see what types of outfits the employees entering or leaving the building are wearing. Or call the company's main number and ask the person who answers the phone what the dress code or preferred attire is for those working there. Always overdress rather than underdress, but don't go so far that you're a total mismatch.

There are some universal rules that apply no matter what environment you're considering working in.

First, *always dress as though you are worth what they are going to pay you.* When I meet a candidate who dresses like a slacker, my first impression is that he/she isn't worth the money being paid. And if someone doesn't have enough respect for himself/herself to dress appropriately, he/she would not be an asset in any job. As a job candidate, all you need to do is analyze the environment in which you'll be working and use common sense. When applying for a corporate job, don't come in jeans. When applying for a job in a grocery store, don't wear a dark blue suit with a tie. Always dress your part. And no matter what, you need to look sharp—neat and clean.

Next, after studying your potential new work environment and deciding what you're going to wear, put on your outfit and look at yourself in a full-length mirror. Start with your shoes. Do they look worn out and soiled? For men: Do your socks match the shoes and the pants? Are the pants clean, pressed, and in good condition? How about your belt, shirt, suit jacket, and tie, if they are appropriate? For women, do your shoes, dress, or suit look like a coordinated outfit? Are your clothes clean, pressed, and in good condition? For both men and women: Are you well put together? Does it all match and represent you? Are you proud of yourself, of being God's creation? If that's the case, your outfit should he appropriate and be of the best quality possible.

I realize when times are tough or money is tight you may feel overwhelmed when looking in your closet, thinking you have nothing good enough, new enough, or of the appropriate style or quality for the job you want to get. If possible, invest in yourself: go out and buy an "interview outfit." When that's not possible, borrow an outfit from a friend. The point is: This may be your opportunity to change your economic circumstances, as well as create a better job/career future, so give it your all.

Remember, for your first interview—and all other interviews that follow—always go in looking like you're ready to do the job you're applying for and will fit right in at the company. That way you'll never be judged or disqualified for the way you dress.

It's also very important to always be well groomed. Trends come and go, such as sideburns, a goat beard, or long hair on men, but one thing that never fades or changes in the professional world is looking clean cut, well groomed, and professional. In the very competitive job market, don't give potential employers *any* reason to kill your opportunity of getting a job just because you can't bear to part with your ponytail or goat beard (if you're a guy), claiming it's a statement about your authenticity. When you are a player in the job market you have to follow the rules in order to win.

Handshake and eye contact

A limp handshake shows no backbone. If a job candidate grasps too hard, it feels uncomfortable for the other person and it can appear that he/she is trying to prove something. Perfect a handshake that is warm and connecting, firm but not too hard and engaging but not wishy-washy.

When it comes to eye contact, look your interviewer straight in the eyes throughout your meeting—unless, of course, they are showing you something, such as a report or a spreadsheet, then give it your full attention. Don't scan the room or look toward the window or down the hallway. People with wandering eyes appear to be not all the way present, which translates to "not really interested or focused." People who don't maintain eye contact also come across as being insecure, which is a liability in the work world, not an asset.

Always keep structure in a conversation

When communicating with a potential employer, in addition to being well prepared, always have a mental structure in your mind about how the meeting should and will go. In this way you can make sure everything that's important to you gets covered. Also, make sure to get to the point fast. If you have nothing to say, don't just talk. It's annoying. People who don't present facts or answer questions directly come across as having something to hide. On several occasions I have presented very strongly qualified and experienced candidates to clients/companies, but for some reason they couldn't get to the point. After an entire hour of social talk, not many facts were conveyed, and the clients didn't feel they learned anything about the person. In essence, the job candidates talked themselves out of job opportunities.

During a job interview conversation, always have a structure in mind and make sure that everything gets covered during the allotted time. Your chances of nailing the job will dramatically increase.

Be confident, but be humble

Few companies want to hire a person who comes across as insecure. But they also aren't interested in the other extreme, a person who is cocky. Nobody likes a person who is full of himself/herself. One quality every company looks for in someone to hire is a person who is balanced—confident and humble at the same time.

Humor is important

In every company environment that I have known humor is key. People with a sense of self-irony are always likeable because they don't take themselves too seriously. A job environment without smiles and laughter is a horrible place to work. Little feels better than having a good laugh. Therefore, job candidates with a sense of humor are much more likeable than a dry person that has a hard time smiling. The stories from the work environment that people remember and tell others are often the funny things that took place. The same goes with when an interviewer meets a well-qualified candidate with self-irony and a sense of humor. Such a person is easy to remember.

Being able to put a smile on the face of the person interviewing you is an ice breaker which gives you an advantage. But don't push it too far by giving the impression you don't take yourself or your job seriously—again, it's all about the balance. Nobody wants to work with a disrespectful clown. And humor can never be at someone else's expense.

From working with people as a life coach and recruiter, I have seen almost everything in regard to humorous episodes—so many that it would be hard to believe. But these events still make me smile, which fills me with happiness. When, I meet people with self-irony, they have a smile that makes you like them right away because you connect on a deeper level. Job candidates with a smile, who have the ability to connect with others, always have an advantage. And, of course, when everything else is in place they're way ahead of the game.

Physical posture in a meeting

When a job candidate enters the room for their interview with bad posture and looking uncomfortable, the impression they make is just as negative as being inappropriately dressed and unprepared. I have even seen high-profile candidates leaning back in their chairs as if they were at home in their living rooms.

It's important when you are in a job interview to sit up straight and behave as professionally as you can. And it is always more engaging if you lean forward a little toward the interviewer as it shows more interest than almost falling off the chair backwards when being too relaxed.

How to follow up after the interview

After someone takes time out of their busy schedule to meet with you regarding a potential job opportunity, it's customary and a courtesy to always send them a thank-you letter or email. This letter or email is very important. It gives you an opportunity to do many things, especially when you are left with the impression that another interview or a job offer may be coming:

- politely thank them for their time and the opportunity to meet with them about the job
- once again state your strong interest in the job
- express that you got a great impression of their company
- tell them you look forward to the next step in the process
- and tell them that if they need any more information from you to please let you know

Even if it was clear at the end of your interview that you and the specific job you were interviewing for weren't a good match, a thank-you letter is still needed to leave the best possible impression. Include in such a letter: thanking them for their time and what a great impression you got of their company. Also say something like: "If there are any future opportunities that come up that may be a better match for my skills, please keep me in mind." After all, there's always a chance that could happen. And even if it doesn't, you could directly or indirectly run into that person again in the future. Always leave a good impression.

When a friend, acquaintance, someone in your network, or a recruiter has given you the job lead or set up the interview, it's important to thank them too. Thank them for the opportunity and tell them you are excited about it. If a job offer comes through, don't forget to let your contact know with another thank you. And if a recruiter arranged your contact with the company that resulted in a fantastic job, send a gift to the recruiter. Always remember: When someone refers you for a job or hires you, they put their own name and reputation on the line. This is something to be very grateful about. Follow-ups, both after an interview and when you are hired, are critical ways to show gratitude.

When the job offer comes through: negotiating your salary

Salary is part of the equation when accepting a new job. It comes down to your expectations versus those of the hiring company, as well as the marketplace. As a job applicant you want to be paid as much as possible, and on the other side the company wants to pay as little as it takes, as long as in ensures that you are happy.

Determining factors will then be a mix of how much you make today or used to make, how much similar jobs in the marketplace pay, and the pay structure of the company. Sometimes negotiations can be involved to reach an agreement on a salary, while other times the numbers are so fixed that you will face a take-it-or-leave-it situation. Smaller companies may be more flexible; larger companies usually have a more fixed pay structure. Other important factors to consider are benefits: health care, 401K, insurance, company car, education benefits, etc. Even though salary and benefits are key factors in deciding whether you want to accept the job, hopefully they're not the determining factors if the numbers are close between your expectations and those of the hiring company.

Be cautious with a company that seems to be unnecessarily overpaying—it may show bad judgment, indicating it could be a high-risk company that could provide you with little job security. On the other hand, many times I have witnessed companies make a sport of paying much less than they can or should—which again is not sound long-term thinking, and it usually backfires. There is some truth in the saying: If you pay peanuts, you get monkeys. When someone is good at his/her job and is underpaid, they will leave at the first opportunity.

When entering a meeting as a job candidate you've got three choices when being asked about your pay requirements:

1) You can say "right now (or in my previous job) I make (made) X amount of dollars."
2) Say a number that is the minimum amount you want or need to get by or cover your bills if this is a job you really need and want.
3) Play hardball and state a fixed number.

Factors other than salary that may be more important to you are the working environment and the potential for where the job will take you. So, while negotiating a salary, always look at the big picture and your true objectives. Ask yourself if this is a company where you can earn enough money by being your true self and following your true passions, where you will be able to learn and grow to become all that you can be. If your primary objective is earning a paycheck, that isn't necessarily a bad thing when you really need a job, as long as your expectations meet the realities of the situation. Know when accepting such a job that you *must* still go into work every day with the commitment that you will give it 100 percent.

Making your job all that it can be

The ideal is having a job/career that is fueled by your passions, enabling you to learn and grow into being your best self while it provides more than enough financial security for you to thrive in the real world. But the reality is that sometimes that's not possible. Sometimes you just need to work for the paycheck. Even then, it's your obligation to always do the best you can do (as in every area of your life) especially if you have a job that doesn't *exactly* feed your passions. It's a matter of honor and a reflection of how much you truly value yourself as a person. Everything in life gets better when your belief in yourself is strong because you know you're always doing your best.

How to be successful once you are on board

Regardless of what job you are going into there are some basic rules that apply if you want to be successful. The first rule is to always do your best with a good, positive attitude.

The second rule is to work hard and smart. In the work world a good worker always hits it hard. Although there are some "job coaches" who tell people they don't need to work hard, just smart, in *A Second Life* you are always striving to be your best, and that includes in the working world, by working both hard *and* smart. Therefore, you are *not* a person looking for shortcuts to avoid duties or expecting someone else to pick up the ball after you've dropped it or are not hitting it. There is no other way to progress except by putting in the time and effort it takes. The harder and smarter you work the better your chances of succeeding. And by doing so with a great attitude you serve as a role model for everyone else in your work environment.

In a reference check one of the questions is: Does/did he/she perform well? When the answer is that the person is/was a dedicated hard worker, then they'll get a gold star. I have never, ever meet or spoken to a company or corporation that was in great need of hiring someone lazy. The truth is, hard-working, hungry people who also work smart usually get very far in life.

Apply all of your God-given gifts and talents to your job/career, always with a great attitude:

- Never arrive at work late, as that clearly shows disrespect. Better yet, arrive at least several minutes before you are supposed to be there.
- Use your mind at all times to come up with new or creative ways to do your job better.

- Push yourself to finish your work and meet deadlines whenever possible, and when necessary to work the overtime minutes needed with a smile—telling yourself you are grateful that you have this job, no matter what the job is.
- Be organized and have your work area reflect who you are and what you stand for—which is being a role model.
- Ask for help, guidance, or assistance when you need it. No one is perfect, or expected to be. There will always be other people who know more than you, especially when you're new to a company. Get comfortable admitting when you don't know something, if you don't. Find out who can best guide or assist you and respectfully ask for their help—but always within reason and when it's not interfering with them doing their own job.
- Offer to help others. We were not brought into this world to live only of and by ourselves. By lending a helping hand you're honoring God—but again, within reason and when it's not interfering with you doing your own job.
- Be serious about your work, but not yourself. Take pride in your work, but don't get cocky. Maintain and use your sense of self-irony or humor, but never at the expense of others.
- As time progresses, measure your knowledge and efficiency to make sure you are progressing forward to new levels at all times. God wants you to evolve in all areas of life, to grow to be all that you can be. He wants you to be a winner living at your maximum potential, which is only achieved when working hard and smart.

I can tell you as a recruiter and on behalf of the major corporations I have worked with that people who do these things are the ones they want to hire, and keep as employees.

Make a good impression from day one and you'll get a good reference when you leave

A determining factor for how well you do in the work world is how the people you report to (your supervisor/boss) and your coworkers in the job environment—both now and in the past—respond to you and perceive you. As long as you always do your very best, follow *A Second Life's* Seven Commandments and treat others as you want to be treated, you will be greatly rewarded—although maybe not at the time, but for sure later down the road. Always know that the people you interact with today you will meet again indirectly or directly at another time in your life. With a clean slate and good standing you can feel confident that your back is clear.

- Don't be an underperformer. Short-sighted thinking is believing that you will get away with being an underperformer. You may get away with it a few times by having good excuses, but in the long run it will come back to bite you. We are all human beings and understand that external factors can hinder our performance at work during difficult times. But this is acceptable only once or, worst case, twice. If someone bases their existence on being a mediocre performer, he or she will be red flagged. Even if such people don't hinder their good performer coworkers, they disrespect God's given gifts.
- Don't speak badly of others. Many people make a big mistake by speaking badly about others. People who complain about others are usually people who are not able to take responsibility for their own faults and prefer to blame someone else. Finding the negatives about others shows a person who perceives himself/herself as better than other people. Every person on the planet has negatives and positives. Assume that for the most part people are doing the very best they can, but because we are all living in our own distorted realities we don't all perceive facts the same way. Also, consider this before you speak badly of others: Perhaps you're seeing something in them that you recognize in yourself and need to correct. To me, criticism most often says more about those criticizing than those being criticized.
- Never complain about your previous bosses or coworkers. When someone complains about their previous boss/supervisor or coworkers it creates mistrust with those they're currently working with. They'll wonder what will be said about them when that person moves on. It's key to remember that your former bosses/supervisors are the people who gave you opportunities for jobs in the past—whether or not you were able to make the most of them. Always speak (and think) in positive terms about them and be grateful for the opportunities you were given. Instead of dwelling on what could have been different or better in previous jobs, focus instead on what was good and stick with the positive thoughts.
- Criticizing your current boss/supervisor or coworkers in public is self-destructive and serves no good. In fact, it can become a huge disadvantage if word gets back to them.

A test to determine how well you're doing is simply asking yourself: How would my former and present coworkers describe me? And more importantly, would my former boss rehire me? If you answer "no" to the latter question, then any reference they might give you would not be good.

Don't take away someone else's opportunity

If someone has a job that they are not grateful for and they don't hold their opportunity and environment in high regard, that person is a rotten apple taking away someone else's opportunity. Such people are not living according to God because they show no gratitude. If these people cannot change their attitudes they are basically destroying everyone else's spirits by undermining the good efforts of others and keeping the right person, who would be fulfilled in their position, out of the job. Rotten apples serve no good purpose. They only spoil an environment that could be positive by limiting everyone else's growth and success.

I have worked in environments where such destructive forces have not only jeopardized the happiness of the work environment but the lives and well-being of their coworkers as well—destroying the greater good. In one particular U.S. recruitment company where I worked, every Monday morning in the elevator an employee would say, "Only five days to go, then it's the weekend." Every day it would be a countdown to the weekend. And to make it worse, there was a loud, daily countdown hour by hour. No matter how positive every worker would be, this one particular person succeeded in killing a great deal of the spirit of everyone else and, ultimately, the entire organization. These people should be removed from their work environment because they serve no good.

Don't be the rotten apple in your work environment—or in any other part of your life! While going through the process of being a job candidate, accepting a job, and once you've landed the job, ask yourself: Would you hire yourself? If you cannot make a positive contribution to the greater good and be a positive role model, don't put yourself in a position where you will be destroying the opportunities of more-deserving people—it's bad for everyone else, and it's bad for you.

View your insecurities as an opportunity for personal growth

Everyone, of course, has insecurities of some kind. Many people are concerned about the impression others have of them if they are working at a job that is not considered by society's standards as acceptable or of high enough status. In other words, they are concerned about what other people think of them. There's a well-known saying that speaks the truth about this: When you're eighteen, you worry about what everybody is thinking of you; when you're forty, you don't give a darn what anybody thinks of you; when you're sixty, you realize nobody's been thinking about you at all.

When it comes to your job/career, your insecurities aren't relevant unless they affect the quality of your work—which they absolutely need not do. If you struggle with insecurities and are having a difficult time overcoming them, it's best to hide them; project confidence even if it is just role-playing. Then, hopefully, this role being played will become so integrated that your fears and insecurities will be overshadowed, and eventually killed.

As an example, many insecure people can't accept a compliment. When someone who believes they are lacking is given a compliment, their may respond by saying, "Really?!" By doing so you reinforce the doubt you have in yourself. The next time someone compliments you, even if you don't believe it, just say, "Thank you." After saying "thank you" enough times you actually will change the way you think about yourself. This can only make you better at whatever you're doing in your job/career and create more success for everyone in your workplace and, ultimately, the company you work for.

Another way insecurity manifests itself is when someone is cocky. Regardless of how insecure you are, exhibiting a cocky attitude in the workplace means you're the bad apple that can spoil everything you touch. The difference between confident and cocky is that confident people go about their business without needing to be praised constantly for every little thing they do, and cocky people are always expressing a need to get credit for their work—which usually has the reverse effect. Having this kind of attitude creates an uncomfortable work environment and puts off your coworkers. It's not easy to diagnosis cockiness in yourself, but the next time you feel a need to require or demand to be recognized, before you do so stop and think about why you're doing it. Cocky people in a work setting must realize that in order to fit in, they need to calm down and be humble.

Every company wants to hire and keep employees who are confident and humble. If you are neither, then play the part until it becomes you. Being truly humble has been described in this way: Don't believe you know everything, as you know so little.

Create a new position for yourself

Creating a new position basically means taking on new or additional responsibilities—usually those of a coworker in order to make it easier for them to do an even better job in their core area of responsibility. Such a mindset is not just important for other people with whom you work, but also clearly shows initiative, independence, drive, and a high degree of responsibility—all traits of a person who succeeds. Taking on new responsibilities also helps you grow by learning and mastering new tasks. But such proactive conduct is beneficial only when your primary assigned job tasks have been satisfactorily completed; otherwise it serves against its purpose.

There is no reason to wait for your supervisor/boss to proclaim that you have added responsibilities. Take the initiative and do it on your own. In most companies it's not too difficult to do. I have seldom been in a work environment that restricted someone's efforts to take on more responsibility as long as it does not intentionally jeopardize someone else's position. Exhibiting a good team spirit means you are concerned not only about your own job, but also the jobs of everyone around you. The most important person whose job you can make easier is your supervisor/boss. By making your boss look good, you will also be viewed more favorably by him/her. Taking on responsibilities or tasks of a coworker may require a mindset of extraordinary stamina and drive, but you can strengthen your position and status in your current company and automatically open doors for future opportunities. The new knowledge you obtain and skills you learn could pay off with a promotion to an entirely new position in the company where you presently work, and they can be used in future jobs in other work environments.

Step Nine: Reevaluate your job/career status according to your timelines

If your job/career targets are not being met according to your timelines and you've encountered roadblocks, then go back to previous steps of this job/career process to reassess what you're doing wrong. Make corrections to get yourself back on course. Then continue to on your path forward toward your goal.

If all approaches you have taken to find a job or improve your current job/career situation have gotten you nowhere, go back to the drawing board and reassess your options. Review the steps you have taken. What is missing? Do you need more training or education? If you already have the necessary skills and talents, do you need an attitude adjustment? There is no surrender—which means there is always a way. The question is how.

If you know in your heart that you are doing everything right and are qualified for jobs you are seeking or advancement in your current company, you need to take more extreme measures.

When you are stuck in a job and can't make career progress, your best first option is to talk with your superior. Offer to take on more responsibilities that could lead to a promotion. This, of course, requires that you have taken the initiative and been a good employee/role model in the company. If your supervisor says there is nothing more in the near future for you in terms of responsibilities and growth that suit your career aspirations or income needs, then it's time to plan on jumping the ship.

When you are looking for a job but can't get into the career field you've trained for or can't get a foot in the door of the companies you would like, you need to take a more targeted approach and do some smart networking.

Here's a game plan: Again, do extensive research on the companies of your choice. Ask to meet with department supervisors to interview them about exactly what they do. This will give you some ideas about what they need that you could provide. If they're definitely not hiring, and you can afford to do so, offer to provide your services to them on a part-time or project basis free of charge—so the company does not feel stuck with you. Tell them that your intention is to prove to them how good you are and how you may be an asset to their team, that there is no risk for them other than getting some important task/project done by you, that they can utilize your talent with no costs or other strings attached. This way they get to know you on a personal level while you get a chance to prove how good you are. Worst case is that they will not have anything for you right then, but they will remember you when you follow up again later. The key is to stand out in a good way; and now you will.

Step Ten: Reassess your job/career values every six months after you are on your path

Now that you are on track, is this still what you really want? There are many ways to measure your success. One way can be to see how you are progressing by taking on new challenges that help you grow—which is a basic ingredient for feeling good about yourself because it means you are evolving. Being stagnant means the opposite. Another strong indicator that you are succeeding, and goes far beyond anything else, is the impact you have on others in a good way. This isn't necessarily a result of direct public service, but can be seen in your everyday work life—and, of course, life in general.

If you're still not where you want to be, decide what it is that you really want. Here's a clue: Your instincts will tell you whether you are doing what you really want to do or if you are doing what you have been indoctrinated to believe you should do. The passion inside is the voice of God showing you the way. All you have to do is learn to listen. You may be surprised by what you hear.

When I was around twenty-two years old and attending university, I got a full-time job as a bellman in a very prestigious hotel in Los Angeles. Having the chance to work in such an environment was a huge deal for me. Employees of the hotel were treated extremely well. We had access to the same great food served to hotel guests and could stay at other hotels owned by the corporation at low rates. Although I knew this was a great work opportunity, it turned out to be a positive experience in many other ways.

Because of the nature of my job assignment as a bellman I saw instant results of my work through the interactions with the hotel guests. At the time my five-day-a-week shift started at 4:30 in the morning, which meant that I got up at 3:45 to get there on time. Every morning I thanked God for having the job, being able to go to school later in the day, and being healthy. Each day I told myself it would be the best day ever. With this mindset I arrived at work happy and energized, ready to do the best job I could every day. Soon I realized that doing a good job and providing good service resulted in people giving big tips. So I'd leave work every day with a lot of extra money. I took great pride in what I did and decided to be the best possible bellman at the hotel. My next goal was to get the most recommendation cards from guests, which were then placed on a wall in the hotel. I never forget for one day how lucky I was to have that job. I felt like I was part of a great team. And never having a reason to feel down, I smiled and hit it hard, every day doing my best.

At the time I remember visiting a friend and when his parents asked what I was doing to earn a living the friend answered before I got a chance, "Christian is temporarily working as a bellman, but has much bigger plans." But I never once felt a need to defend myself and say the job was temporary. Why would I? If I did, it would mean that my coworkers whose jobs were permanent were not respected, as well as saying their jobs were not important—it was judging them. When I eventually left the job because I was moving out of state, I was asked by several coworkers if I had any bad days, because all they remembered was me being happy with a big smile and enthusiasm from day one and for as long as they had known me. As I moved along my path to achieve other goals I thought would give me a great feeling—to make lots of money and reach the high goals that I had set—I never thought of my former coworkers as having lesser goals. Instead, I wanted to make them proud of me.

Ten years later I returned to the hotel for the first time, excited to tell them about everything I had achieved and that I had finally succeeded. When entering the hotel lobby I saw eight of my former coworkers. They were all smiling, genuinely happy to see me and came over to hug me. I could tell their warm greeting came from their hearts and I was truly touched. In those moments I realized that true success was the feeling I felt inside, that I had left such a good impression that ten years later it had stood the test of time. While looking at them, laughing and smiling with them, I felt such positive energy and knew they liked me not because of what I had achieved, but because of the person I was. So I didn't tell them about my achievements and success. Doing so would have been disrespectful to the people I once worked with who were still doing the same jobs ten years later. After all, they were just as good as I remembered them to be, and were happy and content doing what they did.

There were good lessons I learned that day: I realized that my success had been for myself, not to impress anyone else. I was lucky to know these great people I once worked with whose respect for me was measured by who I was and what I had contributed as part of their team.

Success in a job or career, as this story clearly illustrates, can be measured in many ways. But according to God's main belief, each of us is his divine creation and we owe it to him and ourselves to always to do our best and be grateful for whatever jobs we have. How successful you are is greatly impacted by knowing that every job is just as important as any other, and that working together to make a better company, world, and "heaven on earth" is how you will be remembered.

Seeing these people I had worked with ten years earlier, but had not seen since, and they way they all reacted reinforced what really matters. I knew that the monetary success I had achieved was to satisfy my ego. On that day I realized more than ever that true success at a job comes with creating positive energy, always doing your best, and being grateful. By being God's role model you make both yourself and him proud.

Final Step: Be all you can be, but not all at once

JOB/CAREER SUMMARY

- Assess your current job/career situation.
- If it's not all it could be, identify the reasons why, such as:
  - You don't have a job and need to get one.
  - You're afraid you're going to lose your job.
  - You want to feel more secure in your current employment or advance your position.
  - You work too much, causing you to fall short in the other four key areas of life.
- Use the tools you've learned—meditation/prayer/self-programming—to delete the negative indoctrination/brainwashing that has blocked you from mastering the job/career area of your life.
- Devise a game plan for re-creating your job/career situation based on your new reality, including:
  - Steps you will take to get a job, get a better job, secure/advance your current job, or work less in order to devote more time to the other four key areas of your life.
  - Goals and objectives you will achieve.
  - Timelines for enacting or making progress on your plan.
- Execute your game plan:
  - Each day: Systematically set out knowing what you will do to improve, advance, or re-create your job/career situation. Follow through with commitment.
  - Every night: Routinely review your accomplishments and express gratitude.
- Reassess your overall results according to your timelines:
  - If you are on track, are there new goals you now want to reach?
  - If satisfied with your progress and job/career status, be conscious every day of maintaining the changes you have made in order to completely wipe out your old negative programming and establish your new positive reality for the long term.
  - If you have not made the progress you'd planned, go back, reevaluate your situation and find new ways to make your game plan more successful.

ALWAYS REMEMBER: Surrender is never an option. You must find a way to succeed.

Financial

2

Your financial situation is unstable and out of control because you've been indoctrinated and brainwashed by society. This chapter will show you how to break free from the chains of society's mental slavery so you can regain control of your financial situation.

Financial Contents

Introduction

Society's Rules: There are two opposing beliefs about money that permeate society's thinking: 1) The more money you have, the happier you'll be. 2) If you don't have enough money to support yourself, there are lots of social programs—i.e., welfare—you can tap into that will take care of your needs. All you have to do is learn to use "the system" to your advantage.

The Truth: Sure, having enough money is a good thing, but not for the reasons many people believe. Money does not magically solve problems, or even keep them away. In fact, having a lot of money can create problems. It certainly requires that you think about it and learn to manage it well. It can generate fear that it will be lost or run out. Having more than enough money can also tempt you to spend extravagantly or fall into the trap of living beyond what's wise and reasonable. Then you're a slave to your money. Money does not give good health to people who are ill—although it can buy better medical care. Having enough money does not necessarily improve your relationships. Having a lot of money does not mean you're a success. And a lot of money doesn't guarantee that you're closer to God, even if you contribute generously to the church of your choice.

We are indoctrinated to believe that being financially rich is automatically a measure of success, that "rich people" are better than "poor people." By buying into that misleading way of thinking when assessing our own lives and viewing the lives of others, we have become the judges, placing ourselves above God. Not only is this an insult to God—a denial of the individual precious gifts and talents God has given each and every human being—it's a recipe for disillusionment and defeat. After all, how can you live a fully realized life based on your God-given gifts and talents if you accept the idea that society's opinion of your financial status is more important than the true desires and passions burning within you?

Money is just a tool, nothing more, nothing less. Learning to use this tool well is the key to your living a well-balanced, responsible life with purpose while following your true passions to become all that you can be. In that way you'll be able to support yourself financially and contribute to making society a better place for everyone.

Unfortunately, there are too many people living in the western world in the twenty-first century who buy into the belief that if they can't support themselves it's okay to rely on the government to take care of them. Although there may be dire circumstances that warrant temporarily seeking the assistance of government "social services" or accepting financial help from family, the mentality that if you don't have the motivation to take care of yourself financially you're entitled to have someone else take care of you is only traveling further down the road to nowhere. Not only is it a drain on society as a whole, dragging everyone down, it also contributes to an overall feeling of entitlement and lack of motivation. These corrupting feelings usually result in one of three things: false ego gratification by getting away with something when you're not really trying; a defeated ego when you believe you're a loser who can't do what it takes to be a contributing member of society; or in the extreme case, fostering a defeatist attitude that you're not just down on your luck, but out of luck.

Being financially responsible, stable, and successful has nothing to do with luck.

The amount of money you have is not a reflection of how successful you are. The way you manage and use your money is the *only* true measure of financial success.

Any disappointment or disillusionment you feel about your current financial situation is not necessarily the result of lack of trying or desire, but more likely because you are trying to live up to the false standards of society. Has conducting your life based on society's expectations resulted in your financial stability or happiness, or has it made you feel inadequate? Are you able to financially support yourself and the people you're responsible for or are you always terrified about where the next dollar is going to come from? Are you in debt way over your head? Are you unable to routinely save money for a rainy day? If so, you are not alone. Far too many people are living on credit and denying what they know is the truth: nothing in life is free. Far too many people are unable to get ahead financially—or even stay even—because they have an unrealistic relationship with money.

Now is the time to change all of that. By doing the work necessary to erase your indoctrinated programming and activate a new way of thinking you will feel grateful for your *true* talents and gifts and find new ways to apply them as your own personal financial manager. When we no longer cling to society's rules we become more tolerant and respectful of one another, live in the present moments of NOW, enjoying each day for exactly what it is: filled with opportunity. Then everyone is free to pursue their own individual happiness, knowing that they are able to be the best that they can be *because* they are using their God-given gifts and talents for a higher purpose.

God didn't decree that some people will be rich and others will be poor. No matter what economic circumstances or environment you were born into, each and every one of you can do the work to change your current economic status and create a new financial present and future. How can you set yourself free and embark on your true financial path that is a gift from God? Break away from the indoctrinated way of thinking according to society's rules. Begin today by changing your way of thinking. Take the first steps on the journey that is your new, self-fulfilled life in alignment with God. Follow this step-by-step approach to decide on a plan for your financial stability and set out on your new fulfilling life.

TEN STEP ACTION PLAN FOR MASTERING YOUR FINANCIAL LIFE

As you follow each of these steps, do so with the understanding that earning enough money and wisely using the money you earn are the keys to being a successful money manager. The only path to financial security is by not spending more than you earn—no matter how enticing credit offers may seem—and, indeed, actually saving for your future financial needs. Financial management must be approached systematically with dedication, perseverance, and determination. This is not just about having more money to buy more "stuff"; it's about creating financial stability in your life so your mind is free of needless stress and worry that prevents you from being the best you can be in all areas of your life.

If you want to get rich, forget about winning the lottery. Although, obviously, some people do win the lottery, seriously know that the odds are it won't be you. So you've got to devise a reasonable, realistic, alternative game plan based on your financial realities.

Step One: Assess your current financial situation

While assessing your financial situation you must be completely honest with yourself, otherwise you're wasting your time and won't get positive results. Answer these questions:

- Are you financially stable and secure?
- Do you want to achieve financial stability?

- Is your financial situation out of control?
- Are you afraid it's going to get worse or never improve?
- Why are things not working out for you financially, both now and in the past? ("I don't know" is not an acceptable answer! If you can't figure it out, who will?)

Step Two: Assess yourself as the financial manager of your own life

Do you manage your own finances or depend on someone else to do it?

The word "manage" is defined as: to handle or direct with a degree of skill; to succeed in accomplishing; to achieve one's purpose.

Are you the best person to financially manage your own life? Why/why not?

This test will help you determine where you stand today, and also give you important information about what you need to change about yourself. Bottom line: If you're not the best person to financially manage your own life, perhaps that's the reason your financial situation isn't as good as you'd like it to be. Answer these questions as objectively as possible:

- Do you have enough understanding of basic accounting that you know how to balance your checkbook and read your bank account statements, and know the difference between an asset and a liability?
- Have you set aside a specific time of the month to routinely pay your bills?
- Do you have high credit card balances?
- Do you view the ATM machine as what it really is: You can *only* take out as much money as you have put in? It's not free money!
- Do you pay your bills on time or pay late fees and finance charges?
- Are you living from paycheck to paycheck?
- Do you set aside money for a rainy day every paycheck?
- Do you have "mad money" to use just for the fun of it?
- Are you always buying "stuff" you don't need?
- If you are married, do you and your spouse co-mingle your funds or keep them separate?
- Is money, or lack of money, a hot-button issue in your marriage/family?
- If you are married, do you depend on your spouse to handle all the financial matters of your family?
- What would you do if that person were suddenly unable to do so? Do you know enough about what is going on that you could instantly step in and take over?

Even if you are in a position to have a financial manager or leave your family's financial management to your spouse, don't be fooled into thinking that you still don't have to pay attention and be an active participant in how your financial resources are being managed. That's a recipe for disaster—as is made evident by the astonishing greed recently exposed in the news about money managers, hedge fund operators, stock-brokers, banks, and mortgage brokers.

Know one thing for sure: You can't depend on anyone else to manage your finances. You must take full responsibility for your financial management; otherwise you're a sucker who very well might be taken advantage of and end up broke!

What are your financial management skills and talents?

If you've been managing your finances all along and you enjoy good financial health—even if you didn't have any formal education or training—you'll probably continue to do well. But if you're finances are a mess, you're always behind on bills or unable to pay them, or you're in the habit of buying things you don't need and can't afford, it's time to realistically consider a plan B, which most likely would include getting some good advice, assistance, education, or training—or maybe a "reality check" is all that's needed.

To know where you're starting from, make a list of all your financial management skills and talents, including everything you have learned through your education, training, or work experience, as well as things you are able to do well naturally.

Now for your reality check. Take the following $50 Spending Challenge. Carry *only* $50 in your wallet or pocket, as well as a notepad or piece of paper and a pen. At the top of the page write the date you begin this challenge. Then write down every penny you spend, what you spend it on, and the date you spend it until the $50 is all gone. You cannot add more money to the pot or purchase anything by check, credit, or on a charge card until your $50 is gone—you've only got the $50! When the last penny is gone, write down the date at the bottom of the page and sit down to review where your $50 went. What do you see? Anything interesting, enlightening? What can you learn about your financial management skills?

What can you do to improve your abilities?

In order to be a good manager of your own finances you must be completely honest and realistic about your abilities. By answering the questions above and taking the $50 Spending Challenge you should have a better idea of where you are now and how much or little you need to do to improve your abilities. The past is usually a good indication of how the future will be—unless some measures are taken to change your way of doing something. I believe everyone has it in them to greatly improve and radically change any aspect of their lives at any point they choose. It's never too late to get a handle on your finances. No matter how deeply in debt you are or how out of control your finances may be, there is a way to change things.

Step Three: Decide your financial future in specific terms

Create a future view of your financial situation for the following time frames: twelve months from now, three years from now, and five years from now. Various things that could be included are: paying off your credit cards or cutting expenditures and expenses in order to live within your means; or it could be saving for a large purchase, such as a home or a new car, a fun family vacation, or unexpected emergencies. The bottom line goal is: earning more money than you spend, managing your expenditures in a way that you can cover all your financial obligations while still having enough money to enjoy living NOW, and planning/saving for your future financial needs.

When you want something in life it's important to set a clear goal in order to achieve it. First, set a realistic target. When doing so, allow yourself to dream. Set a high goal that requires you to really stretch in order to reach it—this could mean you need to acquire a certain skill set or knowledge. Then ask yourself *why* you want to reach this goal. Is it because you want to test yourself to see how well you can do? Is it because you feel that your new financial management skills or a better financial position will give you a certain feeling of accomplishment or perhaps it will be simply to eliminate from your life the constant stress of financial pressure and uncertainty. Maybe it's because you feel you can better serve a higher purpose by being able to help more people or help them in a better way. The reasons can be many, but it's important that you know *why*, because your reasons are the key to your passions (motivation).

Second, in order to stay motivated you need to set milestones—small goals, with steps to take in order to reach each one of them. My own personal experience is that I would not have reached any of my goals in life if I had not set a clear path to follow. Everything that has taken place in my own life and in the lives of the people I have coached was a result of planning and hard work. Little in life falls into someone's lap unexpectedly. Life planning and time management are needed for each of the five key areas of life, including your finances. Planning for the future does not mean that you stop living for today and start believing that everything in the future will be so much greater. The reason to make plans is to ensure that you get the most of this life.

When planning for your financial future—as well as living the best possible life in the present—remember to shoot for the stars, but never forego the principles of life balance, which are required in order to live *A Second Life.*

Step Four: Decide on a financial action plan and timelines according to your future goals

Once you have set clear goals for your finances you need to decide on a specific plan of action to achieve your future goals and try as best you can to follow it according to your timelines.

- If someone else is managing your finances, do you plan to take over the helm? If so, how will you learn to do so?
- If you are currently managing your finances, will you continue to do so as you are now or learn ways to improve?
- Are you willing to accept someone else's advice and assistance until you are better prepared? If so:
  - Decide on a timeline: How long will it take to achieve your goal?
  - Define your approach: How will you get the assistance and knowledge you need? And how much time are you willing to allocate to doing so?

A belief system that hinders many people from improving their financial situation, opportunities, and growth is that if they've been unsuccessful in the past it's hopeless to even try. No one sets out to ruin their financial situation and create endless stress because they can't pay their bills, save money for an emergency, or comfortably buy the things they need. Very often it's a matter of never having been taught good financial planning and management. It's never too late to get the education you need, either formally or on your own. By being extremely realistic, determined, and having dogged perseverance, anyone can create the kind of financial security that can improve their lives in every way.

Use the tools you learned in Coding to Oneness, Level 1, of this guide—meditation, prayer, and self-programming—to assist you in setting your goals and keeping a clear focus on them as you enact your plans in order to master the financial area of your life.

Step Five: Decide how important financial security is to you

Evaluate how important your financial situation is and how it affects other activities in your life by listing them in order of importance. Then ask yourself how much you are willing to sacrifice in order to achieve financial security. And ask yourself why.

Years ago when there was no welfare, as there is today, or money from parents to get through tough times financially, creating a stable financial structure in life was more geared toward the following order: 1) Survival—money was used to obtain the products and services needed to get through every day—i.e., food, shelter, basic clothing, transportation to work, medical care. 2) Luxuries, toys, and investing—extra money was used only after basics were covered and secure. The adage, "Only invest what you can afford to and are willing to lose," was the creed of the day. But survival mode is no longer predominant in the current belief system. Today people are programmed to a great extent to believe that everything will work itself out somehow; that if there's a will, there's a way. This has left too many people in the helpless position of using credit to purchase things they really don't need when they have no idea how or when they'll be able to pay it back instead of living according to Maslow's Hierarchy of Needs. Today, despite society's standards, Maslow's principles—that clearly indicate our first need in life is survival—still hold true. Then come luxuries, toys, investing, and gambling the financial security of yourself and your family by being unrealistic in the day-to-day management of your finances.

Those who don't work don't deserve food

If someone is healthy with a working mind there is no reason whatsoever that they cannot support themselves financially, which is automatically making a positive contribution to society. If their situation does not allow for them to work at a job they love and earn enough money to get ahead financially, then a temporary job will have to do. You should always have yourself in a financial position so that if your job were eliminated today you would have enough money saved to get by until you find other employment. If it's difficult to secure a job immediately, and if you have money saved, your time could be spent helping people in your community or in a job internship position to obtain more knowledge and experience that would enable you to have a better chance in the job market. The key is to have financial backup so that you can be active in one way or another.

Work builds character

There was a time when teens and young adults had to work for things while growing up. They had duties and responsibilities at home and got jobs during their time off from school in the summer. As a result, they learned discipline, developed character, and understood survival mode. Some needed to work in order to help support their families. Others were encouraged to save at least some portion of the money they earned. A majority of people had to pay their own way through college. Now, unfortunately, there is a completely different mindset.

The baby boomers were born in the United States to parents who had survived World War II and many who remembered the years of struggle growing up during the Great Depression. As a result, they wanted their children to have easier lives, more security, and all the things they never had. When the baby boomers became parents themselves, their liberal attitudes about childrearing, enjoying life, and "going for broke," influenced their children to believe that the sky was the limit in every aspect of life. National prosperity and our nation's financial system encouraged everyone to buy, buy, buy, even if they didn't have the money—credit was freely offered and taken advantage of. But with the slow decline of the American economy during the last several years, and the sudden collapse of our national economic system—which is affecting the global economy—all bets are off and the harsh reality must be faced. Society's indoctrination that a free ride is an option has proved to be an abject failure. It's time to go back to basics, to revert to the old way of doing things. It's time to get back to the work of building character by being responsible.

Every person who commits to doing the work necessary to straighten out and clean up their financial messes by getting serious about really knowing how to manage their own financial life will, in the process, be reestablishing their self-esteem. There's a sense of pride that comes with being able to support yourself and your family, and at the same time be making a positive contribution as a participating member of your community, the nation, and the world. Ultimately you can be in a position to give back, either with your time or money, to make the world a better place. All of this is necessary to live *A Second Life*, to be all that you can be.

Step Six: Determine how your financial security can contribute to making the world a better place by using your God-given gifts/talents

Henry Ford, the founder of the Ford Motor Company, said, "Wealth, like happiness, is never attained when sought after directly. It comes as a by-product of providing a useful service." Unfortunately, the recent economic disaster faced by the automotive industry—as opposed to the extraordinary success Henry Ford created in that same industry decades ago—is a glaring example of how financial stability can be lost when a company's (or a person's) assets are not providing a useful service. The American automotive industry ignored the needs of the public that purchased their products, as well as the product changes they needed to make in order to meet the emerging standards of ecological consciousness of our world today. Their cavalier attitude of first serving themselves has landed them on the brink of losing everything. And, in the process, millions of American who have committed years of their lives to earning an honest wage in support of numerous industries associated with the auto industry are in jeopardy of losing everything as well.

This cautionary tale reminds us that the mistakes of others can serve as our example. Although we have been indoctrinated to believe that it's "every man for himself," and therefore you may not believe that your own financial status has any affect on society as a whole, the reality is that each person's inadequate and uninformed personal financial management takes its toll on everyone else in society.

A story that comes to mind as such an example is that of a man I'll call Malcolm. He was born into a modestly wealthy Northern California family and enjoyed an abundant lifestyle growing up with little expectation that he should ever worry about money. His family paid for him to attend a good university, where he graduated with a business degree but with limited career aspirations because he never felt he would have to work hard to support himself. He enjoyed living for a time as the caretaker of his family's extensive rural property. But by the time his grandparents and parents died, his younger brother—who had also gotten a college degree but entered the business world and pursued a business management profession and was the executor of the family's modest estate—determined it was wisest to sell the family property. This left Malcolm with no home and no job experience that could be applied in the real world.

But through his brother's business contacts Malcolm was able to secure a job as a commercial property manager in Southern California. Because Malcolm was smart enough to do the job and certainly had the education needed to do it well he found an adequate degree of success but did not excel beyond an entry-level position. Always in the back of Malcolm's mind was a longing for the leisure, easy-going lifestyle of living on his family's rural estate. During his off work hours he wiled away the hours reading, enjoying walks along the beach, and dining with friends. He bought a modest house and made just enough money to get by, but didn't concern himself with saving for the future because he knew his brother, who managed the family trust, would provide him with backup funds whenever needed.

When the company Malcolm was working for was sold to a conglomerate, staffing changes were made, including upper level management and lower level employees being laid off. Still, Malcolm was not concerned. His brother made sure he had enough money to get by while he searched for another job. But Malcolm wouldn't take just any job. He didn't think it was unreasonable to want a low-pressure job with high enough pay to support his modest lifestyle. As the months went by and the "right" job didn't come alone, Malcolm relied more and more on his brother to provide him financial support out of the dwindling family trust. Eventually, when there was no more money available to Malcolm from the trust, and his brother could not personally provide financial assistance because of his own financial obligations in support his family, Malcolm lost his home.

Believing that his brother was selfishly withholding money, Malcolm cut off all contact with him and chose instead to live in his car, which he did for a year. During that time he relied on the generous homeless assistance programs provided by a coastal city in California. There he got free meals and was offered counseling services, which he declined. But after a year he had become so depressed by his circumstances that he finally agreed to take advantage of the programs offered to help the homeless get off the streets. During group counseling sessions he was convinced to move into a group home, where daily programs were provided to help the homeless learn how to get jobs and eventually live independently again. Malcolm was a good student. He followed the rules and participated as required to obtain financial assistance from the city. After a year in the group home his social worker encouraged Malcolm to take the next step: find an apartment. Again he did the work required and managed to find an apartment owner who would rent to him, with the city paying most of his rent as long as Malcolm found a job.

The city had agreements with numerous merchants in the area to hire people in their homeless program, so Malcolm visited each one until he found one willing to hire him. It was a minimum-wage job as a store clerk and salesperson, but the pay was enough to get by because his rent was subsidized by the city. He went to work each day, was qualified to go to the food bank every week and get free food, and eventually was even able to afford cable television. But instead of being grateful, Malcolm complained to his social worker that standing on his feet all day at his job was too difficult, that he was too tired in the evening when he got home or on his days off to even clean his apartment. So the social worker arranged for him to have a cleaning woman come to his apartment once a week. Still Malcolm was not grateful. Instead of using his time off to help out at the homeless shelter, he hung out around his apartment building complaining to his neighbors about everything that had gone wrong in his life. He bragged about the city subsidizing his rent, and that the weekly cleaning woman's services were "free" because the city was paying for it. Malcolm didn't seem to understand that his neighbors were actually paying for his lifestyle through their taxes, that none of them could afford a cleaning woman, and many of them were scrimping and saving in order to pay full rent and stay in their own apartments.

Malcolm's story is a clear example of how every person's personal financial situation can help or hurt everyone else's. People who live by the indoctrinated creed, "every man for himself," are taking advantage of everyone else, and certainly not giving back. They are simply draining the system that could be helping those who truly need assistance.

Instead of the mentality: How will you reward me if I do [such and such]? the opposite way of thinking is to take responsibility for the financial stability of yourself and your family. Thereby everyone else will benefit. Every person who lives with this attitude clearly shows a team spirit, that you are not a person driven purely by the ego, but by something greater than yourself. Your goal is not to feed your ego by always looking for what "the system" can do for you. True fulfillment comes by getting yourself together enough that you are able to have the time to find ways to be of service to others.

Make God proud—Give back

God didn't say: I'm giving you all the potential in the world. Now go use it for your own personal gain and to feed your ego. Forget about everyone else. Don't even think about the other guy. Just get the most you can for yourself.

Each of us has been provided with unique gifts and talents that are endlessly beyond anything we can grasp—resources we need to tap into and develop as much as possible. By doing so you will be able to find ways to give back to others and serve a higher purpose, which is the true meaning of life.

The reality is that many people feel just "keeping it together" financially seems like a huge challenge. They barely have enough money, time, or energy to maintain their existence. Clearly, how we use our time makes all the difference. When it comes to our finances there will always be choices to make about how we use our resources. These choices are based on how we view our assets in perspective to our entire lives. Is your financial stability a part of *all* that your life should be? Or does it define *everything* that you are?

No matter what current financial situation you are in, always make God proud. Do your very best to take steps to improve your financial stability and status and, most especially, be grateful that you are healthy and able to work. By being grateful you show respect to the greatest gift of all—life—knowing deep inside that you are doing your best to be all that you can do in life. You will not be truly admired because of the "things" you have or your standard of living, but rather by how much effort and commitment you put into being a contributing member of society. Respect comes through these things, not by what you are able to get at the expense of other people. The people who take responsibility for their own lives, who possess positive traits, are the ones who make other people feel good and hopeful; they enlighten the days of others by being good examples. They leave the impression that true happiness and success in life is possible. These are the people who, no matter where you find them currently, will succeed because nothing can stop them when they are living according to how God wants them to live.

Step Seven: Learn the realities of the financial world

One of the first truths about the financial world that can be learned in Economics 101 is that there are always cycles in the economy; therefore, a smart money manager accumulates money during the good times in order to be covered during down times. It's also a law of physics: What goes up must come down. By ignoring this truth you're setting yourself up for financial disappointment, hard times, failure, or even disaster, over the long haul. It's imperative to plan for the future while dealing with your day-to-day financial situation today in order to protect yourself against the inevitable downswings to come. Get your financial situation straightened out for a better NOW, and for the future, always have backup.

Knowledge is power. By acquiring the right knowledge and skill set, devising a realistic, efficient plan, and following it, you can more effectively manage your financial situation. But securing or maintaining your financial status isn't enough. You must view your own financial management as an ongoing task in your life that is necessary in order to grow that aspect of your life, which contributes to your being a fully realized whole person. Many people believe they don't have time to study on their own or attend school to expand their base of knowledge or skills. The truth is, most people do have the time, but they've decided to use it on non-productive activities, such as watching television. Life is about priorities and how you use your minutes on earth. You can invest them by learning, growing, and evolving or you can choose to waste them.

Educate yourself. Instead of watching television or wasting your valuable minutes hanging out with losers, take advantage of your time by reading about your chosen career or areas of interest, attending classes, networking with others in your field, or brainstorming with other smart people or with yourself while taking a walk or getting some healthy outdoor exercise. Arm yourself with knowledge about money; learn how to master it. There are lots of good books and Web sites that provide information you can use to build your knowledge. Your opportunities to learn and grow are as limitless as your potential.

The educated differ from the uneducated as much as the living from the dead.

Aristotle

Learning and growing = utilizing our God-given gifts to the fullest—which is why he blessed us with our mind and body. By wasting time we are disgracing God's gifts. Our duty is to live a balanced, whole life by being all that we can be, which we do by constantly learning throughout life in order that we never stop growing and discovering our full potential.

Step Eight: Execute your financial action plan to get where you want to go

Getting savvy as your own personal financial manager

Becoming a savvy manager of your personal finances requires taking what may be a difficult look at the details of your money management skills to date and asking yourself this question: If your finances (or your family's) were a business and you were the COO (Chief Operating Officer), would you keep yourself in that position or fire yourself immediately? Of course, that's a trick question, because no matter how good or bad you've been at the job in the past, now you're going to do things differently. The reason many people don't do well as their own personal financial managers is because they were never told what the job entails or taught how to do it. This step-by-step action plan will take you through the process:

Know where you're starting from

No matter how overwhelmed you may be, no matter how many bills may be stacked up or hidden unopened in a drawer, your financial situation is not going to get any better unless you're proactive. Every good story has a beginning, a middle, and an end. This is your financial management story. Call it *The Balance Sheet* (defined as a snapshot of your financial condition). Right now is the beginning of your story. Make two lists:

- **List A:** On a sheet of paper or in a computer program make a list of your current monthly income from your job or other sources, or an average if your income is variable but reliable.
- **List B:** Then make a list of all your financial obligations and expenditures every month. Include the cost of your housing (which should be fixed), averages of your utility bills, automobile/transportation costs, insurance (both auto/truck and health), food, schooling, cell phone, Internet, cable/satellite television, entertainment, etc. Also include your credit card payment obligations, with your total balance, current amount due (including past due amounts), and the interest rate you're paying (for your mortgage, credit cards, lines of credit, etc.).

- Add your total monthly income on List A and your expenditures and obligations on List B. Compare the two totals.

If the total on List A (income) is greater than the total of List B (obligations), you're off to a good start. You've got enough money coming in each month to pay your bills. And, as you'll learn shortly, you have a great opportunity to do some fabulous money management to improve your financial stability.

But if the total on List B (obligations) is greater than the total on List A (income), then you've got to buckle down and get to work, pronto! Somehow you've got to get more money coming in than you need to spend each month. If you don't have a job, you need to get one (see the previous Job/Career chapter). If you have a job, you can get a better job making more money, get a second job, or create other ways to add to your income. Or you can cut your monthly expenditures and obligations—or even better, cut both!

Facing the truth that you're in a bad financial situation—even if deep down inside you've known it but are in denial—is one of the hardest things to do. Choosing to be proactive and do something about it takes courage and fortitude. But the payoff is huge!

Increase your income

There are a few strategies you can apply to increase your income:

- If you currently have stable employment that is fulfilling, review your situation and decide if it's feasible to discuss with your boss/supervisor the possibility of getting a raise. But be smart about using this strategy. Don't jeopardize your status, standing, or potential future advancement for monetary gratification today.
- If your current job is not fulfilling for you, either personally or financially, update your résumé and discreetly get it out there to start looking for a new, better job. (Again, see the previous chapter for more guidance.)
- While you're either working hard and smart at your current job that you want to keep or looking for a better, higher paying job, consider also getting a part-time job to increase your total monthly income. Such a part-time job can be viewed as temporary, or could be one that can be built into something full time or permanent. But it's important to keep the rest of your life in balance at the same time. Don't create a situation where you're working so many hours at two jobs that the other key areas of your life are suffering.

- Start a side business that can be conducted during your off work or free time. There are a multitude of possibilities that can be investigated—through networking, on the Internet, or trade publications. But there are also a multitude of schemes and scams that would be a waste of time for you to become involved in, so again, be smart about this. The first criteria for starting any kind of business—whether it's part time or full time—is that you feel a passion for it, which creates your motivation. Think of things that you love doing and are good at, perhaps a service you could provide to others, and figure out if there's a way to turn that into a successful business enterprise. But be aware: If your reason for starting a part-time business is to create income, be realistic about making *any* financial investment—that would be counter-productive. And figure out a way to still give enough attention to the other key areas of your life.

Cut your monthly expenditures and financial obligations

Spending less money than you earn or need to spend may not seem easy at first, but it basically comes down to creating new habits. Saving money may even be accomplished by eliminating a lot of small, wasteful expenditures—which is a strategy successfully used in business and by many other people in their personal financial management. You may already have a clue about how and where you're wasting money after taking the $50 Spending Challenge. Review your results and think about where you spend your hard-earned dollars and see what you come up with.

Also, make a list of all of your expenditures during the last six months (excluding necessities such as housing, utilities, insurance, and medical) according to categories—which will be particularly easy to do if you've been putting them on your credit cards, paying by check, or if you kept receipts. Categories where there could be room to immediately save money include: food, beverages, tobacco products, entertainment, toys and gadgets, sport and fitness activities, beauty products and services.

Food: Immediate monetary savings can result from reducing food expenses, but I don't mean to eat cheap, poor-quality food or less than you need to be physically healthy. (We'll talk more about food in the upcoming chapter on Physical Health/Wellness.) What I mean is instead of going out to lunch every day, pack a lunch at home and take it with you to work. This can offer you multiple benefits: you'll be eating better quality, more nutritious lunches, as well as have time during your lunch hour to take a walk and get some fresh air, and save money.

Eat out less often. Going out for a nice dinner instead of eating at home should feel like a special occasion, not an excuse to not cook at home. And actually, a home-cooked meal is usually more healthy and nutritious, as well as less expensive.

Don't go to the drive-through. Although it may be tempting to stop at the drive-through on your way home after a long day of work or shuttling kids around, those once economical and nutritious fast meals have turned into high-priced junk food that drains your health and your wallet while adding pounds of fat to your body. Keep handy, nutritious snacks, such as nuts or fruit, in the car to tide you or the kids over until you get home and prepare a quick, nutritious, economical meal.

Beverages: Although it's not a bad thing to support the economy by spending in your local shops, it doesn't make good economic sense to stop at a coffee shop every day to buy a cup of coffee or a latte when you can brew your own at home. Add up how much you've spent at a coffee shop during the last year and then decide how you could have better used that money.

Alcoholic beverages are another habit that's a drain on your wallet. Although red wine has been touted as having positive health benefits and, indeed, even limited daily consumption of other alcoholic beverages has recently received the same accolades, the truth is that alcoholic beverages are addictive and are just as likely to have a detrimental effect on your health (and your weight). Plus, whether you favor beer or champagne, all alcoholic beverages are expensive.

Tobacco products: No one still needs to be warned about the negative effects tobacco products have on your health. Although cigarettes get the worst rap, cigars are more likely to cause deadly throat or mouth cancer (as is chewing tobacco). Besides wasting a lot of your hard-earned money on a habit that could kill you, you're also alienating and offending a large percentage of the population that lives, works, and walks around you when you blow stinky smoke where they want to breathe fresh air.

Entertainment: The indoctrinated belief of society created by advertising states that every household must have cable or satellite television with premium channels. You should immediately delete this indoctrination from your consciousness and replace it with the harsh truth of reality: If you can't afford to pay your other bills or put a little money aside for a rainy day, if your relationships are suffering because you're too absorbed in watching the tube to pay attention to your loved ones, if you are overweight from eating too much junk food while surfing your 300 television channels, then you must immediately turn off the TV, put down the remote control, go directly to the telephone to call and cancel your cable/satellite service, then run—don't walk—out the door and get some healthy exercise! No discussion!

While you're out, stop off at a local library or video rental store and pick up a feel-good movie with a positive message that you and your family can watch together. Stop wasting money and at the same time sacrificing your relationships by watching television! And if you say you only watch public television or National Geographic shows, much of that programming is free on over-the-air television or can be borrowed from the library or rented for a modest fee.

Or, when you get home, dig deep into the game cabinet, pull out and dust off the old Scrabble or Monopoly games and gather around it with your family for a night of entertainment that also has some value in terms of expanding vocabulary, your ability to understand strategies or handle money, all while enhancing your personal relationships and saving you money.

And don't overlook the obvious: Parks, playgrounds, beaches, lakes, rivers, streams, mountains, well, most of the great outdoors offer free, healthy, stimulating entertainment environments—plus opportunities to exercise.

Toys and gadgets: There is no reason on earth that you have to be told this, but I'll say it anyway: You don't need to have the latest toys and gadgets that hit the stores, despite how attractively they may be portrayed by advertisers. Know one thing for certain: the *newest* and *latest* models of computers, televisions, cell phones, and other electronic gadgets are *all* obsolete the minute you buy them! You will *never* have the *newest* or *latest* because manufacturers will *always* bring out something newer next week. So don't waste your money.

Perhaps the largest drain on your wallet and unnecessary purchase is a new car. Again, understand that the only reason they keep bringing out newer models of cars is because they want you to waste our hard-earned money buying them—they're not necessarily better or safer, they're just newer. If the recent economic crisis has taught us anything, it's that the liberal credit approval standards for people wanting to buy new cars—which most don't *need*, but *want* because of ego gratification—has resulted in many of those same people now being unable to afford the monthly payments. Show gratitude for what you already have by taking good care of it and it should serve your needs for years. When you really do *need* a new car or truck, buy a good quality used model with a warranty. Stop being a victim of the indoctrination of society's consumer advertising that appeals to ego gratification.

Sports and fitness activities: Staying active and fit are key components of being healthy and enjoying every day to the fullest. But you don't have to belong to a gym or a country club to participate in either. Sure, both are nice and offer an environment where you can meet and hang around like-minded, positive people, and even network. But when times are tough you must consider whether the cost to your financial stability is worth the price you must pay. There are lots of free sports groups who are always looking for new members to join their activities. There are public golf courses, pools, and gyms you can join for a modest fee in most communities. And when it comes to fitness, evidence shows pretty strongly that the benefits of working out with little or no equipment (which I'll cover in the Physical Health/Wellness chapter) are just as great, or greater than going to the gym. Not to mention that the best way to stay in shape and healthy is by simply doing good, hard physical labor, such as mowing the lawn, raking the leaves, trimming the bushes, weeding the garden, cleaning house, etc.

When it comes to sporting activities that you love that require equipment, again, remember that it's a consumer market with the survival of manufacturers depending on coming out with a *new* or *improved* model of everything for you to buy. When you're on a reduced consumer diet and you already have the equipment you need—whether it's golf clubs or a bicycle—forget about getting anything advertised as the *latest, newest,* or *better* product. Keeping using what you've got until you truly can afford to splurge.

Beauty products and services: It's interesting that Barney's, the high-end department store, reported that sales were down in every department of their stores during the 2008 holiday season, except the cosmetics/skin care department. Cosmetics/skin care is a billion dollar industry in the United States *only* because of advertising. Women and men are targeted by companies that have always suddenly discovered miraculous new ingredients to put in products that will make people look more attractive, healthier, vibrant, glowing, younger, or even turn back the hands of time. But apparently those products are not working because people who can afford to do so are still going in for invasive or noninvasive medical cosmetic procedures to make them look like the latest celebrity they see on television, magazine covers, or on the movie screen.

The saying, "beauty comes from within," does not refer only to the fact that when you're a beautiful person it shows, but also that when you live a healthy lifestyle, take good care of yourself, find happiness by giving back to others, and being the best that you can be your true God-given beauty comes through. Now that's something all the cosmetics companies can't bottle and the cosmetic medical community can't inject into your skin. So don't waste your money on every new product that's advertised.

Making your financial situation—past, present, and future—all it can be

View your past financial missteps as learning experiences. Whether you made honest mistakes, got in over your head, or were "suckered in" by unethical lenders, credit brokers, or credit card companies who offered you low initial rates, then raised your rates after you accumulated a high balance, get over the unfairness of it all. Now's the time to stop buying into society's indoctrination and start operating based on your new belief system. If someone tried to take advantage of you—whether or not you knew or suspected the deal was too good to be true—and you took the bait, you are the fish on the hook. You have no choice now but to do the work necessary to get yourself off the hook, survive, and thrive.

If you've started reducing unnecessary and wasteful daily spending, whether or not you've managed to increase your monthly income, and your balance sheet is looking better, you've reached the middle of your story and are ready for the long second act. Here's where your perseverance and determination will pay off big time!

Credit cards: Decide that you're going to at least pay down, or perhaps pay off, all of your credit cards. Although paying the minimum amount due on time is better than skipping a payment, seriously consider whether you can pay more than the minimum. For incentive, do a little math. Write down the total balance of charges on your credit card. Now divide that amount by the minimum amount due this month. How many *years* will it take you to pay off your balance by doing it this way? I'll bet it comes out to decades. In other words, you're going to have an ongoing relationship with that credit card company every month for all those years! Do you like them that much? The quickest way to uninvite them from your life is to pay them off, close the account, and throw away the card.

In the meantime, try to get them to reduce your interest rate. Call each credit card company you're doing business with and simply ask them to lower your interest rate. If you're a good customer they're likely to do so. If the customer service representative you speak with refuses, either ask to speak with a supervisor or hang up and immediately call again—another person may be willing to help. While you've got them on the phone, ask if they would offer you a better interest rate and waive any fee if you transfer your other credit card balances to them. But be warned: If they agree to do so, they'll send you a new piece of paper with the terms of your agreement. Read the fine print *carefully* to see how long the better rate lasts, if there are any surprises hidden in there, etc.—you don't want to have them increase your interest rate three months down the road.

As an alternative to dealing with the credit card companies, if you're a member of a credit union, ask if you can get a personal loan to pay off your credit cards. Or ask your local bank. If either will do so and the interest rate they'll charge you is good, you can use the money to pay off balances on credit cards with higher interest rates.

Other strategies are to transfer balances from cards with high interest to those with low interest; pay off the balance with highest interest rates faster while paying the minimal on all other cards.

If you set out to pay off your credit cards in any of the ways mentioned, it's best to put away all of your cards until you've wiped out your debt. If you're not carrying a card with you, you're less likely to use it. Instead, carry enough cash for your necessary expenditures on days you need to go shopping. Once you've got everything under control you can carry one card for emergencies. But after doing the hard work it'll take to pay off your cards, don't fall for the credit card company indoctrination that using cards is a convenient, smart way to use your money—it's a trap!

One caveat and cautionary note: Don't renegotiate your home mortgage to a higher rate to get equity out and pay off other debts. This is a trick. Despite what too many lenders have recently encouraged borrowers to do, your house is not an ATM machine. If you've got a good, fixed-rate mortgage and equity in your home, leave everything exactly like it is; keep paying your interest and paying down your principal, keep paying your taxes and insurance. Protect your asset!

Smart shopping: Consider whether shopping at big box stores is really saving you money. Sure, you can buy large quantities of items you regularly use, but are you actually paying more per item than if you got a smaller quantity at the local grocery store? Take a handheld calculator, notebook, and do the math. Plus, going to big box stores that also carry clothing, books, CDs, electronic toys and gadgets, etc. may be too tempting. If the individual prices of larger quantities of items actually are a good deal but you don't have storage space at home, form shopping clubs with friends or neighbors who use the same products. Have one member of the group make the large purchase, then divide it up among the others, with each paying their share. This way not only is everyone benefiting from saving money and saving time, but you're forming groups of like-minded of people who are helping each other.

You can save a substantial amount of money each week by always making a list of what you're going to buy *before* you go shopping and take the list with you. How many times have you gone to the store to buy one thing and come out with a lot of stuff you didn't plan to buy? When you get to the store with your list, walk directly to the items on your list as fast as possible. Never wander around stores, browse, or go up and down every aisle of the grocery store, although you might want to glance in the aisles of other items you regularly buy and see if they happen to be on sale or specially priced. If the savings is substantial and you've got the extra cash, it's smart to pick up the item even though it's not on your list.

Don't hang out at the mall or go window shopping. Why torture—or tempt—yourself? Spend free time on more satisfying free activities that are good for you, your finances, and your relationships. Hang out in the park, ride your bike, go to the library where you can get books to read or DVDs to watch with your family or friends. Work in the yard or garden. If you have a family, get everyone out there to work together and enjoy some fresh air. It's good for your health, your relationships, and your wallet.

When is a bargain a bargain? Two women were shopping together in the kitchen supplies department of a large department store. They would wander away from each other, pick up an item to buy, and return to put it in a basket they were sharing. One of the women came back to the basket with a pasta strainer. Holding it up to show it to the other before putting it the basket, she said, "This is a great deal. Look how cheap it is. Why don't you get one too?" The other woman said, "I don't need a pasta strainer." The first woman replied, "Me either, but it's on sale. It's such a bargain." The second woman said, "But if you don't need one, it's not actually a bargain is it?" The lesson is that no matter what a great deal you can get on something or how much money you can save, it's not actually a bargain unless you need the item. Save that money or use it for something you actually do need.

Save for a rainy day: Even if you are tempted to use every last dollar to pay off your debt, decide how much you can pull out each week to save. It could be only $10 or $20, but it will add up fast. You could open a savings account at your bank or credit union, but if you stash the money somewhere safe at home you'll have the pleasure of counting it every week and seeing how much progress you're making. Keep this under the mattress if you like. But don't be tempted to use *any* of the money. At the end of the year put it in a bank account that earns interest. You won't believe the feeling of security it will give you to have that kind of backup.

Save money for a splurge: It may be a fancy dinner out, a new television (if you really need or want one), or a family vacation. Again, either keep it in a safe place at home (not with your rainy day money) or put it in a separate bank account.

Keep your résumé updated and in circulation: Always be on the lookout for a better job. Consider starting a part-time business during your off hours—but again, be wary of scams or schemes that want you to invest or buy something to get started.

Go to school part time to acquire new knowledge or skills that could help you become all that you can be.

Periodically consider asking your boss/supervisor for a raise—particularly if your performance is good and you're an asset to the company. Keeping a good attitude, willingly doing more than you need to do, and being a team player who helps out others will keep you in good favor not only with your boss, but your coworkers as well. Even if it doesn't pay off with better pay in your current position, there's always the great reference you'll get when you apply for the next job.

Think long term and save big time

Even if you have the money, that doesn't mean you have to spend it. Learn to distinguish *want* from *need*. Before making any purchase beyond necessities, ask yourself *why* you want the item, and, if the word *need* does not genuinely apply, consider holding off on the purchase—at least for a while—and revisit the idea at a later time. Usually if you're savvy about your long-term financial situation it will be easy to get off the consumer bandwagon and ride instead on the saver's train to a secure future.

Your home: Think about your expenses based on Maslow's Hierarchy of Needs. Sure you need shelter, food, clothing, etc., just to survive, but go one step further. Take an honest look at how much you are spending on those things and whether your expenditures are too high. For instance, the best financial advisors will tell you that your average monthly housing needs should cost no more than 28 percent of your monthly gross (meaning before taxes) income—19 percent is in the safe zone. (By the way, these were the standards to be met in the past when banks/lenders considered whether to give someone a home loan—before the lowered standards resulted in brokers and banks making millions at the expense of buyers who were kidding themselves.) If you own a house and your mortgage payment, taxes, and insurance equal more 28 percent of your income, you're definitely in a danger zone. Seriously consider downsizing for big-time savings and long-term financial security. If you're renting, apply the same formula and solution. Don't be house rich and wallet poor—it affects everything else in your life.

Your car: Do you really need more than one car/truck or a gas guzzler? Can you drive less, take public transportation, or walk where you need to go?

Your relationship with money: Never stop learning ways to create a more functional relationship with money by realizing that your old indoctrinated dysfunctional relationship with money has resulted in your financial situation not being all that it can be.

Your retirement: When you start accumulating extra money, don't forget about your retirement future. What are you contributing to your 401K or other retirement package? If you have no retirement plan, set up one now. Put away at least 5 percent of your pay initially and try to increase it by at least 1 percent each year. If your employer matches your contribution, then contributing to your 401K may be better than paying off credit card debt. Another option—which may be a bit more difficult because it is not automatic—is to save a small amount each week and put it into your IRA. Start by doing some research on your retirement savings options, talking with the human resources department at your job or attending free seminars or lectures on retirement savings.

Step Nine: Reevaluate your financial status according to your timelines

If your financial targets are not being met according to your timelines and you've encountered roadblocks, then go back to previous steps of this process to reassess what you're doing wrong. Make corrections to get yourself back on course. Then continue on your path forward toward your goal.

If all approaches you have taken have gotten you nowhere, go back to the drawing board and reassess your options. Review the lists you made for the steps above. What is missing? Do you need more knowledge and skills? Do you need more income? Do you need to cut expenditures even more? Do you need an attitude adjustment? There is no surrender—which means there is always a way. The question is how.

If you know in your heart that you are doing everything you can but still can't get your financial situation straightened around, or you haven't been able to make enough progress to feel comfortable that you can work everything out eventually, then you may need to take more extreme measures.

When all else has failed and you just can't get ahead no matter how hard you try, consider bankruptcy. Many bankruptcy attorneys will have a short initial meeting with you for free. And although you can go through the legal process of bankruptcy without a lawyer, most have reasonable fees or are willing to work with you.

Bankruptcy is the dirty little secret that no one is talking about over lunch, around the water cooler at work, or at family dinners. Most people don't admit that they've gone through bankruptcy, so you may feel like you're the biggest loser of everyone you know to even consider it.

Only by experiencing financial hardship is it possible to truly understand what it means to feel helpless. When there is nowhere to turn for help, people learn that they are the only ones who can make a difference, and that difference comes from their own actions. Almost everyone has felt financially strapped during a temporary situation in their life, but there are a growing number of people who are standing at the edge of the cliff facing bankruptcy.

> *The only man who never makes a mistake is*
> *the man who never does anything.*
>
> Theodore Roosevelt

In my early twenties I took on a high amount of debt through credit cards, in addition to student loans, that made my life difficult to master. The debt was not from lavish spending, but merely as a way to survive—to help keep me going during college as well as for unforeseen expenses. It became impossible to make even the smallest minimum credit card payment or meet my other financial obligations, plus I did not have the necessary means to cover my most basic needs, such as food and shelter. Naturally, I had to do something, but what, I wondered. The situation was very overwhelming and scary. There were moments when I felt like the world was going to end. I didn't know where to turn, but I pulled myself together, knowing I had to make some difficult choices about my financial future.

Being a responsible person, I wanted to do the right thing and thought I could pay off my debts over time. The first thing I did was to gather the few belongings I had that were of any value and take them to a pawnshop to sell. But the pawnshop didn't give me very much money for them. No matter how good my intentions, survival had to be my prime objective—which meant paying for food and shelter, with no money left to make payments on my debts. Because I had excellent credit before this unfortunate situation occurred, my choice was even more difficult. My pride told me to find a way to make things right, but I just couldn't see a way to make it happen.

A part of me wanted to ignore the problem and pretend that it didn't exist, hoping it would go away on its own or that some miracle would magically make everything different. But I realized I couldn't let things keep going on the way they were by denying the problem existed. I had to figure out a way to get out of the financial rut and get back on my feet.

Then one night sitting in the dark of my empty apartment after going through the piles of bills that I was unable to pay, I was exhausted from many sleepless nights worrying and feeling miserable and helpless, like my world was crashing. In my mind the financial burden had turned into a life-and-death situation. With very little hope left for resolving my problem, I prayed to God for help, asking him to show me a clear way out of my despair. Finally I went to sleep. After sleeping almost twelve hours, I woke up the next day fully rested and with a new perspective. My first thought was: Did someone die? If not, then the problem can be fixed. That bit of wisdom was a saying my father would repeat when people got too caught up in their problems and needed to see things more clearly and in a more realistic perspective. Next thought that came to mind was another one of his sayings, "Sometimes we feel guilt just because that is how we've been taught to feel, which distracts us from making the right decisions. It's only when we listen to our hearts that we know the real truth."

Because of the wise guidance my loving father had given me years earlier, my state of mind changed in a matter of minutes. With full clarity I finally knew what to do. I realized that what had made me feel trapped and unable to move forward had been guilt of failure. I realized that my financial situation was just another challenge to overcome in life and not fatal to any extent. I decided to write on a piece of paper all the pros, cons, and options that I had. The note with my scribbling went something like this:

- Do nothing
  Con: Problem will increase.
  Pro: Can temporarily trick myself into believing everything is fine.

- Make a payment plan and find a way to meet it no matter what
  Con: Based on the fact that I already have +100K in student loan debt that needs to be paid off no matter what, I will struggle financially for the rest of my life and never be free.
  Pro: I could ensure a great credit history in the short term, which could help me later when needing credit to buy a home, car, etc.

- Personal bankruptcy

  Con: Bad credit for next seven years, making it difficult for me to obtain credit. When applying for a job some people might view me as not being as responsible as someone with a stronger credit score.

  Pro: All debt, except government student loans, would be wiped clean, leaving me free and clear of all financial obligations.

I decided that based on my list I would make the most objective decision I could, free of self-judgment and criticism. It became clear to me that more than anything else I needed and wanted a new start in life, a second chance, where I could have a new beginning with less pressure. The only option that allowed me this was to declare bankruptcy. A big factor weighing in was my young age and not having any assets of value. Looking at my timetable, I realized that my credit would be restored right after I turned thirty, which gave me plenty of time to learn to live without credit and spend only what I made, leaving me free of debt. In addition, I would have time to save up for a good down payment for a home, as well as for a nice car. During the next seven years I could focus on my career and live a less pressured life because I was getting a second chance in life.

That same afternoon I called lawyers specializing in bankruptcy, got a price quote from a few of them, went for the one with the lowest price, and set a date for a meeting. Shortly thereafter I went to court. Sitting in the city courthouse, hoping that none of my creditors would show up, was a challenging experience. To keep it together I kept telling myself, "Nobody died, so it's all good." The judge declared me bankrupt and I walked out of the courthouse feeling like a new person, with a big weight off my shoulders.

As planned, I did buy my first home and car in my early thirties, and the experience of not having personal credit also taught me to never spend money I did not have on luxuries or unnecessary consumption.

Looking back on how I ended up in that difficult financial situation and the decision I made, experiencing the hardship was how I learned and evolved, so I am grateful. If I were back at the same place and time, I would make the same decision again. Based on circumstances and where I was in life at the time, it was the best solution and right thing to do. I learned a great deal from the experience, and it never stopped me in any way from achieving financial success later in life.

My father's saying, "Did somebody die? If not, it's fixable," has saved me from being a prisoner of my own negative thoughts many times in my life by putting things in perspective.

When the mind steers into negative thinking, it makes you feel out of control. It's necessary to know that there is no reason to feel trapped because there is always a way to work everything out. Everyone deserves a second change and a fresh start. If you decide to go the bankruptcy route, remember what you've learned for the past and set out on a new financial course better prepared to be the best manager of your own personal finances that you can be.

Step Ten: Reassess your financial values every six months after you are on your path

Now that you're on track financially, is this still what you really want? A lot of people work hard, have a beautiful home, a fancy car, and pay all their bills on time, but they still don't feel happy and fulfilled. They may feel as though they're working for the "stuff" instead of for a higher purpose. When you're on the path you had set as a goal and everything is turning out the way you'd planned, there's nothing wrong with thinking about whether it's still what you truly want. Some people decide that's not what they want after all. Perhaps they'd prefer to have more free time to travel or pursue new areas of interest. Some people decide to move to another area of the United States, or even to another country. Some just want an adventure and take off to sail around the world. Others join the peace corps.

You don't have to wait for retirement to live today as though it's the last day of your life. If your life right now is not all that it can be, then figure out what you can do to change it. God didn't give you the gift of life with the expectation that you'd acquire financial assets that end up making you a prisoner to your own financial success. An asset only serves a higher purpose if it enables you to live more fully, giving back to others in ways that make the world a better place.

Never let society's indoctrinated expectations motivate you to do things you truly don't want to do or live in a way that is not truly satisfying to you. Tap into the unlimited potential that God has gifted to you as you move through life.

Always remember that money is just a tool given to you by God. Learning to properly use that tool can give you access to an unlimited array of life experiences and opportunities to make your world a better place. Life is not about getting rich—although there's nothing wrong with that. Life is about using your riches well in ways that honor yourself, everyone else in your community, your state, your country, even the entire world, and God. By being the best personal financial manager you can be you make God proud.

Final Step: Be all that you can be, but not all at once

FINANCIAL SUMMARY

- Assess your current financial situation.
- If you are struggling financially, identify the reasons why, such as:
  - You monthly expenses/expenditures are more than your monthly income.
  - You've made large purchases with long-term payments, such as a house or vehicle, or used your credit cards so much that now you can't pay on time.
  - You know you need to cut your expenses and spending, but you don't know where to start.
  - Your work hours have been cut, you may be laid off or lose your job.
- Use the tools you've learned—meditation/prayer/self-programming—to delete the negative indoctrination/brainwashing that has blocked you from mastering the financial area of your life.
- Devise a game plan for re-creating your financial situation based on your new reality, including:
  - Steps you will take to increase your income, reduce your expenses/expenditures, even begin to save money for the future, a fun vacation, or luxury items.
  - Goals and objectives you will achieve.
  - Timelines for enacting/advancing your plan.
- Execute your game plan:
  - Each day: Systematically set out knowing what you will do to improve and re-create your financial situation. Follow through with commitment.
  - Every night: Routinely review your accomplishments and express gratitude.
- Reassess your overall results according to your timelines:
  - If you are on track, are there new goals you now want to achieve?
  - If satisfied with your progress and financial status, be conscious every day of maintaining the changes you have made in order to completely wipe out your old negative programming and firmly establish your new positive reality.
  - If you have not made the progress you'd planned, go back, reevaluate your situation and find new ways to make your game plan more successful.

ALWAYS REMEMBER: Surrender is never an option. You must find a way to succeed.

Physical Health/Wellness

3

Your health and body are not in top condition because you've been indoctrinated and brainwashed by society. This chapter will show you how to break free from the chains of society's mental slavery so you can regain control of your physical health/wellness.

Physical Health/Wellness Contents

Introduction

Society's Rule: The human body is like a machine, with moving parts that serve a specific function. When a part breaks down, then all we have to do is go to a doctor and have it repaired. In other words, if you don't take excellent care of your physical health each day and something goes wrong, modern medicine can fix you.

The Truth: Although the human body is the most efficient, miraculous "machine" God ever created, it is also the home in which your soul, your connection to God, resides. Because your body is the foundation that supports your entire life, your obligation is to honor that home/connection and keep it in the best possible condition. You cannot build a strong house on a crumbling foundation.

Your body is the foundation for everything else in your life. Not only does your body carry you around in life, it is also a vehicle through which your God-given gifts speak to you. When the body is in a state of wellness and balance, it provides a vital service as an instant and ongoing barometer of whether you are living your true passions, which feed and motivate you, or if you are entering a state of indoctrinated fear and denial, which affects everything in your life, including the health of the physical body. Because the body doesn't know the difference between imagined fears, anxieties, denials, and real difficulties, it's imperative that everything possible be done to keep the mind clear of the stresses that affect the health and proper functioning of the body, while being fastidious about honoring the body's physical needs.

If your body is not currently in the best condition it could be, it is not necessarily the result of lack of trying or desire, but more likely because you have been disconnected by society's indoctrination from the true purpose your body serves. Only by deleting that false programming, gaining renewed understanding of *all* that your body can do for you, and taking steps right now to bring your body into alignment with it's full potential as given by God will your life, health, and connection to your true purpose begin to manifest.

How can you heal your relationship with your body and set yourself free? Break away from the indoctrinated way of thinking according to society's rules. Begin today by changing your way of thinking. Take the first steps on the journey that is your new, self-fulfilled life in alignment with God. Follow this step-by-step approach to improving your physical health and wellness and set out on your new fulfilling life, *A Second Life*.

TEN STEP ACTION PLAN FOR MASTERING YOUR PHYSICAL HEALTH/WELLNESS

As you follow each of these steps, do so with the understanding that getting your physical body back into shape/good working order is work! It must be approached with dedication, perseverance, and determination. This is not just about eating the right foods and getting enough exercise, it's about honoring the God-given gift that is your body, which supports you and enables you to fully develop every part of your life in alignment with your God-given gifts. It's about making God proud by being the best you can be. Only then will you be able to maintain your physical health/wellness with passion and enthusiasm and benefit from the multitude of rewards offered in the other four key areas of your new life.

Step One: Assess the current status of your physical health/wellness

While assessing the current status of your physical health/wellness, you must be completely honest with yourself, otherwise you're wasting your time and won't get positive results. Answer these questions:

- Are you physically healthy?
- Do you have good habits that support and enhance excellent physical health/wellness?
- Do you want to improve your health or maintain your good health?
- Have you had health challengers or a health crisis?
- Are you afraid you're building up to a health problem/crisis?
- Why has your health suffered both now and in the past? ("I don't know" is not an acceptable answer! If you can't figure it out, who will?)

Step Two: Assess yourself as the caretaker of your own health and wellness

Would you trust yourself to be in complete control of your physical health/wellness?

Of course, this is a trick question. When it comes to your own physical health/wellness there is no one else who can be responsible for it, and no one who could even try to be, if you're not doing what's needed to improve or maintain your health. More than in any of the other four key areas of life, when it comes to your physical health/wellness, the buck starts and stops with you!

So if you don't trust yourself, ask why or why not. Is it because you've let your physical condition/health deteriorate and feel unmotivated to do anything about it? Is it because you feel you've truly tried and still haven't gotten the results you'd hoped for? Or is it just because you don't know what to do?

How much do you really know about what's needed for good health/wellness?

This test will help you determine where you stand today, and also give you important information about what you need to change about yourself. Bottom line: If your physical health is not the best it can possibly be, then you've got to start right now to delete any old programming that's standing in your way and embark on your new physical health and wellness plan. The benefits go way beyond your looking better and feeling better. Because your physical health is the foundation of everything else in your life, the rewards of good health are limitless.

Answer as honestly as you can these questions about the key components of good physical health/wellness:

Nutrition

- How much do you know about basic nutrition?
- Do you understand the health benefits of nutritious, well-balanced eating?
- Is it important to be conscious of what you eat and whether it's nutritionally beneficial, as opposed to just eating whatever's put in front of you, whatever's available, or whatever you crave?
- Are frequent or regular fast food meals on the run as good for your body as homemade, well-balanced meals prepared with nutritious ingredients and love?
- How does eating nutritious food in the right amounts benefit your overall physical health/wellness?
- How can honoring daily mealtime as a sacred gathering with your family—if you are married and/or have children—enhance your relationships?

Exercise

- How much do you know about healthy exercise?
- Do you understand the health benefits of the right kinds of exercise?

- Is it important for healthy exercise to be part of your daily/weekly routine?
- Is going to the gym for a workout as good for your health as outdoor exercise?
- What benefits can be derived from outdoor exercise activities with your family?

Understanding what your body is telling you

- Can you recognize when you are hungry, have eaten enough, or eaten the wrong things?
- What signals does your body send when/if you don't eat properly?
- Are fad diets good for your body and overall health?
- Do you know how your body expresses a need for you to get up and move around?
- What signals does your body send if your exercise choices are harming, rather than improving, your physical condition?
- How does the right amount of proper exercise enhance or improve your overall physical health/wellness?

Stress reduction

- What signals does your body send that indicate you are feeling stressed?
- Is stress *always* bad for you?
- What methods or techniques do you use for stress reduction?
- Can exercise reduce your stress?
- Does eating poorly add to the stress your body feels?
- How can you better reduce negative stress?

Rest and relaxation

- What are the benefits of rest and relaxation?
- Do you get enough rest and relaxation?
- What can you do to enhance your rest and relaxation efforts?

Many people believe they can answer all of the questions above. If you believe you can, a final question would then be: Do you apply what you know? If so, you would be in excellent health, fit and full of energy.

What are you willing to do to maintain or improve your physical health?

If you are in excellent health and already have an effective, consistent health maintenance plan that you follow religiously, then you're on the right track. Stick with it.

If you're not in excellent health, fit and full of energy, then either you don't really know the answers to the questions above, you're not doing the right things to honor your body's health/wellness, or you don't really understand how important these things are in order for your health—and your life—to be all that it can be.

Improving your physical health/wellness is not a complicated process, but it does take determination, perseverance, and a desire to succeed. As you embark on this step-by-step program to mastering better health/wellness, you must realize that much of what you may be doing incorrectly is not your fault. The way you eat, how much you exercise, and what type of exercise you get, even your "body image," all are the results of your indoctrinated programming since birth. No one sets out to eat food that's bad for them or not exercise and ignore the signals or symptoms from their body that are telling them something is wrong—and may contribute to suffering with an illness, disability, or even an early death! By deleting the destructive programming that's gotten you where you are today and taking a proactive approach to re-program yourself by changing bad habits to good, you're on your way to an entirely new you and a future of unlimited possibilities. Although the past cannot be changed, most people can undo any obvious damage or potential hidden damage brewing under the surface of their physical health. You must start today to live with integrity in alignment with the God-given blessing of a magnificent body by honoring this gift and treating it with reverence as the sacred vessel in which your soul dwells, which it truly is.

Step Three: Decide your health and wellness future in specific terms

Create a future view of your physical health/wellness for the following time frames: twelve months from now, three years from now, and five years from now. Various things that could be included are better habits (such as eating only nutritious foods most of the time, getting regular exercise, rest and relaxation, and better managing your stress) or making specific improvements to your health (such as quitting smoking and/or drinking, eliminating excessive sugary or fatty foods from your diet, etc.).

When you want something in life, it's important to set a clear goal in order to achieve it. First, set a realistic target, but when doing so, allow yourself to think big. Set a high goal that requires that you be really dedicated in order to achieve it. This could mean you need to learn more about health in general or more about your specific health challenges. Then ask yourself *why* you want to reach this goal. Is it because you want to test yourself to see how well you can do? Is it because you feel that your focus on improving your health/wellness will result in a longer, better, more fully lived life; that you'll have a certain feeling of accomplishment; or perhaps it will eliminate from your life the constant guilt you feel about not taking better care of yourself.

Maybe it's because you have children you want to be with as they grow up and future grandchildren you want to be able to fully enjoy. Perhaps it's because you feel you can better serve a higher purpose and set a better example to others by living a healthier lifestyle. The reasons can be many, but it's important that you know *why*, because your reasons are the key to your passions (motivation). When planning for your physical health/wellness future—as well as enjoying the present—remember to shoot for the stars, but never forego the principles of balance in all five key areas of your life, which are required in order to live *A Second Life*.

Step Four: Decide on a physical health/wellness action plan and timelines according to your future goals

- When will you begin a program to improve/maintain your physical health/wellness?
- What are your exact goals?
- Decide on a timeline. How long will it take to achieve your goals?
- How will you know how well you're doing?

A belief system that stands in the way of many people successfully breaking bad habits that are detrimental to their health, or embarking on a health improvement program, is that they want to see results instantly. (Perhaps this is the reason we've become a pill-popping society, with people choosing vitamins, over-the-counter medicine, and even prescription medications to cure their ails instead of making lifestyle changes that will eventually result in elimination of their ails altogether.) When it comes to health improvements, immediate gratification is not always possible. It's taken a long time for you to get into the physical shape you're in—supported by your indoctrinated negative programming—and perseverance is a must in order to establish new positive habits and reverse health challenges. If you have a plan and stick with it—and also learn to interpret the messages your body is sending you—you *will* experience positive results within days. The longer you stay with your plan, the better you'll feel and the healthier you'll be. This is not about enjoying one new day, but about living to the fullest an entirely new life!

In order to stay motivated you need to set milestones—specific periods of time when you'll consciously reassess how you're doing. All of the goals I reached in my life were because I set a clear path to follow. Everything that has taken place in my own life and in the lives of the people I have coached was a result of planning and dedication. Few good things in life happen unexpectedly. Conversely, when it comes to your physical health/wellness, if the unexpected does occurs it's usually not good—and could have been avoided. Don't allow your indoctrinated bad habits continue to feed the destructive volcano of illness boiling inside your body—which eventually will erupt into disease and perhaps an early death! As with the other four key areas of your life, planning and time management are needed, particularly when it comes to your health. Planning does not mean that someone stops living for today and starts believing that everything in the future will be so much greater. The reason to make plans is to ensure that you make the most of this life today, and create opportunities for the future.

Set up a system to keep track of your progress. To begin with, you need to know where you're starting from, so take the "One-Week Health Challenge."

For one week write down the following:

- *everything* you eat, including meals and snacks, and how much of each
- *everything* you drink, including water, healthy beverages, unhealthy nonalcoholic beverages (you know the ones), and alcoholic beverages of any kind, and how much of each
- every time you exercise, including what type of exercise and the duration of such activity
- what you do to relieve stress
- how much you rest, relax, and sleep

Be totally honest. Remember: If you cheat on this challenge, no one will know but you, so you're only cheating yourself. At the end of the week look at the details that create the picture of how you treat your body. Do you respect and honor yourself? Or are you slowly, systematically undermining your own best interests by damaging your body—which could become permanent. You'll clearly see the areas where you need to make changes immediately.

Now decide on your timelines for reassessing yourself and your progress as you enact your new healthy lifestyle changes. During the first six months retake the same One-Week Health Challenge once a month (during the same week of the month is best, perhaps the first week of the month or the last week of the month so you'll easily remember your schedule). After six months—if you've been genuinely dedicated and are feeling and seeing the dramatic improvements and results that you're capable of achieving and expect of yourself—begin retaking the Challenge every six months to make sure you're staying on track.

Whenever you retake the Challenge, compare your current results with those from the most recent past Challenge. Give yourself credit for your hard work and dedication as you improve, becoming healthier and healthier! To really give yourself an emotional boost as you progress, compare your most current results with the first time you took the Challenge. How proud of yourself are you? If you're not getting the results you're capable of and you're not proud, then you'd better buckle down and do better. After all, it's only yourself you're disappointing. Ultimately you're the one who will suffer.

Define your approach. What will you do to get healthy or maintain your good health? Here's a clue: As with everything else in life, balance is the key. Because every aspect of the five areas that need to be mastered to achieve good health affects the others, a five-pronged physical wellness approach must be embarked upon.

If you fall into the category of the 65 percent of Americans who are overweight or obese and list losing weight as one of your goals, you've probably already tried various "food diets," or even "fad diets." Did you achieve the results you'd hoped for—meaning, long-term weight reduction and stabilization?

While living *A Second Life* your weight is not a measure of your physical health/wellness. Whether you're treating your physical body with respect and regard, how you're caring for it and nurturing its well-being, those are the goals. When you delete your old indoctrinated negative programming that has gotten you into the physical condition you're now in and begin to live in alignment with your body's true needs, your physical weight will automatically change and adjust to its correct level—whatever that may be in pounds.

What your body needs is not to weigh a specific number of pounds, but to be nourished with the proper food and hydrated with the proper liquids. Your body needs to keep moving to stay strong and flexible. It needs to feel comfortable, at ease and free of negative stress. It needs the proper amount of rest and relaxation. Only when all of these needs of your body are satisfied and maintained will you *thrive*, feeling enthusiastic as you embark on each new day living the life you were meant to live.

How much time are you willing to allocate for your efforts?

As with every other area of your life, time, effort and dedication are required to change old destructive habits and establish a new health-supporting lifestyle. Your initial efforts will take up more time than you're presently spending on your physical health/wellness, but as your new lifestyle takes hold it will become automatic. In time you'll find that by living a healthy lifestyle you actually have more time to do the things you love doing and enjoy them to the fullest. So the time you invest initially will pay-off big time in the long run.

Can you do it on your own or do you need guidance and support?

This *A Second Life* guide provides all the information you need to embark on and establish a health improvement/maintenance lifestyle. As you read further in this chapter it may seem as though what you're being told is somewhat different than other "experts" are saying, because you're not expected or encouraged to calculate how many calories you're eating, stick to a specific eating plan, or join a gym to work out or take fitness classes.

An important component of *A Second* Life's health improvement/maintenance belief system is that your body will provide the guidance you need. As you delete your negative indoctrination and learn to understand what your body is telling you it truly needs, you must then respond to those needs for your physical health to automatically improve. But if you need external support, turn to other people in your life. Encourage them to join you in creating the best physical health/wellness they can. Support each other in your efforts and celebrate and enjoy your new, healthy lifestyles together.

Also, use the tools you learned in Coding to Oneness, Level 1, of this guide—meditation, prayer, and self-programming—to assist you in setting your goals and keeping a clear focus on them as you enact your plans in order to master your physical health/wellness.

Step Five: Decide how important physical health and wellness are to you

Decide what is important to you in regard to your physical health/wellness by listing those things in order of importance. Do you want to feel better, have more energy, and look better? Do you want to eliminate habits that are detrimental to your health and/or live a more vital, higher quality, long life?

The motivation for many people may go back to Maslow's Hierarchy of Needs. It's a primal need of every human being—just as it is of animals—to first do whatever it takes to survive. But since human beings, as opposed to animals, have been given the gift of conscious thought, analysis, and the ability to make choices, we have learned through our indoctrination that it's possible to survive without actually doing everything that's best for us. The question is: Do you want to just survive or do you want to *thrive*? There's a huge difference. You will feel the difference by the choices you make.

Thriving is such a higher state of being and way of living that it's almost impossible to imagine, much less discuss, how your life will be different when you're *thriving*, as opposed to just surviving. But just for the fun of it, think back to *your best day ever*. Remember how you felt when you woke up and jumped out of bed. Remember the spring in your step as you went through your day. Remember how clearly you were able to think and respond with excellence in everything you did. Can you remember how it *felt* to be living life to the fullest at your ultimate capacity? Were your self-esteem and self-confidence at their highest levels? Were you better able to be considerate of others and interact with them in ways that were beneficial for everyone involved? Did you feel like a different person living a better life? This is what you will have and the way you will feel when living *A Second Life* as a person whose optimal physical health contributes in a positive way to every other aspect of your life in alignment with God's gift to you.

Step Six: Determine how you can contribute to making the world a better place by being physically healthy

"The *I* in illness is isolation, and the crucial letters in wellness are *we*," is a quote by an unknown author used by Mimi Guarneri in her book *The Heart Speaks: A Cardiologist Reveals the Secret Language of Healing.*

How does being physically healthy transform your "*I*" view of the world to the "*we*" view? By deleting your old indoctrinated destructive habits and replacing them with a positive, consciously healthy lifestyle, you are honoring God's gift of life every day by accessing your true self, the person God intended you to be, the person with unlimited opportunities and happiness. Your life becomes a marvelous adventure you are prepared and willing to engage in fully, without the restrictions imposed by not being in optimal physical condition. If you must, do it for yourself first—even if it's only for selfish reasons—and soon you will see that when your body is not constantly demanding your attention because it is feeling unwell, undernourished, and ignored, your world will open up to *everything* around you, transforming you into a person who just as automatically thinks of others as well as yourself. Then, in addition to being a role model, you are living in a way that makes God proud!

Step Seven: Learn the realities of physical health/wellness

When it comes to physical health—just as in every other area of your life—knowledge is power. The basic rules that must be followed in order to become physically healthy and maintain good health are really quite simple. And once you've mastered the basics and put them into practice you'll begin to feel and see the rewards immediately.

The problem is that many people have been indoctrinated to believe that they can get away with not taking good enough care of their physical health and that they'll escape any dire consequences for a very long time. Even though deep inside everyone knows this is a false and destructive belief, they continue to buy into it because they are too afraid to face the reality that the repercussions of not being physically healthy go beyond undesirable body fat that makes them feel sluggish and unattractive. Underneath the surface of their bodies is a volcanic disaster brewing that could explode to the surface at any time.

The 2007 statistics reported from the Centers for Disease Control and Prevention show that the greatest health risk for Americans is the high prevalence of people with unhealthy lifestyles and behaviors—such as insufficient exercise and being overweight. Both are dramatic risk factors for many chronic diseases and disabilities, including heart disease, diabetes, hypertension, and back pain. And despite the health and fitness trends frequently highlighted in the media, it's an unfortunate fact that there continues to be an increase in the numbers of children and adults who are overweight because of physical inactivity and harmful dietary habits.

Instead of following sound nutritional and dietary guidelines, too many people cling to unhealthy eating habits that not only limit the quality of their lives, but also shorten their lives. No matter how often people are told that they need to eat a well-balanced, nutritious diet of fresh foods, fast food and processed foods still permeate their diets. No matter how many times people are encouraged to get off the sofa, turn off the television, and get some healthy outdoor exercise, people aren't getting the physical exercise needed to keep their bodies in a healthy, vital condition.

In 2004, life expectancy for the average American was seventy-eight years. That's a long time to suffer with a debilitating, preventable health problem—before it finally kills you! The leading cause of death continues to be heart disease, which is avoidable for the vast majority of people who eat a healthy diet and exercise on a regular basis.

The most significant effect on people's health status and predictor of their future health are their lifestyle choices and behaviors. Heavy and chronic alcohol consumption = increased risk of numerous diseases and physical injuries due to accidents. Yet statistics show that consumption of alcoholic beverages has increased! Cigarette smoking = increased risk of lung cancer, heart disease, and breathing disorders. Although for a period of time the percentage of Americans who smoked was declining, now that decline has stalled! Obesity = increased risk of heart disease, diabetes, and stroke. Yet overweight and obesity rates continue to steadily increase!

Conversely, regular physical activity = reduced risk of disease + enhanced mental and physical functioning. Yet statistics show that only 20 to 33 percent of adults engage in even regular leisure-time physical activity—forget about routine vigorous physical activity!

These facts and statistics are just the tip of the iceberg that is the total picture of how Americans today are failing to honor the God-given gift of a magnificent body—the vehicle that carries every person through life. Where do you rank among these statistics?

Another known fact is that negative, nagging stress kills. It affects *every* part of your body, eating away at your nerves, organs, and muscles. Still, the majority of Americans do *not* routinely use to their best advantage simple techniques that have been *proven* to reduce negative, destructive stress. And when it comes to rest and relaxation—which should be a natural part of every person's daily routine—most people are too busy rushing around in their status-driven lives and their minds are too preoccupied with unimportant, unproductive thoughts to settle down long enough each day to renew and restore their bodies. How are you doing when it comes to managing your stress and getting enough rest and relaxation?

In addition to following this guide to bring your lifestyle and habits into alignment with the way God expects you to take care of your physical health, learn to notice and pay attention to any signals or messages your body might be sending you. By responding in informed, efficient ways you can maintain your physical health/wellness and enjoy a full, vital life and thrive!

Step Eight: Execute your physical health/wellness action plan to get where you want to be

The belief system of *A Second Life* is that when you honor the needs of your physical body—by first deleting your indoctrinated programming in order to be able to feel and understand what your body truly needs—your physical health will automatically improve. Whatever excess weight you are now carrying around that your body does not really need will fall away, your energy and vitality will be awakened, and you can enjoy life to the fullest every day. This commonsense approach to excellent health and vitality is based on what science has told us the human body needs to be healthy and function optimally. Master these five components of physical health/wellness and enjoy a life of unlimited potential:

Nutrition

You will not be told in this life manual what specific foods to eat or be prescribed a specific food plan. What's most important in *A Second Life* is that you learn the types of foods that are healthy for you to eat because they nourish your body and generate good clean energy for you to use in pursuit of being all that you can be. What you eat is the key to excellent health and wellness. Without proper food and nourishment everything else you do will never be enough.

You are what you eat

This old adage is often repeated because it's true. The next time you gorge on a dozen donuts or a bucket of fried chicken, don't be surprised to look in the mirror and see a donut of fat padding around your waist or fat hanging over your belt. This is not to say you shouldn't have a donut every now and then—unless, of course, you have a genetic diabetic condition or other health problem that would prohibit eating one—or occasionally enjoy some good fried chicken. I'm saying that overdoing *anything* is never the wisest choice. And we are talking about choice here. Even though you may have learned to eat unhealthy foods during childhood—and don't even *think* of blaming your parents or grandparents for that, because they were only doing what they were taught—now that you know why you thought it was okay to do it, *you* must make the choice to change. No one will be force-feeding you a dozen donuts or a bucket of fried chicken. From this moment forward, if you go there, it's your *choice* to do so.

Food cravings and addictions

Accept the fact—and personal responsibility—that if you're craving donuts and other sugary foods or highly fatty foods, you have an addiction. Eating the foods you crave is like getting your "fix"; it makes you high . . . temporarily. But then comes the crash. Your blood sugar plummets, you feel weak, perhaps a little dizzy, and you've got to sit down. You can't think clearly or go about doing the things you need to do. Yes, you're an addict.

But just as with any addiction, you have the power to stop right now! Don't buy into society's indoctrination that you must wean yourself off of your "habit." Instead, use the tools at your disposal to delete the indoctrinated programming that got you addicted in the first place. Through self-programming you can change the way your mind thinks about what foods your body wants. And as you change your mind, your body will follow. The cravings will stop. As you substitute healthy foods that feed your body and your soul—instead of unhealthy foods that feed your addiction—soon your new habit will be healthy living with the unlimited potential that is your God-given gift.

Forget fad foods and diets

The multimillion dollar diet/fitness industry would have you believe that their products and services will cure all of your body weight/health problems. Again, this is indoctrination through advertising. Not only that, but it's false advertising. If it were true that any of their products and services cured body weight/health problems, why are 65 percent of Americans overweight or obese?

To make matters worse, many of the "diet" foods they want you to buy may actually be bad for you. Take diet soda, for instance. Maybe they leave out natural sugar, but instead they put in low-calorie artificial sweeteners. Just because it's low calorie, does that mean it's better for you? From my way of thinking natural is always better than artificial. If you want fewer calories when drinking sodas, just drink fewer, or none at all. And don't be fooled by "diet" food products. Reduced fat usually means reduced flavor. So in order to make the food taste decent they add salt, or "flavorings," some natural, others artificial. Not to mention the fact that they have to add back in vitamins to give it the nutritional value it lost during processing. Answer this: Would you rather eat a "reduced fat" food that has more sodium that you should consume—sodium that, by the way, may make you feel fuller because of the water weight you're accumulating, which is bad for your circulation and your kidneys—or would you rather eat a freshly prepared meal of wholesome food?

Even though frozen food meals have been around since the 1950s, to me they still fall into the category of "fad foods." They give the impression that they are healthy, economical, and quick. But, again, check the labels. What's in them? Particularly check the sodium content. And economical? Well, figure out how much it would cost you to prepare the same meal at home in the same quantity contained in the frozen variety. Certainly if you microwave them they are ready to eat sooner than if you a prepare the same meal from scratch (which could take an entire 20 to 30 minutes), but then answer this: Do you quickly eat the microwaved meal directly out of the plastic container it was cooked in, and then rush off to do the next busy thing you must do? Or worse yet, sit down in front of the television and eat? Or do you then put the microwaved food on a nice plate, sit down with your family, and savor the experience of enjoying a good meal over good conversation?

And where's the proof that "diet" pills/supplements or diet meal programs or regimented limited food programs actually work—besides the spokespeople who swear by them and show off the results on television? All of the diet pills/supplements have side effects. Secondly, although the people who write an entire book to tell you how to eat only twenty-one specific foods in order to get healthier may actually believe what they're telling you because it worked for them and their particular body, but how will it work for you and your particular body?

All of the advertising and marketing of these products is playing on the false hopes of people who are indoctrinated to believe that there's a magical way to get healthy.

A well-balanced diet and moderation = a healthy body

Here's a radical idea: Revert to the basics. No, not the old indoctrinated basics of the U.S. government Food Pyramid's recommendation of eating lots of refined grains and carbohydrates (think flour), starchy vegetables, high-fat foods, and sugars—all of which turn you into an addict. Revert back to the new basics. Eat pretty much what you want, but make sure you eat a well-balanced diet of food that's as fresh as possible, not processed, and includes lots of colorful foods. In fact, the more color the better because foods with color have more nutrients. Needless to say, the most colorful foods are vegetables and fruits, which also happen to contain fiber, which in addition to being good for your digestion also fills you up—they're called calorie-dense foods in nutritionists' lingo. That's not to say that the traditional mostly white and beige meal on Thanksgiving (i.e., turkey, dressing, mashed potatoes, gravy, with a little green beans and cranberry sauce on the side) is forbidden. I'm just saying don't make it a habit.

Along with fresh vegetables and fruits, include whole grains and legumes (beans). Whole, of course, means all the nutrients aren't processed out of them. When grains are processed to make white flour for bread, pasta, cakes, donuts, etc., they have to add vitamins and minerals back in. Even flour used to make wheat bread is usually processed. Such grains, as well as sugars, are called refined carbohydrates. They're the addictive kind. That's why you want to look for the word "whole" on grain products. Food in its more natural state is always the most reliable and beneficial source of nutrients and energy. Fresh vegetables, fruits, whole grains, and legumes—called complex carbohydrates—give you good clean energy, not fake, jittery energy like too much caffeine or refined carbohydrate consumption, but real, sustained, focused energy.

And don't forget to eat enough protein. Muscles need protein to stay strong and build strength. There are various types of protein to choose from: plant protein (usually soy or whey mixed in protein drinks by athletes), animal/fish protein, eggs, and dairy protein. Since it's not really good to eat too much animal fat—which makes you sluggish because it slows down the digestion—the animal proteins with the lowest fat are chicken, turkey, and fish. Shellfish is high in cholesterol, so if you need to watch that, then limit your consumption. Many people limit eating red meat to once a week or every couple of weeks, depending on the cut and how it's prepared. If you want to eat bacon, ham, pastrami, salami, pepperoni, and cured meats, do so infrequently because any cured meat has high sodium content. Eggs are fine, but probably not every day, as is cheese in small quantities. Although every person's protein needs are different depending on how muscular they are, how much exercise they get, and what their body type is, the general rule is to have your protein serving per meal be the size of your closed fist.

How food is prepared is just as important, too. Needless to say, avoid fried foods, including hamburgers and fish sandwiches (except occasionally and then preferably grilled), particularly deep-fried foods—chicken, fish, eggs, potatoes (French fries), zucchini and other vegetables, and cheese (sorry, mozzarella marinara lovers). Opt instead for grilled, baked, broiled, or boiled.

Now that you've got a beautiful plate of colorful fresh vegetables and a closed fistful of protein, sit down—with friends and family whenever possible—be grateful and slowly savor each delicious bite. But then, stop eating *before* you get full! If you feel full, or worse yet, stuffed, then you've eaten too much. Forget about the indoctrination of being a member of the "clean plate club."

Beverages = hydration, bad beverages = addiction

What you drink can either be beneficial for your body and your health or detrimental. Good clean water, of course, is the beverage of choice. Even though you'll hear that you should drink eight to ten glasses of water a day—and most people don't—think about the amount of water you drink this way: If you're thirsty, you're already dehydrated. Of course, your level of thirst can be influenced by what you eat—salty foods—and how much you sweat during exercise or hot weather. You need to rehydrate after sweating because dehydration can dramatically affects how your body functions, particularly your heart. And when eating salty foods your kidneys will be working overtime to filter the sodium out of your system, so hydrating can help them better function. (Obviously you don't want to be constantly taxing your kidneys by eating too much salty food or foods containing lots of sodium.)

Bottled and designer water is expensive, but preferred by those with a refined pallet or some extra cash. But many people who are concerned about the health of our planet are now opting to no longer purchase water in disposable (even if they are recycled) plastic bottles and containers. If you're not convinced, consider this: In the middle of the ocean between the continental United States and the Hawaiian Islands is a place where the currents flowing in from various directions creates a huge vortex of swirling water. Environmentalists have recently observed that that vortex is now *filled* with plastic! They call this the North Pacific Gyre. The currents carry plastic trash—bottles, containers, plates, cups, bags, shoes, clothing, toys, toothbrushes, even used condoms, you name it—to this area, where they are sucked into the vortex and swirl endlessly round and round, now creating a giant plastic-filled cesspool the size of Texas. The extent of the effects this is having on the planet's marine life and ecosystem are not completely known, but it's very, very bad news. Thirty years ago the bottled water industry barely existed in the United States; now Americans spend $15 billion a year on bottled water—more than Ipods and movie tickets. Are we making our planet a better place by buying and using disposable plastic?

Plastic soda bottles and sports drink bottles are also found in abundance in the North Pacific Gyre. Even though you wouldn't imagine that soda and sports drinks would have anything else in common, actually they do: Both can be equally bad for your health. Although having a soda or sports drink isn't necessarily a bad thing, drinking a lot of either definitely is. Soda (all kinds) contains phosphates, which leach calcium from your bones, and lots of sugar. Diet soda contains various artificial sweeteners, which recent studies have suggested are addictive and actually contribute to the obesity problem in this country. So you're not doing yourself a favor if you're trying to lose weight and drinking "diet" anything. Sports drinks were developed to rehydrate athletes who sweated a lot. But now they've become a "fad" beverage that can actually be harmful to your body if you're not sweating a lot and need to rehydrate. They're high in sugar, sodium, and potassium so much that they could throw off your proper sodium, and potassium balance, which is necessary for your heart to function properly.

Also trendy are bottled high-caffeine drinks that give you a "rush" of energy. Drinking them is like quickly having several cups of strong coffee or tea, with the effect being that you get a buzz; your heart starts racing, your mind zooms . . . and then you crash. Not only are they addictive, they also dehydrate the body. Caffeine drinks, including coffee and tea, even some cola drinks, are best consumed in moderation; otherwise they can have a detrimental effect on your body.

Enjoying alcoholic beverages in moderation can have a positive effect on your health. But they can also have some negative side effects. Most alcoholic beverages have a high calorie count (not that we're asking you to count calories), which can create extra body fat, and are converted to sugar by the body. This can take a toll on your pancreas (not a good organ to irritate) and, as is well known, the neighbor organ to the pancreas, your liver (also not a good organ to irritate). Plus, alcoholic beverages can dehydrate your body—perhaps it's the salty food you snack on while drinking—and can be addictive; and they're a depressant.

Drinking fruit juices in moderation can be good for you when it's pure fruit juice, but many have added sugar. Even those without sugar added can have naturally high sugar content, as does most fruit. Although fruit juices often contain the same nutrients as the actual fruit, most juices don't have the fiber. Not only is fiber essential for good digestion, it also helps the body metabolize the fruit sugar. Ultimately it's better to eat the whole fresh fruit than just drink the juice—and drink a nice tall glass of clean, fresh water.

Exercise

In addition to eating proper food and drinking proper beverages, you must keep moving in order to get your body into tip-top condition and maintain that level of physical health.

Usually when people hear the word "exercise" they think of going to the gym, working out, or jogging. But in *A Second Life* exercise is any type of physical movement that keeps your body strong and flexible. Of course, this could include going to the gym, working out, or jogging, but it could also be playing tennis, mowing the lawn (*not* on a riding mower), vacuuming, and cleaning windows, or even washing the car. The point is to *use* for body for what it was designed to do: move!

Aerobic and anaerobic exercise

Technically there are two types of exercise: aerobic and anaerobic. Although there is a physiological distinction in terms of how energy is used by the body, put simply: aerobic exercise is good for the heart and circulation; anaerobic is good for building and keeping muscle strength. In fact, your body needs both! Keeping your heart and circulation strong has a beneficial affect on *every* other part of your body, and it also gives you energy. Aerobic exercise is when you get your heart beating fast for a sustained period of time (at least 20 to 30 minutes) by exerting yourself. For most people this happens with these types of sporting exercise: jogging, running, tennis, basketball, swimming, roller skating, etc. (By the way, an increased heart rate due to stress and anxiety is *not* healthy aerobic exercise!)

Anaerobic exercise requires resistance to strengthen your muscles and bones. Muscle strength develops and is maintained when the muscles contract and then release in short-lasting, high-intensity activities. Many people work out with weights for such an effect. Other activities that have the same results by having your body weight provide the resistance are: jumping rope, hill climbing or hiking, old-fashioned calisthenics—such as push-ups, etc.

There are also types of movements that can have both aerobic and anaerobic effects on your body, such as fast walking, stair climbing, sprinting, and bicycling—alternating between moderately fast and steady for an extended time for aerobic and short bursts or uphill at the fastest speed or with more exertion for anaerobic.

The American Heart Association recommends at least 30 minutes of moderate to fast exercise three to five times a week—which can be simply taking a brisk walk—to keep your heart healthy. But *A Second Life's* belief system is this: Whenever possible, keep moving. Move as much as you can as often as you can. Of course, the best kind of exercise doesn't focus on whether it's aerobic or anaerobic, but fits into two other distinct categories:

- Good old-fashioned physical labor, such as vacuuming, window cleaning, washing the car, building a deck, mowing the lawn, trimming a tree, carrying your neighbor's groceries into their house from their car, etc. That's exercise with a purpose!
- Sporting or outdoor activities with family and friends. That's improving and maintaining your relationships, as well as your physical health/wellness all at the same time!

Besides keeping your body as healthy as it can be, with specific types of exercise training and a lot of discipline you can also re-create your body to be and do whatever you desire. Anyone can run a 10K marathon if they feel passionate enough about doing so by setting their goal and working (training) to achieve it. Anyone can train their body to have the right muscle development and cardiovascular endurance to ride in the Tour de France. Anyone can sculpt their body as though they're Michelangelo creating a sculpture, as I did. Even though I was once a tall, skinny young man, I felt a passion to transform my physical body from skinny to muscular. First I set a clear goal, and with determination and discipline I was dedicated to my training: working out and providing the correct nourishment described in this chapter. After achieving my goal at age eighteen, I kept sculpturing as well as maintaining my body.

The key to successful preservation is maintenance.

Christian Schoyen

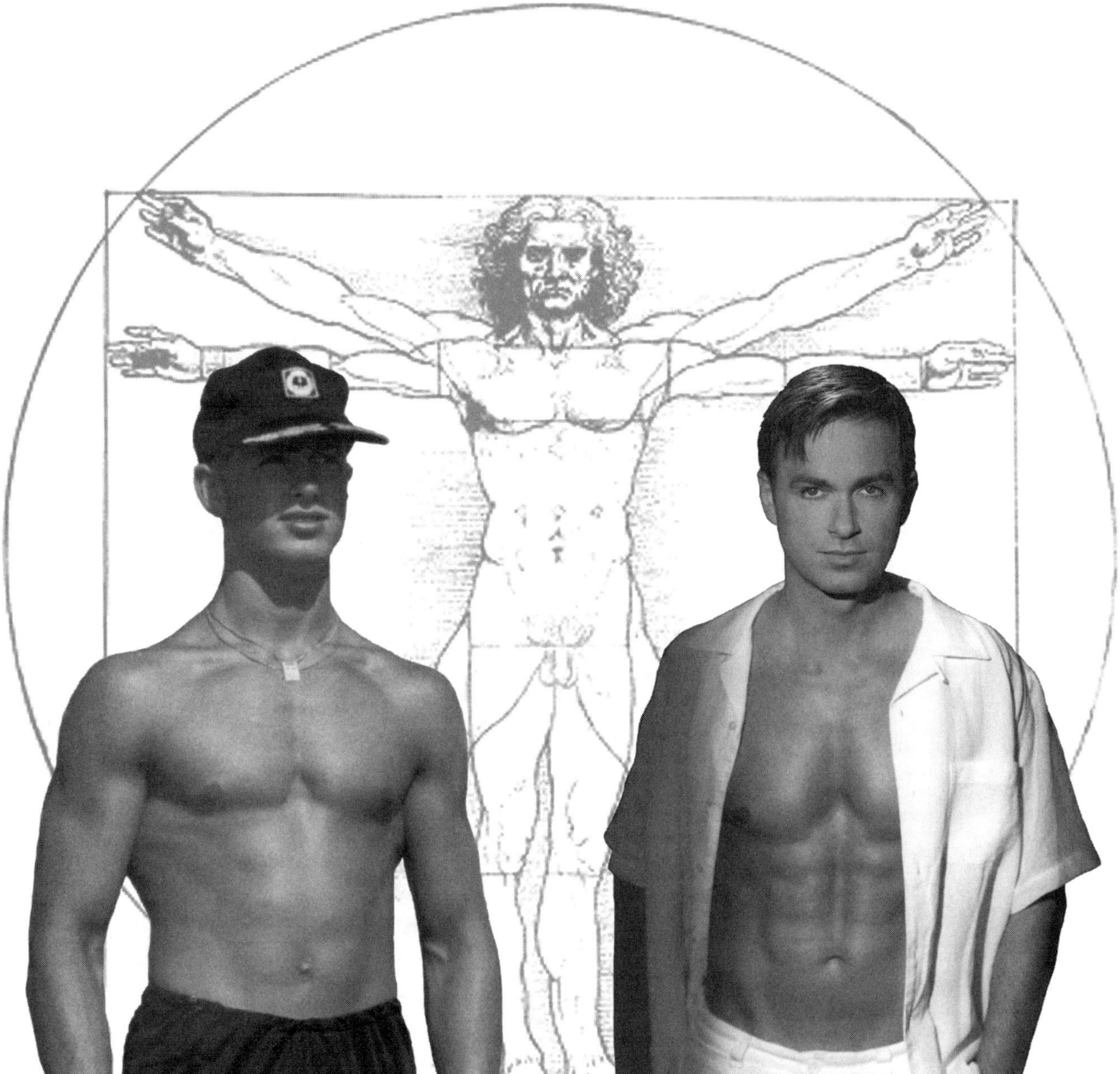

Christian at 18 years old, 178 pounds

Christian at 43 years old, 178 pounds

As with everything else in life, you want to clearly envision your goal in your mind—meaning as soon you mentally become the change you want, so it will happen. Even though it takes work, it's never considered difficult because you are One with God and creating something like an artist does on a blank canvas. The exciting thing about going through the process of achieving a physical goal is that you can see and feel the changes in your body each day. But whatever applies for physical also applies for everything else in life: *a clear target + the right formula + strong dedication and endurance = achieving your goal.*

Everyone can change their physical body if they desire to do so, because we are all created in image of God; just as the Vitruvian Man, we are all perfect. It doesn't matter what you start with, your greatest tool for creating anything you want in life is your mind, which can create any reality you desire, whether it's a certain physical appearance, strong financial foundation, better self-worth, or defining and integrating your higher purpose. Although your mind can be your worst enemy while society's indoctrination still has a hold on your thoughts, once you are free from your indoctrination you become the creator of everything in your own life. When re-creating and maintaining my new physical body, I learned as an awakening process that it was important to do so for myself and not others—meaning taking care of myself was merely respecting God's gift, life, the best I could. Taking responsibility for the health and condition of my physical body for as long as I live is one way I show respect for my body (and myself) as it is the same as respecting God.

Wherever your passions lead you, no matter what your goal, you too can achieve it through hard work, discipline, and being all that you can be.

Understanding what your body is telling you

Your body is communicating with you at all times. Another key component of excellent physical health/wellness is learning to notice the signals and messages your body is sending you and then responding to them.

Nourishing food/beverages = a happy, healthy body

Your body will let you know when you eat food or drink beverages that aren't good for you. You may have stomach pains or nausea, a headache, feel a rush followed by a crash; you may feel sluggish and lack energy; you could crave more of that bad thing you consumed; or you could even feel depressed and unmotivated. These are all messages from your body that must be noticed and not be ignored. Notice how you *feel* after you eat or drink something. If it makes you feel bad and out of sorts or *toxic*, it's not good for you. Worse yet, if it makes you physically ill, you must avoid it!

On the other hand, after eating the types of foods that are good for your body and drinking the proper beverages, notice how nourished, energized, or relaxed you feel. If it makes you feel *nourished*, then it's good for you.

Stop eating before you're full

Your body will also tell you when you eat too much, even if it's too much of the good stuff. Just because your plate is filled with food, that doesn't mean you have to eat it *all*. That's old indoctrinated programming from your childhood—to be a member of the "clean plate club." Sure, you've heard it: "The children starving in Africa would love to have that food." Even though that may be true, you know there's no direct link between helping the starving children in any part of the world and continuing to eat the food on your plate even though you're already full. There's another saying, "Save yourself first; only if you're alive can you set out to save other people."

Once you master being able to push the plate away from you when you're full—even though there's still food on it—then you can start working on learning to recognize when you're *almost full*. It takes about half an hour after you stop eating for you stomach to recognize that you've had enough food. That means if you stop eating when you're *full*, you've eaten too much.

Portion control is a device used by "diet gurus" to trick people into eating less, thereby reducing their calorie intake. But if you learn to listen to what you're body is telling you, you'll automatically put less food on your plate, begin to recognize when you've had enough—even when you don't feel full—and not feel "stuffed" half an hour after you've left the table. (By the way, automatically putting less food on your plate also means your food budget will be reduced, which gives you some extra money to save and donate to an organization that helps to feed people who really don't have enough food. Now, that's truly giving back!)

Take time to eat nourishing food

You must always have the same concern for yourself as you feel for people who are starving because they don't have enough food. Honor your own body by feeding it the proper food, and also by taking the time to feed it properly. Of course there will be times when you're doing something so important that you can't stop the minute you want to and have a nourishing meal. But losing the balance in your life by ignoring the need of your body to be nourished because you're overworking, overplaying, or just too lazy is disrespecting your body!

Move me! Give me a break!

When your body is feeling stiff or you're feeling restless, those are definite signals that you need to get up and move around. The only way to keep your body flexible and vibrant is to keep moving. On the other hand, if you're feeling pain because you've overdone it, give your body a rest. Again, moderation is the key, but some kind of daily exercise is mandatory; otherwise your body will start wasting away, because it was designed to move.

Stress reduction

If your body is feeling all pent up, almost frozen, then you're not managing negative stress well. Not all stress is bad. Stress is a motivator. It can push you to be your best even when you're not sure you can do something. But negative stress is a different thing entirely. Negative stress breaks down your immune system and body parts, contributing to ill health and even disease. Not only does negative stress affect your body, it also affects your thinking, your reasoning, and your ability to make good choices. Until you've deleted all of your old indoctrinated programming and have your new belief system established, negative stress can also cause you to revert back to believing that society's rules are your reality, instead of knowing that God's truth (your truth within) is what must be followed in order for you to be the best you can be.

It's mandatory not only to release and relieve negative stress, but also to avoid imposing undue stress on your body. Meditation, prayer, and self-programming—which help you to delete the old indoctrinated programming that's holding you back in life—also help you release and relieve negative stress. Eating proper food nourishes, feeds, and supports the health of your body—instead of placing demands on your body to work harder to digest and eliminate the toxic effects of bad food. And exercise is an excellent stress reducer. It's proven to reduce blood pressure and release feel-good chemicals in the brain while keeping your body in good operating condition.

Don't forget to exhale

When you get overwhelmed by everything going on around you, or by your own thinking, and begin to lose focus on your true purpose, it's time to slow down, sit down, stop, and breathe. Take several slow, deep breaths. And don't forget to breathe *out* as well as in. Many people forget entirely about exhaling but mostly inhale or even hold their breath. Breathing out is very important. In fact, breathing out for a longer count than you breathe in for 30 minutes a day is a proven technique for people with hypertension to naturally reduce their blood pressure.

You've got to be joking

Probably one of the most effective ways to reduce and relieve the ongoing stress that nearly everyone feels is by not taking yourself too seriously. When you look at yourself from the perspective of God, how big is your problem or how important are the things that you're stressing about? This is not to say that you should go through life with a cavalier attitude and approach. But, indeed, there's a fine line between giving everything you do your best effort and being so intense about it that you believe one misstep will result in the end of the world. When all five key areas of your life are in balance, no one thing will feel so important that it can ruin your day, much less the world. And if you begin to feel that it could, stop and think about how ridiculous that is—then have a good laugh at yourself!

Humor and laughter are the miracle cure given to us by God. Laughter clears the mind. A good belly laugh shakes up the entire body, vibrating through every cell, stimulating healing and renewal. And at the same time feel-good chemicals are being released by the brain, lifting our spirits and our energy.

Try to find humor in difficult or challenging situations. Laugh freely and often. Not only will humor and laughter help you stay physically healthy, they'll enhance the quality of your relationships and create a positive atmosphere in the space you occupy, making the world a better place for everyone you interact with or encounter.

Rest and relaxation = renew and restore

Not only does your body need to feel well nourished, flexible and strong, comfortable and at ease, and free of negative stress to function at its ultimate level, it also needs to renew and restore through rest and relaxation. Although it's sometimes difficult to find time to relax during the twenty-first century when everyone's lives are so busy, scheduling downtime is just as important as getting enough sleep.

During sleep is when the body slows down and restores and renews itself. During relaxation is when the mind does the same. Relaxation means something different to every person. For some it's being entertained by reading, watching television, going to the movies, or viewing sports events. For others it's casual outdoor activities in natural, pleasant environments where they can immerse themselves in the wonders of nature.

Still others find it relaxing to hang out with friends or family; having stimulating conversations with colleagues; attending classes, conferences or conventions; participating in sports leagues or hobbies such as boating or golf; doing yoga or tai chi; tending a vegetable garden in the backyard. Discover what you personally find to be fulfilling, relaxing activities and make it your goal to schedule time to do them.

And at the end of each day, no matter what—whether you've completed everything on your "to do" list or not—have a designated time that you will go to sleep so that you can be certain to get enough rest. Numerous studies have shown that adequate sleep every night—either seven or eight hours—is required for the body to have time to regenerate, restore, and renew itself. God entrusted you with the gift of a magnificent body; it's your responsibility to keep it in the best condition possible.

Making your efforts all that they can be

Everyone has pushed the envelope at some time in life, not getting enough good quality sleep or rest or relaxation or exercise or food. And if you're completely honest with yourself you have to admit that even if the sacrifices seemed worth it at the time, ultimately they weren't as important as the precious gift of excellent health and vitality. Only when all key components of your physical health/wellness are fulfilled and in balance will you *thrive*: be full of clean energy and feel enthusiastic as you embark on each new day living the life you were meant to live.

Step Nine: Reevaluate your health/wellness status according to your timelines

Reassess your health/wellness status by retaking the One-Week Health Challenge according to your timelines—or once a month during your first six months, then every six months when you are on track with your health/wellness improvement plan. If you have not achieved the level of physical health/wellness you set as your targets or if you've encountered roadblocks, then go back to previous steps of this physical health improvement/maintenance process to determine what you're doing wrong. Make corrections to get yourself back on course. Then continue on your path forward toward to your goal.

If the approaches you decided upon still don't get your physical health/wellness to the level it needs to be, go back to the drawing board and reassess your options. Review the lists you made for the steps above. What is missing? Do you need more training or education? If you already have the necessary information but are having difficulty sticking with your plan, perhaps an attitude adjustment is in order. Always remember: You only get one body in this life; if you don't properly care for it, nourish it, and honor it, you're dooming yourself to a limited life—which is unacceptable! There is no surrender—which means there is always a way. The question is how.

Step Ten: Reassess your health/wellness values every six months after you are on your path

Now that you are achieving your goals, were your standards set high enough? Or is there more you can be doing to improve and maintain your physical health/wellness? There are many ways to measure your success. One way can be to see how you are progressing by taking on new challenges that help you grow—which is a basic ingredient for feeling good about yourself because it means you are evolving. Being stagnant means the opposite.

Another strong indicator that you are succeeding toward being all that you can be, and goes far beyond anything else, is the impact you have on others in a good way. This isn't necessarily a result of showing people how much your dedication and discipline have paid off by transforming your body and your health. Look around at the other key areas of your life and notice how your better health is contributing to making you a better employee/boss; how your ability to think clearer has enabled you to better handle your personal finances; how your new level of energy has enabled you to work harder and at peak levels; or how much energy you have left at the end of the workday to spend quality time with your loved ones.

Several years ago I began to hear stories that gave me an additional reason to keep my physical body in optimal condition. I realized that the human body, like a robot, is made up of hundreds of parts that may not be used up when our time on earth ends. Instead of "the corpse" being disposed of as though it no longer has any useful purpose, I signed up to be an organ donor after my physical death, so any parts of my body that are still usable will be given as replacement parts to someone in need. By keeping your body in the best condition possible you too have another way to serve a greater purpose with your life—even after your minutes on this earth have ticked away.

If you've gotten your physical health/wellness on track and stuck with it, sometimes changes/adjustments still need to be made in your plan of action to take you even further. When you learn to listen to yourself, your instincts will tell you whether you are doing everything you are capable of doing. The passion inside is the voice of God showing you the way. All you have to do is listen to what your body is telling you.

Final Step: Be all that you can be, but not all at once.

PHYSICAL HEALTH/WELLNESS SUMMARY

- Assess your current physical health/wellness.
- If you're not as healthy as you could/should be, identify the reasons why, such as:
  - Your eating, exercise and other daily habits are not health enhancing and may even be detrimental to your health and well-being.
  - Your solution for feeling tired, unmotivated, bored, anxious, or stressed is to escape into unproductive activities, such as watching television or partying, or consuming addictive substances, foods, or drinks.
  - You work too much, causing you to feel stressed out most of the time, and don't get enough proper rest and relaxation.
- Use the tools you've learned—meditation/prayer/self-programming—to delete the negative indoctrination/brainwashing that blocks you from excellent physical health.
- Devise a game plan for restoring your physical health/wellness based on your new reality, including:
  - Steps you will take to eat more nutritious foods in the proper amounts, get moving or exercising in adequate and healthy ways, make lifestyle changes that will help you reduce stress or handle it better, and make time for rest/relaxation.
  - Goals and objectives to achieve, and timelines for enacting/advancing your plan.
- Execute your game plan:
  - Each day: Systematically set out knowing what you must do to improve your physical health/wellness. Follow through with commitment.
  - Every night: Routinely review your accomplishments and express gratitude.
- Reassess your overall results according to your timelines:
  - If you are on track, are there new goals you now want to reach?
  - If satisfied with your progress and health status, be conscious every day of maintaining the changes you have made in order to completely wipe out your old negative programming and firmly establish your new positive reality.
  - If you have not made enough progress, reevaluate your physical health/wellness situation and find new ways to make your game plan more successful.

ALWAYS REMEMBER: Surrender is never an option. You must find a way to succeed.

Relationships (with yourself and others) 4

You have difficulties in your relationships (with yourself and others) because you've been indoctrinated and brainwashed by society. This chapter will show you how to break free from the chains of society's mental slavery so you can establish a genuine connection and feel fulfilled in your relationships.

Relationships (with yourself and others) Contents

Introduction

Society's Rule: Success in relationships is achieved when you are fulfilling everyone else's needs and making them happy.

The Truth: Most people living in the western world in the twenty-first century are given the impression from the time they are young children that they will be popular, well loved, and happy if they put everyone else's needs ahead of their own. This belief system that judges people by external circumstances creates an illusion that a person's value as a human being is based wholly on what they do for others, regardless of their reasons for doing so. But such a mentality corrupts our society by creating people-pleasers who don't understand that they will feel personally fulfilled *only* when their actions come from the heart.

We are indoctrinated to believe that being popular and well liked, even loved, is the only measure of success in relationships. This encourages people to do whatever it takes to make other people happy, even if it means foregoing their own wishes or desires—which is a recipe for disillusionment and defeat. After all, how can you live a fully realized life based on your God-given gifts and talents if you accept the idea that society's opinion of who you are in relationship to others is more important than expressing the true desires and passions burning within you? By buying into that misleading way of thinking we are simply self-dramatizing—acting out a part we were taught to play. Most people are not even aware that they are role playing because they are indoctrinated in such a way that they are unable to get to know themselves intimately or learn to understand what is truly important to them as individuals. Therefore, instead of consciously expressing themselves through words and actions that are based on deeply held truths, they automatically engage in erratic emotional drama that destroys their ability to honor the beauty of their inner selves.

Only by deleting our indoctrinated programming that encourages us to engage in such self-defeating behavior and learning to become one with ourselves will we have something of genuine value to offer other people in relationships.

Ultimately, the relationships you have with others are a reflection of the love you feel for yourself and God. Take responsibility from this moment forward for every relationship you have. From now on, the degree to which *any* relationship you have is high quality and worthwhile begins and ends with you!

> *Change will not come if we wait for some other person or some other time. We are the ones we've been waiting for. We are the change that we seek.*
>
> Barack Obama

When your relationships do not currently feel satisfying and fulfilling, if you constantly experience difficulties and drama, or are unable to connect or bond with people on a deep level, it is not necessarily the result of lack of trying or desire. Most likely you are among the millions of people who have been indoctrinated by society's rules to believe it is wrong for you to place your relationship with yourself before all others. The fact is, there is no way you can *ever* develop or maintain substantive, deep relationships with anyone else until you truly know who you are and understand what you have to offer others from your heart. Putting your relationship with yourself first is the same thing as putting your relationship with God above all others. When coming from that place while interacting with anyone else, the best of you will be fully engaged and involved and genuine connections will easily develop and be maintained.

All of this is possible only by deleting your indoctrinated false programming, gaining renewed understanding of *all* that you have to offer in relationships, and taking steps right now to bring your relationships with yourself and others into alignment with your full potential as given by God. Then the true purpose of your personal connections can begin to manifest, they can feed your soul and enable your relationships to have true value.

Has conducting your life based on society's expectations resulted in your happiness or feelings of success in relationships? How can you heal your current relationships, create new better relationships, and set yourself free? Begin today by breaking away from the indoctrinated way of thinking according to society's rules and changing your way of thinking. Take the first steps on the journey that is your new, self-fulfilled life in alignment with God. Follow this step-by-step approach to improving your relationships and set out on your new fulfilled life, *A Second Life.*

TEN STEP ACTION PLAN FOR MASTERING YOUR RELATIONSHIPS (WITH YOURSELF AND OTHERS)

As you follow each of these steps, do so with the understanding that a complete change in the way you view relationships—most especially starting with your relationship with yourself—is necessary! Shifting your consciousness must be approached with an open mind, an open heart, and dedication to a new way of thinking.

This is not just about putting your own needs and desires first, it's about first understanding how your special God-given talents can be used to make the world a better place through every kind of relationship you have. By recognizing your special gifts, you gain understanding of what you can offer others. By truly knowing yourself you become free of the emotional ups and downs that result when you react to others; instead, every one of your actions will be based entirely on your own God-given truth. Only then can you have complete self-assurance and confidence to interact honestly, kindly and from a place of genuine love—no matter how or why others behave as they do toward you. In this way you are honoring and respecting yourself and know you have the support of God that enables you to fully develop every part of your life in alignment with your God-given gifts. It's about making God proud by being the best you can be by developing and maintaining relationships with passion and enthusiasm, and benefiting from the multitude of rewards offered while living in the NOW that is your new life.

Step One: Assess your current relationship with yourself

While assessing your relationship with yourself you must be completely honest; otherwise you're wasting your time and won't get positive results. Answer these questions:

- Who are you?
- Do you have a good relationship with yourself?
- How do you behave in ways that are supportive and respectful of yourself?
- Do you fearlessly honor yourself and your inner truth?
- Are your relationships with family, loved ones, and friends mutually supportive and respectful?
- Do you want to have better relationships?
- Are you afraid of losing important relationships in your life if you change the way you interact with others?
- Why are your relationships not working out both now and in the past? ("I don't know" is not an acceptable answer! If you can't figure it out, who will?)

Step Two: Assess yourself as a participant in your relationships

If you were someone else, would you want to be in a relationship with you? Why/why not?

Step back and view yourself and how you interact in a relationship from the perspective of someone else. This person might be someone who is either currently in a relationship with you or it might be someone who is considering entering into one. This test will help you gain some perspective on what you offer in a relationship with yourself or someone else today, and also give you important information about what you need to change about yourself. Bottom line: if you would not want to be in a relationship with yourself, you've got a lot of work to do. Answer these questions as objectively as possible:

1) Do you believe honest, thoughtful communication is the cornerstone of all successful relationships?
2) Are you a good listener who is interested in the ideas of others?
3) Are you dependable, reliable, and trustworthy?
4) Do you give consistent attention to your relationships?
5) Are you even-tempered and kind, even during situations that are emotionally challenging?
6) Are you able to control your feelings, reactions, and actions, rather than be controlled by them?
7) Are laughter, humor, and play elements of your life each day?
8) Have you mastered a balance between your work and personal life?
9) Do you use your energy to promote your strengths, rather than defend your weaknesses?
10) Do you deserve to have a good relationship with yourself and with others?

If you answered "yes" to all of the questions above, you should be happy to be in a relationship with yourself and find your relationships with others to be harmonious and worthwhile. On the other hand, if you answered "no" to any of the questions or were uncertain about how to answer, you need to examine yourself and your behavior further and make changes as soon as possible. Even though many people accept relationships with themselves and others that are less than ideal, these same relationships—which are plagued by doubts, uncertainty, and insecurity—do not encourage people to be the best that they can be. Living with acceptance of a less-than-ideal life is cheating yourself, as well as everyone else with whom you interact, and disappointing God. Only when you develop your best self can you enjoy genuine and deep relationships that are truly fulfilling.

Create a Relationship Résumé for yourself, which sums up the relationships in your life so far. The saying, "A man who doesn't learn from the past is doomed to repeat it" provides inspiration to sit down and perform this very insightful—and fun—learning exercise.

Your Relationship Résumé

1) List the most important and significant relationships you have had during your life. Just as on a career/job résumé, include:

- the length of time each relationship lasted/has lasted (don't get caught up in counting the days and months, just approximate, estimate, and round off)
- the nature of the relationship (family, romantic, marriage, friendship, career/work)
- the good things about the relationship
- the challenges in the relationship
- if the relationship ended, why did it end

2) List the special qualities you brought to or exhibited within each relationship. These are the special qualities and abilities you have already developed and nurtured that you can offer as a participant in a relationship—such as, are you a good listener, interested in other people's points of view, consistent and reliable in your words and deeds, even tempered and considerate, etc.

3) List the ways you can improve your interactions with others in relationships. Even if you feel confident that you are engaged in mutually fulfilling relationships with others, there is always room for growth. For most people the success—or failure—of past relationships can serve as learning experiences when they are viewed with a detached perspective.

4) Now focus on your relationship with yourself and make two lists: one containing the positive qualities you exhibit in your self-with-self relationship. Then list the ways you can improve your self-with-self relationship.

Before anyone can expect to feel fulfilled and truly happy in relationships with others, they must first develop and nurture the best qualities in themselves and exhibit those qualities in their most personal of relationships: self-with-self. After mastering your self-with-self relationship you are then fully prepared to engage in genuine and truly giving relationships with others.

Step Three: Decide the future of your relationships in specific terms

Create a Relationship Bio/Résumé for the following future time frames: six months, twelve months from now, three years from now, and five years from now.

When you want something in life, it's important to set a clear goal in order to achieve it. First, set a realistic target. When doing so, allow yourself to dream. Set a high goal that requires you to really stretch in order to reach it—this could mean you need to acquire new skills (such as better ways to communicate) or knowledge (understanding more about the subjects/topics that are important to loved ones). It may mean you need to first work on your self-with-self relationship and develop it to the fullest before embarking on relationships with others that can be truly meaningful. Then ask yourself *why* you want to reach this goal. Is it because you want to have relationships that are models of your parents' or other family members you admire? Or is it because you feel that as a unique person your own relationship goals can be very different in order to be fulfilling for you personally? Maybe it's because you feel you can better serve a higher purpose by being in relationships that help other people directly with your gifts or make the world a better place through your time and commitment to causes or endeavors. The reasons can be many and varied, but it's important that you know *why*, because that is the key to your passions (motivation to grow as a person).

Second, in order to be realistic you need to set milestones—small goals with steps to take in order to reach each one of them. Little in life falls into someone's lap unexpectedly. Life planning and incremental management of your goals are needed for each of the five key areas of life, including your relationships. Planning does not mean that you stop living for today and start believing that everything in the future will be so much better. The only reason to make plans is to ensure that you keep a focus on where you're going in order to get the most of this life right NOW. Life isn't about finding yourself; it's about creating yourself and being all that you can be each day.

When developing your self-with-self relationship and mastering it in order to have more to offer other people in relationships, remember to shoot for the stars, but never forego the principles of life balance, which are required to live *A Second Life.*

Step Four: Decide on a relationship action plan and timelines according to your future goals

- Do you plan to do whatever is necessary to better know yourself and improve your relationship with yourself?
- What things can you do to improve all of your relationships?
- What do you hope to achieve by improving your relationships?
- Do you believe changing the way you interact with others will change the way they react to you?
- Can your current relationships with others be improved based on your actions alone?
- If not, how will having a better relationship with yourself change your perspective on the challenges in your current relationships with others?
- What new or different qualities will you look for or find appealing when forming and developing new relationships?

A belief system that hinders many people from changing their existing relationships or forming and developing new healthier relationships is their indoctrination about the roles everyone needs to play in specific relationships. As children we learn that because mommy and daddy are the boss it's wrong to question what they say, and that we must live up to their expectations. We learn how to keep people happy by not "rocking the boat" with our own opinions or desires, but instead, "going along with the program" that exists. We grow up in a family structure with a hierarchy that we hesitate to question or challenge—even when all evidence points to the fact that the structure is misguided or not beneficial for everyone involved.

When it comes to romantic relationships, we are indoctrinated by a wide variety of different and conflicting messages. The traditional and idyllic roles of romantic relationships as portrayed in children's stories—where love conquers all—create in us a strong desire to find a mate who will fight against all odds to be with us, rescue us, or protect us from dangers. Yet the rocky and high drama emotional tenor of relationships portrayed in films and on television—especially on soap operas or novellas—create in us a desire for the excitement of dysfunction. And the examples of how romantic relationships can or can't work that we see in the role models in our own families can create further false beliefs or false fears. Sorting out all of these emotional mixed messages and drama by thinking through and analyzing what we would prefer to have in our own lives on a daily basis can be frustrating. Worse still is blindly following our physical attractions to a person who turns out to be less than perfect or supportive and may even be destructive to us as individuals. And blind loyalty to a person or relationships that isn't worthy of our time or love is foolhardy at best, and self-destructive at its worst.

Again we return to the reason why you must first know yourself and develop the strongest possible you-with-you relationship before you will be capable of developing and mastering strong relationships (particularly romantic) with other people. Only when we come from a place of self-knowing, assurance, and confidence about who we are and what special gifts we have to offer other people and the world will we be able to form relationships that completely support us being the best we can be. And that, after all, is the ultimate goal, to make God proud that your gifts and talents are having a positive effect in every aspect of life and on everyone you interact with or encounter.

Use the tools you learned in Coding to Oneness, Level 1, of this guide—meditation, prayer, and self-programming—to assist you in setting your goals and keeping a clear focus on them as you enact your plans in order to master your relationships.

Step Five: Decide how important your relationships are to you

When you evaluate what is important in your life you find that the success of your relationships affects all of the other four key areas of life. Some people may feel that putting family relationships higher on their priority list than their job/career relationships is most important to them. Others may feel that development of personal relationships can be put on hold temporarily until they establish secure job/career relationships that can be built upon for a bright and prosperous future. Everyone's assessment of what is most important to them is different, and for most people there will be a shifting of importance from one of the key areas of life to another during different phases or cycles of life. Still, good-quality relationships are important in all five key areas of life:

- Your job/career success depends as much on your ability to develop and maintain good working relationships as it does on your other skills, knowledge, and talents. No matter how talented or even brilliant you are at your job, if you're not able to effectively interact with your peers, coworkers, employees, bosses, or clients you'll go nowhere fast in your career. The ability to develop and maintain good working relationships is key to being part of a successful team in any work environment.

- Financial stability or instability can be a source of reassurance and comfort in your relationships—either personal or business—or it can cause a great deal of stress and anxiety, which has the potential to overshadow much of the other good things in relationships. Worries about money have even been listed as one of the leading causes of divorce. And strong relationships are imperative for any business to survive. Therefore, the importance of maintaining strong relationships cannot be overstated, especially during difficult financial times.

  Everyone faces financial challenges or financially related stress at some point in their lives—even those who have more money than they need to pay their bills. By having a strong self-with-self relationship, you feel confident and self-assured no matter what financial situation you encounter. By developing and nurturing strong personal and business relationships, you create team energy, with everyone working toward the same goals. Just knowing that you are not alone in your struggles makes the difficult times feel more manageable. And successes and triumphs become even more meaningful when they are shared with others.
- Physical health/wellness can only be achieved and maintained long term when a person is relaxed and happy. The nature of your relationships absolutely has an effect on your health. Good relationships create a sense of certainty and calm; they offer companionship to help you get through tough times and special people with whom to engage in fun, relaxing activities and share laughs.
- Having a highly developed relationship with yourself is key to being able to form and maintain good relationships of any other kind. Without first knowing who you are and what you can offer other people or the world, there's no way to be a positive, cooperative, contributing member of any circle of other people—whether it's family, friends, a company, or a community.
- Spirituality that supports you and feeds your soul is based on your connection to God and your feeling of oneness with everyone and everything else in your life. This develops as a result of truly knowing yourself and understanding that you do not stand or walk through life alone but are an integral part of all other things. Even if you envision yourself as only a single wave in the ocean, you know that without you (and millions of other waves) the continuous movement of the ocean could not exist.

Step Six: Determine how you can contribute to making the world a better place with healthy, vibrant relationships

> *How far you go in life depends on your being tender with the young,*
> *compassionate with the aged, sympathetic with the striving*
> *and tolerant of the weak and strong,*
> *because some day in life you will have been all of these.*
>
> George Washington Carver

Whatever your current age, status in life, or state of mind, you are on a journey during which you will visit and experience a variety of conditions and circumstances. Much of what you have encountered or become so far in life is not of your own making, but rather as a result of your indoctrination by society's standards. But now you have a chance to change all of that and re-create your life in ways that offer you opportunities to do truly remarkable things. From this moment forward you have a *choice* to become the type of person who touches others on a truly genuine level, whether it is during casual encounters, through established long-term personal and family relationships, or in your job/career environment. This change is possible because you now know that by developing a sincere, reverent relationship with yourself you create a foundation upon which all other relationships can be developed and maintained with the same honor and dignity you will be showing yourself.

This one simple change in the way you view life—through having a different connection with yourself—will magically transform everything else. Everyone you encounter will be touched by your attentive presence in the moment and your calm self-assurance. They will feel a special connection to you through the way you convey a feeling of oneness with them. In these ways you will be giving back naturally, as well as serving as a role model to others, inspiring them to also reach out to others with kindness, thoughtfulness and love.

> *Spread love everywhere you go.*
> *Let no one ever come to you without leaving happier.*
>
> Mother Teresa

In 2004 my business partner, Christin Tellefsen, and I made a feature documentary film that originated from a human behavior case study. *Living The Dream* (distributed by Paramount Pictures) is about how belief systems can corrupt and destroy people's

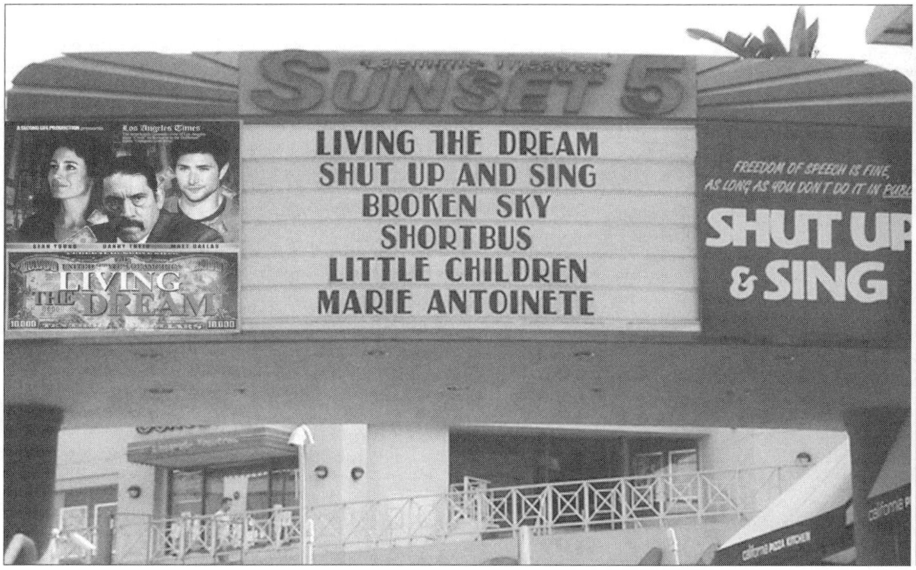

LEFT: The opening theatrical release of Living the Dream *at the well-known Laemmle movie theater chain in Hollywood, California, on Thanksgiving weekend in 2006.*
RIGHT: Ron and Christian during the filming of Living the Dream, *May 2004.*

lives. All of the characters have different types of back stories that show how they have been victims of indoctrination to such an extent that even the good people become corrupt. The goal of the film is to expose how lives are wasted, and that there are no happy endings when one cannot free oneself from society's negative belief systems.

During the initial days filming in downtown Los Angeles, a homeless man was watching from the sidelines. When he showed up to watch every day we invited him to eat with us. His name was Ron. As we got to know him and learned his story we found that his downward spiral and the events that caused him to be where he was in life were the results of him being a victim of a belief system.

Ron's kind spirit made us look beyond his downtrodden exterior without judgment and see him for who he really was, a person just like us. But he had great difficulty mastering life's challenges—which was the theme of our docudrama. So we invited him to play a part in the movie, as well as work on the crew, being paid like everyone else. His dedication and good heart touched us all and we become friends with him. Because of who Ron was as a person and what he had experienced in life, we also trusted him to fulfill key functions for making *Living the Dream* become a reality.

The donation ceremony on December 22, 2006, that took place at the Los Angeles Mission's Christmas lunch where 3,000 homeless were gathered (with Los Angeles Mission's CEO Herbert Smith left, and Christian Schoyen and Christin Tellefsen).

When I asked him how he felt inside and about life, he answered, "Christian, I have experienced hardships like everyone else. I have not been as strong as others who have been able to get back on their feet again. But I know that there is a God who is watching over me and making sure that I'm okay and that everything will work out. I tell myself every morning that I'm happy to be alive and I smile at life. During my hardships I have experienced love and support from others when I needed it. And being a part of this project, something greater than myself, has given me a feeling of doing something special and having a purpose."

Having the chance to get to know Ron and see someone with so little still have so much gratitude and goodness inside reminded me once again, like so many other times in life, to never ever judge a person for what work he/she does or does not do, how they dress, or their life situation. The true value of a person can be found in the goodness of his or her heart.

After we had finished filming the docudrama, I asked Ron where he got his positive spirit. His reply: "I get a feeling of goodness from people who show kindness to me and reach out their hand with compassion, not pity, and treat me with respect as an equal human being. How can I not see hope when these acts of kindness takes place?"

He told me about the Los Angeles Mission, where he had found assistance and support. Ron expressed how crucial their work was for helping people in unfortunate situations, especially those who needed someone to be there for them as they were trying to regain control of their lives. "Not only do they offer a place to eat and sleep," Ron said, "but counseling is available too. And that is an important element for people who need to change how they think about life in order live a better life." Inspired by what Ron told us and showed us, my business partner and I discussed how we could help other people like him. The final dream therefore became giving a donation from the profits of the film to the Los Angeles Mission.

Many of the people who worked on our film crew were reluctant to have Ron join our team, but our interactions with him were a great lesson. Ron taught everyone not to be fearful of helping a stranger who on the surface appears to be different than yourself, because while you're helping that person they can help you learn that inside we are all the same. Never let a person's skin color, sexuality, religion, or age discourage you from engaging in a conversation with an open mind and open heart; that person might have something to teach you.

> *The value of a man should be seen in what he gives*
> *and not in what he is able to receive.*
>
> Albert Einstein

Step Seven: Learn the realities of creating and maintaining good relationships

There are innumerable books and theories about how to create and maintain good relationships. In fact, an entire multimillion dollar industry is based on helping people improve their relationships. Included in this industry are a variety of psychological "experts" who offer "professional" advice and assistance to people whose relationships have gone so badly astray that they are desperate for any type of help whatsoever. When talk therapy and counseling don't work, people turn to prescription medications and over-the-counter medicine to numb their pain and anxiety; legal drugs (such as alcohol and cigarettes) to self-medicate; illegal drugs to escape; overeating to cope, etc., etc. When all of these things fail, legal professionals benefit by facilitating divorces, court hearings regarding child custody and support, or civil suits over financial or business miscommunications, misunderstandings, or misconduct. The list and progression goes on and on . . . with the same result: Everyone wants to be heard, to prove they're right or "wronged," to get their due (recognition). What no one seems to understand is that all of these "solutions" to relationship problems are treating the symptoms instead of the root cause.

All of the difficulties people experience in relationships are based on—and supported by—false beliefs and indoctrination. Like robots following around behind each other, it's the blind leading the blind. Not knowing the difference, we believe what other people have told us, or have shown us, is the basis for good relationships. Because that is all we know, that is what we do.

But here, again, is where your relationship with yourself is so important! The only truth about how to create and maintain good relationships is very individual and must come from within each of us. What's good for me may not be so good for you. What makes you feel fulfilled may not be the same for me. What feeds my soul may not feed yours. We are each individuals blessed with our own strengths, talents, and special gifts. Therefore, only by truly knowing yourself and recognizing the God-given gifts and talents you are intended to nurture and share with the world will you achieve remarkable, worthwhile relationships that enable you to be all that you can be.

Forget about what everyone else is telling you, has told you, or will tell you. Look for the answers inside yourself. Find your own passion and follow that.

You must begin by eliminating everything you currently believe based on the indoctrination and false programming that has prevented you from truly knowing yourself and what is best for you. Use the tools of meditation, prayer, and self-programming to delete society's beliefs that you have until now accepted as your own. Focus on what "feels" true to you. Your body is a powerful barometer of your specific truth. Learn to listen to the messages it is emitting. When something "feels" wrong, your body will tell you so. At first the signal may be weak and difficult to distinguish, but as you learn to recognize what your body is telling you the signal will become clear and strong. For some people it will be a gut reaction—literally a feeling in the stomach. For others the feeling may be in the head: pressure, buzzing in the ears, twitching of the eyes or lips, an itchy nose. Everyone will receive signals from their bodies in different ways. Find your way. Learn to listen to your own truth and follow it.

Step Eight: Execute your relationships action plan to get where you want to be

Whatever your specific relationship action plans, in some ways or others you'll either be setting out to improve your current relationships to be more in alignment with your true self or to form new self-aligned and supportive relationships. These basic beliefs of *A Second Life* can provide inspiration and guide you along the way:

Choose yourself over all others

You are not your mother, father, grandparents, aunts, uncles, siblings, or any other relative who cared for you while you were growing up. Although you will treat them with the respect they deserve and honor their efforts to care for and nurture you—if they did so—it is *not* your obligation to think like them, behave like them, or have the same goals as they do in life. Understand that the beliefs they have taught you and shown you were the best they could offer you based on their own indoctrination. Never blame them if their efforts now fall short in your new view of life. But while honoring their best efforts, you are not obligated to abide by their beliefs or teachings. Your obligation is *not* to *them*, but *to yourself and God*, to develop and freely express your own gifts and talents in the world by being all that you can be. You are now evolving into the unique individual you were intended to be.

> *With realization of one's own potential and self-confidence in one's ability, one can build a better world.*
>
> Dalai Lama

This is a *choice* you must make immediately! Use the tools of meditation, prayer, and self-programming to delete all limiting indoctrination that has kept you mentally enslaved until this time. Release yourself from your mental prison. Wake up, take a deep breath, and open your eyes. See that the world is a very different place than you have believed it to be. Look around and see the unlimited possibilities that life has to offer as you set yourself free to live the kind of life that is *your* true desire and potential. By doing so you do not disrespect those who did their best for you in the past, but rather honor their efforts by becoming your own true best self.

As you set out on this new journey *by choice*, you will see every current relationship in your life in a new way. Some will seem better in ways you never even noticed before. Other relationships and circumstances that you have previously embraced and accepted may now seem startlingly or shockingly unacceptable. But do not panic or recoil. Taking action in haste or out of fear is not productive and will not resonate with your true self—the person who fearlessly faces life's challenges and calmly attempts to develop the magical potential in all circumstances.

Practice being your own best self

When you are in touch with your true self and connected to a power greater than any human power, your need for melodrama and negative, unproductive emotionalism no longer exists. Your habit of participating in such a way now needs to be broken and replaced with a new positive way of interacting with others. Although initially you will need to make an effort to detach from such situations and resist the impulse to participate as you did before, with practice your new way of being will become natural.

Your world will be remarkably transformed when you begin to act in concert with your deepest God-given truths. This may inspire you to spring forward, instantly changing everything about your life. While in the long run your entire life *will be* different, not every element of it will necessarily be changed or even need to be changed—some things can just be improved. So, during the initial period of transformation, small steps should be taken as you gather information and insights based on your new way of thinking and observing the world. Before leaping ahead, stand still, assess the entirety of your life and the details of your relationships to get a clear view of what is truly in alignment with your highest self, what needs improvement, and what might be unacceptable as you move forward into your new life.

While doing so, practice being the new person you are becoming. Just as toddlers bounce around while learning to walk, surging forward, seemingly about to fall, then regains their balance, you may feel unsteady on your feet at times. When this happens it is important to stop, steady yourself, and reconnect with your power within. Until your transformation is complete, with the indoctrinated drama of your emotional actions and reactions replaced by genuinely calm, steady full engagement in every aspect of life, pretend that you have already achieved such a state. By doing so you will be informing your mind and your body that this is the way you will be operating from now on. Soon enough your mind and body will recognize that this is the more natural, relaxed, invigorated way of being, and you will automatically embrace this way of living naturally.

Allow others time to adjust

As you are developing and nurturing your relationship with yourself, sooner or later it will become obvious to those with whom you interact, and especially those who are in relationships with you, that something different is happening with you. They may be accustomed to your emotional responses or overreactions, or perhaps you have shut them out and rarely respond at all. While giving yourself time to transform and adjust, it's only fair that you also give the people with whom you are in relationships a chance to get used to your new way of thinking and behaving.

You may be surprised by the reactions you elicit from others when you suddenly change. Some people may be immediately delighted with the new person you are becoming. Others may feel threatened and insecure. Understand that the way any person reacts may not be a true indication of who they genuinely are or how they will relate to you after a period of transition. Many people who are operating from their own indoctrinated programming will instantly react defensively because they will feel their habits, values, and way of life are being threatened by your new way of thinking or being. Fearful reactions or responses would not be surprising as they may feel their very survival is at stake.

When you have been interacting with people within a drama-based emotional environment or relationship for as long as you've known each other, to have you suddenly "unplug" and not react as before could propel them deeper into their own individual drama role. If this should happen, make no snap decisions or judgments about the true nature of this person or whether they are capable of changing in response to your new way of being/behaving. Use such opportunities to practice patience and tolerance with a loving spirit and give the situation or relationship time to sort itself out while you become more practiced as your true God-centered self.

Communicate your new philosophy and belief system

When the time is right, discuss with the important people in your life why you are changing and how you envision a better life for yourself and for them.

Perhaps they will be with you on this journey from the beginning. If so, you are lucky to be part of a team of like-minded achievers. The discoveries you will make together and support you can provide each other will result in a quicker transition into a life of unlimited potential.

If you have begun this journey alone or others in your life do not wish to join you or resist discussing your new life philosophy or belief system, then back off. Proceed on your path with dedication and perseverance regardless of their reactions. But do so humbly. Do not preach to them or criticize—either mentally or verbally—their lack of insight or agreement. Soon enough they will see the evidence of how the changes you are making are positively affecting your relationships with them. It's not always possible to change the circumstances of your life, but changing how you react to them can make a huge difference. The people who truly love you will welcome your becoming a more loving, nurturing, tolerant person in their lives, regardless of the reasons why you are doing so.

Communicate honestly and thoughtfully

Even if your efforts to discuss your new philosophy of life and belief system are not welcomed or embraced, continue to communicate honestly and thoughtfully.

When someone attempts to drag you back into an old pattern of emotionally charged exchanges or confrontations, respond simply and calmly with truth—respond, but do not confront. Respectfully inform them that you hear what they are saying and understand their point of view. If you disagree, say so, but do so kindly and without judgment. Your mission is not to make others wrong in their beliefs, but to *show them* through your actions that there is a different, better way to interact and relate. In that way you are not only improving your relationships, but also serving as a role model for others. Discussions that are productive and informative are constructive, but arguments only escalate emotionalism and reinforce the fears that create unresolved conflicts that no one can win.

In routine interactions and conversations always say what you mean and mean what you say—but being truthful does not give you license to say things you know will hurt another's feelings. Learn to communicate at all times in ways that are kind and not charged with emotional drama. As you consistently maintain this new standard for all of your conversations, people will quickly see that you are serious about this new way of being and view you differently. Consistency is also important in all of your actions because it builds trust. When you agree to do something—either one time or routinely—you must follow through and do it. Consistency is also a component of living with integrity, which means your quality as a person can never be questioned and your intentions will always be clearly understood as being only for the good.

Act, don't react

When you are grounded in your beliefs and guided by your God-given truth, every action you take will come from that place. You will no longer be reacting to what someone else does or says. To be *acting,* not *reacting,* is a powerful confirmation of the assurance you feel because of your new way of living. Changing this one thing about how you interact with others will reinforce everything you know to be the truth of who you really are and how you are meant to live. It will provide ongoing evidence that your new belief system and way of living make your life better and better each day.

Notice each day how you can *choose* not to react to people, things, or even your own old habits.

Conduct this experiment to determine if it is your habit to waste time sitting in front of the television surfing the channels when there's nothing interesting to watch. Settle in on the sofa, turn on the TV, and start channel surfing. Likely you'll stop at a channel here and there, then automatically surf on past to another and another. Now stop and *feel* what you're doing. You're plugged in, right? You're reacting to some impulse in yourself that says, "There's got to be something interesting to watch," or "I'm going to miss something if I don't keep looking." How does that feel? Are you in control or are you being controlled by something else?

As another experiment, the next time you're driving through town, notice how you *react* to other drivers and the way they behave. When someone cuts you off in traffic do you automatically get upset, perhaps honk your horn or curse at them? This automatic reaction is not uncommon, especially when encountering people who are rude or inconsiderate. But when you *react* to the other driver's rudeness, it actually triggers a fear response in you when there's usually no real danger. This type of reaction is called a fight-or-flight response—when the adrenaline pumps through the body in order to give you instant energy to do whatever is necessary to survive. Although some may consider this a normal reaction to feeling threatened and in danger in traffic, in the reality of normal, everyday driving when this commonly happens, such a reaction is a conditioned response based on a competitive ego need to selfishly keep the space that you consider yours and not let the other guy get the upper hand. Of course, defensive driving is always wise during these times when people are distracted by all sorts of things while operating heavy, powerful motor vehicles that can cause serious injury to people or damage to property. *But choosing to allow someone else to trigger a reaction from you is giving away your real power.* Instead, see how it feels to *act* by being calmly prepared for whatever might happen and feel confident that you will be able to control the outcome.

These experiments illustrate whether or not you have deeply developed your relationship with yourself to the point that you feel confident that every action you take is based on your best interest, not on something someone else prompts you to do.

The true test of your connection with your inner strength and self-assurance will come when you apply this type of calm rationality while interacting in relationship with other people. As you condition yourself to stop *reacting* to others you'll find that your *actions* toward them will be remarkably different. People cannot belittle you or offend you with an offhanded remark—whether it's intentionally or unintentionally insulting—if you truly know yourself and feel confident about yourself. Even those who in the past have been able to "push your buttons" will lose their ability to trigger your emotional reactions. Instead, you can smile inside knowing that the old saying is true: words and deeds can't hurt you unless you let them!

When your relationship with yourself is strong, there is no need to *react* based on ego or in self-protection; instead, you can *act* in whatever ways are most satisfying and fulfilling for you personally.

If everyone would apply these principles in every interaction or relationship they have with other people, the world would be a completely different place.

Changing the way you interact with others will usually change the way they respond to you

As you become more grounded in your beliefs and new way of living, the benefits to your relationships will become obvious to those who are open and loving. Despite any initial fearful reactions they may have, stick with your new way of being. In time they will adjust and truly appreciate you for being the catalyst for change that will transform their lives as well.

When you take more responsibility for the small things in relationships that seem to mean so much to another person, everything changes.

Remember as a child when your mother had to nag you about taking out the trash? Of course, being a child who was always distracted by other things, you probably didn't follow through on this small chore that actually took hardly any time at all. What's the big deal? you thought. Even though the reasons mother would get so upset that you didn't do it don't really matter, the fact that she would get upset seemed at the time to confirm that you had a great deal of power over her. In that case, it was the power to make her angry or disappointed or whatever she felt. Imagine, though, if the tables were turned and you actually had routinely taken out the trash without being asked. The same power you had to upset her would have delighted her and made her proud! And all for doing a small thing that took a few minutes: taking out the trash without being asked.

This type of thinking can be applied to almost any aspect of your interactions with other people. It's called being thoughtful. And it's easy to be thoughtful toward others when your mind is not constantly spinning with thoughts and questions about who you are and what you should be doing and if you're doing the right things and whether doing certain things will get you what you want or need. When you feel confident in who you are, your mind is clear and you are able to live in the moment, noticing everything that's going on around you and giving your attention to things other than yourself.

Having a solid, well-developed relationship with yourself frees you up to enjoy to the fullest extent everything you encounter in life, as well as share the unlimited generosity from your heart. When you are generous with your thoughts and your actions, other people notice. And it is a natural impulse for people to respond in kind.

When your current relationships cannot be changed by your actions alone

Even though most people will recognize positive change and welcome living a better, more fulfilling life with more harmonious relationships, the truth is that some people may not respond as you would hope. They may not know what to do or how to behave differently, even if they are willing to change; they may be too afraid to change, or simply to stubborn or unwilling to embrace change; or resentment and anger could be so strong in them that they are incapable of even understanding that change is possible.

If there are people in your life who cannot adjust to the changes you are making in yourself and your relationships with them, if they remain too fearful or stuck in the old ways your relationships operated, then you cannot let that be your concern. Although this may be sad, it is a reality that you may have to face. As you do the work and dedicate yourself to change it will be necessary for your relationships to change as well; otherwise you will not feel fulfilled—which is no longer acceptable. Eventually people who cannot appreciate all that you now offer will withdraw from you and the relationships will prove to be of no value to either you or them.

> *If at the end ... I have lost every other friend on earth,*
> *I shall at least have one friend left,*
> *and that friend shall be down inside of me.*
>
> Abraham Lincoln

This is not to say that there is any specific time frame for gauging whether it is still worth making honest efforts toward transforming relationships that have potential for improvement. If there is a possibility for change, if you see any progress at all, when there is value in your relationships, then you must stick with it, stay dedicated to acting on your beliefs based on your true self and work for change as best you can.

There may be some relationships that cannot be changed as much as you'd like but still have some limited value to you and your life. These relationships are often with family members or in work environments. When kept in perspective and understood for what they are, this can be an acceptable alternative for you. It is not an assault on you personally, or your beliefs, for you to agree to having limited satisfaction and fulfillment in a relationship. As long as you understand the realities of the limitations and accept the terms, the choice is yours.

The calming and reassuring effects of humility

During the transition from your old indoctrinated self to your new self-directed, inspired self there may be times when you feel anxious to progress more quickly and other times when you will want to savor your feelings of pride for all you are achieving. Acknowledging your successes within your own thoughts during your journey helps to keep you on track as you reach mini-goals you may have set. But bragging about how well you're doing is never appropriate. If someone notices the changes in you and says, "You seem so different. What's going on with you?" certainly you can share with them *A Second Life's* belief system and your experiences during your journey. But do so humbly.

When you privately congratulate yourself in your thoughts, also remember to express gratitude to the higher power accompanying and guiding you toward this new life of unlimited potential. Such gratitude reinforces your accomplishments and reminds you that it is not without assistance that you are able to transform your life as you are doing. As you believe more and more strongly each day that you truly do *deserve* every wonderful thing you are choosing to have in your new life, always remember that these gifts you are accepting are given to you for a purpose by God. It is now your obligation to give back by using your special talents and gifts only for good and the benefit of others.

Still, there may be times when you become too full of yourself because of your accomplishments and the abundance you enjoy during your new life. After all, you are still a human being. When these thoughts come into your head, even if they are only fleeting, stop and notice. Smile inside and laugh at yourself, then remind yourself that it is only because of God that you are lucky enough to be in a position to do the work required to receive and embrace all that you are given.

Keep things light with humor, fun, and laughter

Although making radical changes in your relationships with yourself and other people is serious business, a stern, heavy attitude will only drag you down and hold you back. Feeling or behaving as though the world will end if you can't immediately get things right or if other people can't get with your program is counterproductive. Keep everything in perspective. Remember the saying: What's important in life is the journey, not the destination. And this is a journey that's intended to be enjoyed.

Besides learning to laugh at yourself, lighten up the mood during challenging times of change by finding the humor in life and engaging in fun activities. Plus, fun, humor, and laughter are proven methods of defusing physical tension, as well as emotional difficulties in relationships. But use humor wisely and appropriately. When it comes to the relationships you're trying to improve, there will be other people involved who may be frightened or feel insecure because of the changes the are experiencing that you are initiating. Never make fun of them, or anyone else for that matter (although, on second thought, it's probably okay to laugh at the idiot driver that cuts over in front of you in traffic or won't let you merge into their lane). And feel free to make fun of yourself.

Remember that laughter is God's medicine. It shakes up the body, releasing pent-up stress, tension, fear, and anger. It creates feel-good chemicals in the brain. It heals wounds and feeds the soul. Laughter and smiles are contagious, so generously share God's medicine with others. By bringing a smile or a laugh to another you will ease their transition, as well as your own, into the new relationships you are creating. And, during the process, you can contribute to making the world a happier, more positive place for everyone you encounter.

What new or different qualities will you look for or find appealing when forming and developing new relationships?

This question is very thought provoking and may not be easy to answer. It may be a matter of trial and error as you meet new people and consider whether you want to have a relationship with them—whether it's a personal relationship, a friendship, or a job/career relationship.

You may notice an automatic impulse to consider forming new relationships with people who are similar to those with whom you currently have relationships or have had relationships in the past. But once you test the water it could be very surprising for you to find that the qualities you thought would be appealing to you based on your past experiences no longer appeal to you at all because now you've become a different person. Indeed, now you *are* a different person and what you want and need are likely to be different as well. Discovering that this is true can be an astonishing and delightful confirmation that all of your hard work and dedication to developing your self-with-self relationship is paying off big time. Isn't it amazing?

When looking for people with whom to form or develop new relationships, it's important be realistic. First look at yourself and see what qualities you have—even make a list of what you believe you can now offer in a relationship and where you still have room to improve. Keep that list in mind as you meet and get to know new people. The most successful and fulfilling relationships are between people who share common values, goals, and attitudes toward life, and are supportive of each other's continued growth and development—making them a good match.

Step Nine: Reevaluate the status of your relationships according to your timelines

Go back and review your Relationship Bio/Résumé for the future in Step Three and see how you're progressing toward your goals according to your timelines.

If you've encountered roadblocks or not made the type of progress you'd projected, go back to previous steps of this process and reassess what you could be doing differently. When it comes to matters of the heart—which relationships, even those that are job/career related, definitely are—as you change your relationship with yourself your heart's desire absolutely changes as well. It will be interesting for you to see if your future relationship goals have changed since this process began and your self-with-self relationship has grown stronger.

If your goals still resonate for you but progress has not been made as you'd hoped based on the approaches you've taken, then go back to the drawing board and reassess your options. It may help to review your Relationship Résumé in Step Two and see if your perspective has changed on any ongoing relationships that still exist in your life. You can also add to your relationship résumé any new relationships you may have formed or developed.

When you have been doing everything you know to do to improve your existing relationships and make them more fulfilling and worthwhile but have been unsuccessful and are finding it difficult to let them go, perhaps it is time to consider whether changing the nature of those relationships could make a difference. Particularly when it comes to romantic relationships, when people view them as "all or nothing at all," they are often cheating themselves out of something that could be more valuable to them when viewed through a different lens. Many married people could be better off as platonic friends and some platonic friends could be wonderful romantic partners if they had the courage and were willing to take the chance of making such changes. Shifting your perspective on the nature of a relationship is something to consider.

If changing the nature of an existing relationship is not an option and improving it has not been possible, perhaps it's time to take the dramatic step of cutting it loose. Of course, if it's a marriage you've been working on improving and there are children involved, the situation can seem very complicated and heart tugging, especially when the welfare and best interests of children are mandatory. It may be helpful to make a couple of lists about the relationship to gain new perspective. One list can have all the positives of staying in the relationship, despite it being less than fulfilling, in one column and the negatives in another. The second list would have the positives and negatives of separation or divorce in the two columns. When it comes to the psychological welfare of children, there are a lot of excellent resources, particularly those based on child development studies, which are available to provide more information and guidance for making such tough choices. And ultimately, talking with your children and finding out how they feel about mommy and daddy not getting along so well could provide the valuable information you need to make decisions that are best for everyone involved.

When you are deciding whether to stick with any relationship that you are having difficulty improving, there is a danger of stubbornness setting in and spinning your wheels endlessly. Loyalty and devotion are admirable attributes, but they do not replace the true happiness and satisfaction that every person deserves as their God-given gift. Many people spend their entire lives trying to perfect situations that will always be imperfect because their expectations are too high or the people involved in the relationship simply aren't right for each other in that particular way. Personal relationships are too vital for living a happy, fulfilled life to settle for less than the best for you.

Step Ten: Reassess the values of your relationships every six months after you are on your path

Now that you're on track, is this still what you really want? There are many ways to measure your success. One way can be to see how your relationships are changing and growing, and you are growing within them—which is a key ingredient for feeling good about yourself, because it means you are evolving; being stagnant means the opposite. Another strong indication that you are succeeding at creating better relationships with yourself and others goes far beyond anything else: it is the impact you have on others in a good way. How have the changes you instigated and worked to achieve in your relationships improved the lives of the other people with whom you relate? Whether or not they've joined your mission and are in agreement with everything you are doing to create a fabulous new life, *A Second Life*, do they at least exhibit signs that they have benefited from your efforts and are generally happier because of them?

If you have achieved everything you set out to achieve according to your action plan, but are still not feeling fulfilled or that your relationships are truly worthwhile, then you need to decide what it is you really want. Here's a clue: Your instincts will tell you whether you're following your heart's desires or if you're still trying to live up to your earlier indoctrinated programming by society's standards. The passion you feel inside is the voice of God showing you the way. All you have to do is learn to listen. You may be surprised by what you discover about yourself and other people.

Final Step: Be all that you can be, but not all at once.

RELATIONSHIPS (WITH YOURSELF AND WITH OTHERS) SUMMARY

• Assess your relationships (with yourself and with others).

• If your relationships are not all they could be, identify the reasons why, such as:

  - Your relationship with yourself is not fully developed; therefore you cannot be your true self in relationships with others.
  - You are afraid other people in your life will reject you if you do not sacrifice your own desires and happiness to please them and make them happy.
  - Your relationships are not fulfilling; therefore they are less important and receive less attention than other key areas of your life.

• Use the tools you've learned—meditation/prayer/self-programming—to delete the negative indoctrination/brainwashing that has created your false self, limiting your ability to truly know yourself and master your relationships (with yourself first, then others).

• Devise a game plan for developing more fulfilling relationships based on your new reality, including:

  - Steps you will take to recognize who you truly are, what you need to feel fulfilled so that you can be more present and genuine in relationships with others.
  - Your goals and objectives, as well as timelines for enacting your plan.

• Execute your game plan:

  - Each day: Systematically set out to better understand yourself and your role in fulfilling relationships with others. Follow through with commitment.
  - Every night: Routinely review your progress and express gratitude.

• Reassess your overall results according to your timelines:

  - If you are on track, are there new goals you now want to reach?
  - If satisfied with your progress, be conscious every day of maintaining the changes you have made in order to completely wipe out your old negative programming and establish your new positive reality for the long term.
  - If you have not made the progress you'd planned, reevaluate yourself and your relationships to find new ways to make your game plan more successful.

ALWAYS REMEMBER: Surrender is never an option. You must find a way to succeed.

Spirituality

5

Your spiritual life is lacking or not all it could be because you've been indoctrinated and brainwashed by society. This chapter will show you how to break free from the chains of society's mental slavery so you can develop a spiritual life that can support you and guide you in *A Second Life*.

Spirituality Contents

Introduction

Society's Rule: Who you are as a person is defined by the values of the family you were born into, and those that are conveyed to you and through you as you grow up. You must embrace, observe, and honor their beliefs for the rest of your life or else you are an ungrateful traitor.

The Truth: Your birthright is the unlimited potential unique to you personally. Who you become and what you do in life must be based on your connection to God within you regardless of anyone else's expectations for you. Living in a state of Oneness means being fully in tune with your true self and free from the mental slavery of the negative belief systems that attempt to control you.

You were born as an uncut diamond—God's divine perfect creation. When you started this life journey you were meant to be the creator of your own life, using all of your imagination and bountiful hopes and dreams. Your senses were strong and life in your mind had no limits. For a little while you were so alive that you saw God in everything, including yourself. You felt blissful and connected to your true self and were the total opposite of what many of you later became, a disconnected "flat-liner," programmed and conditioned to a life filled with fears.

Everyone wants to be the dreamer and the artist of their own life. In order to restore your birthright, to live this life in Oneness, with anything and everything being possible, you must re-activate your connection with God within and re-claim your rights as the creator of your own life. In this state of existence you no longer search for ways to fill the void you feel. Instead, you realize that what you are looking for can't be found externally, but already exists within you. In this state of Oneness you don't just think or believe that you are connected to God, you *know* that it's true. When you live this reality there is no need to search for meaning in life. You have arrived at your final destination, which is NOW.

The inner peacefulness and contentment that give your life true meaning are waiting to be discovered under layers of negative programming. Once you delete that

St. Michael the almighty Archangel—The Commander of God's army who fights evil

indoctrination and re-connect with your true self you will be totally present in your life each moment, which will be the only moment that exists. You will be free of the past. You will no longer look forward to a future time when you will be truly happy. You will be truly happy NOW, which is all that matters.

Oneness is all there is.

Oneness is the spiritual goal for every human. Being in a state of Oneness means being fully in tune with your true self and free from the mental slavery of the negative belief systems that have controlled your life.

Oneness means that you have finally arrived home by genuinely re-connecting with God within yourself. This new life is *A Second Life*, where love is everything and the real truth is found within, not dictated by anyone else. In Oneness you have left behind the person you once were and emerged like a butterfly from the prison of your cocoon to fly free in a new heightened state of reality. Ego gratification no longer matters. Instead you *know* that the well-being of humanity is of far greater importance than yourself. You learn to follow the passion inside you on a life path with your heart aligned with your intent to fulfill your God-given potential. Your actions always reflect the truth in your intentions.

Mastering the principles of *A Second Life* frees you from society's mental slavery by empowering you through a connection with the unlimited power of God. By living in Oneness you are a co-creator of heaven on earth. You are free to live and enjoy the life God intended you to live. In your new reality there is no separation of your true self from the higher power that guides you and supports you. You master inner peace and acquire the ability to be objective, fully detached from the indoctrination of society that has limited your existence and your happiness. You will not be controlled by grudges toward those who have held you back (unknowingly or knowingly) or fears (created by your negative programming). When you have achieved Oneness, you will be free from judgment toward yourself or anyone else.

All of this is possible only by deleting your false programming, re-connecting with God within yourself, and taking steps right now to live only based on your true passions and unlimited potential. Then the true purpose of your life can begin to manifest in all that you are and everything that you do. Begin today by breaking away from the indoctrinated way of thinking according to society's rules. Take the first steps on the journey that is your new, self-fulfilled life in alignment with God. Follow this step-by-step approach to living a spiritually powerful life, *A Second Life.*

TEN STEP ACTION PLAN FOR MASTERING A SPIRITUALLY POWERFUL LIFE

As you follow each of these steps, do so with the understanding that a complete change in the way you view your existence is necessary! Shifting your consciousness can be achieved with an open heart and dedication to re-connecting with God and the true you within.

Step One: Assess the current status of your spiritual life

You must be completely honest with yourself as you assess the current status of your spiritual life by answering the following questions; otherwise you'll be wasting your time and missing an opportunity to elevate your life to the next level.

- Do you wake up in the morning with a smile on your face, feeling blissful inside, excited about the moment of just BEING?
- Do you look forward to the day ahead, knowing it's going to be the best day ever and that there are no problems, only opportunities?
- Do you set out each day knowing that you can accomplish anything you choose because you are the creator of your own life—as opposed to just trying to get through each day unharmed and unphased?
- Do you go to bed at night filled with gratitude, thanking God for the amazing day you just had and how blessed you are—as opposed to lying in bed counting the hours available for you to rest before beginning another identical repetition of the day before?

Most people cannot answer "yes" to the questions above, which means neither their hearts nor their passions are the center of their lives. Instead, they are living the lives they have become programmed to live, not living in alignment with their true desires and passions of their true selves.

Step Two: Assess how you participate spiritually in your own life

An underlying goal of *A Second Life* is for you to be an active participant in your own life in a way that resonates with your true self and your connection to God within. As such, you conduct your life deliberately and with purpose.

Many people are only going through the motions most of the time. They aren't the leading man/woman of the movie that is their life. Their actions don't move the story forward. Instead, they are bit players participating in a drama that is being directed by everyone else. They go along with what someone else wants to do, they are *reacting* to situations in response to others instead of *acting* based on their own beliefs, or they are behaving in ways that someone else says is acceptable. In essence, they believe what someone else says is true instead of listening to their own inner voice of truth. They don't even realize that they are not making their own choices or decisions in life.

In order to begin living a spiritually powerful life in alignment with your true self, you must:

1) Learn to recognize when you are living according to society's rules or someone else's standards.
2) Truly understand how your indoctrinated programming is controlling you.
3) Learn to recognize when your responses to situations in life or to other people are based on your "conditioned indoctrination."
4) Develop the ability to know whether you are in touch with who you truly are.
5) Distinguish whether you are making choices based on pleasing others or because it resonates with your true self.
6) Always exhibit your status as living in Oneness in your everyday actions and approach to life.

Take this assessment test to gauge whether you are living in Oneness and are conscious of your actions and behavior. Begin your day by asking yourself these questions. Allow the questions to remain in your thoughts and observe yourself as you go through your routine for an entire day. End your day by asking yourself the same questions and see if your answers and view of yourself are different than in the morning.

Your Oneness Assessment Test

- Do you feel vibrantly alive?
- Are you motivated to do things based on:
  - the standards others set for you
  - ego gratification and false pride
  - what resonates with your inner truth/consciousness
- Can you recognize the difference between the three types of motivation above?
- Are you afraid to disappoint others by not going along with what they believe?
- Are you afraid to admit that others disappoint you by insisting that what they believe is the absolute and only truth?

- Do you feel it's necessary to confront others about their wrong thinking and influence on you?
- Do you know that you deserve to live up to your true potential and create your own life according to what you believe inside, as opposed to the beliefs of others?
- Are you afraid it will be necessary to walk away from people in your life whose expectations for you are actually stopping you from realizing true happiness and fulfillment?
- Do you notice, observe, and appreciate the miracles being displayed all around you each day:
  - the way the light illuminates colors, shapes, and shadows
  - the perfection of nature, the sky, and the earth
  - integrative, genuine interactions with others
  - feeling as though you are part of everything going on around you
- What has stopped you from mastering a spiritually powerful life of Oneness?

Step Three: Decide the future of your spiritual life

In order to decide where you are going, you must first know where you are starting from and why. Therefore, you need to understand how the spiritual foundation of your life was established in order to gain perspective on whether it is of your own choosing. *A Second Life* defines spiritual foundation as your sense of self as a unique, special being entitled to choose how and why you exist in the world. Only through thoughtful observation of yourself will you see how you need to change in order to create a reality that honors your true self and begin to live a life of Oneness.

Reflecting on your childhood provides the clues to the origins of why you interact as you do in the world. The purpose is not to be critical of others who indoctrinated you with their beliefs and programming. Placing blame on others—whether it's your parents or family members, teachers, pastors, priests, or other authority figures—is a useless waste of time. Whether the people who programmed you with an incorrect/separate view of yourself did so with good intentions or with malice, the fact is that they were only conveying what they were indoctrinated to believe. Blame, revenge, or being judgmental are all dark and negative energies, which are evil. Thereby, to destroy the dark forces within it's of great importance to not fall into the trap of feeding the darkness, but rather, always forgiving, as this will bring in the light.

When most people look back in time at childhood to reflect on what they were taught and how it relates to why they did the things they did, they will understand that they felt a need to please others by being a certain way or were driven by fear of not being good enough. Too many people will remember that someone said or did something at some point in their life that crippled them with fears and instilled in them a motivation to behave in ways that went against the needs of their true selves. Again, blame is not necessary or constructive and will only feed the dark forces inside. During the process of re-connecting with your true self and God within you, remember that there exists no judgment in God's kingdom. Those who caused you to feel badly and separate from your true self did so only because they themselves were going through life feeling fearful and inadequate because of their own wrongful programming. You must always remember that people who said or did hurtful things to you during your life's journey are the ones who are truly crippled with greater problems than you. When you meet these people and feel assaulted by their negative and destructive energy, never judge them; instead, sympathize with them, knowing they are lost and disconnected souls. By doing this you will always stay connected to the good energy inside you that is a reflection of God. Remember that these people are human beings with great potential, just like you and me, but they are trapped within great pain and suffering from their fears and feelings of self-doubt and inadequacy—which are negative energies, evil, controlling them in a life of mental slavery.

Forgive your enemies, but never forget their names.

John F. Kennedy

Now that we have grown to be adults, we no longer need to allow our feelings or actions to be controlled by other people. Our lives no longer need to be based on the ideas and expectations of other people. It is our choice to act on our own true desires and passions. But it's a sad fact that for many people their childhood programming and indoctrination killed the excitement and passion that once burned inside them—which gave them the feeling that they could do anything and be anyone they choose as the artist and creator of their own life. Instead, we go through each day acting out automatic robotic behavior intended to meet the expectations of other people. Therefore, it is essential to use meditation and prayer to delete the old programming and indoctrination that is holding you back from creating a truly powerful spiritual life, discover the passions and excitement of your true self, and self-program your new life of unlimited potential into existence.

A Second Life requires that each person is obligated to discover what connects him or her to God and inspires him or her to create a life lived in Oneness.

In the other four key areas of life, it is best to set specific goals for growth and improvement, with milestones to be reached along the way in order to track your progress. But that is not the case when re-aligning your life to be spiritually powerful. For this area of life you must begin now to immediately live in alignment with the passions and desires of your true self and integrate with the rest of the world in Oneness. No one will be perfect on day one, but the attention you give to the goal must be as though perfection is expected and already achieved. When you know that you are One with everything you encounter, that what you do and who you are affects everything else, your sense of fairness and responsibility will not allow you to give less than 100 percent. Your attention to everything must be immediately elevated so that you are acutely conscious of how everything you do affects something or someone else. When you are able to conduct your life in concert with all that there is to experience, you will feel an obligation to always do your best, be your best, and contribute to making everything/everyone else better as well.

So, now you understand that deciding on the future of your spiritual life means beginning right in this moment to live from your passions, giving it your all. Each day you will become more conscious of how things have changed. Each day you will get better and better at being your true self. Each day you will see and more greatly appreciate the miracles all around you. At the beginning of each day, you will delight in the adventure that is in front of you. At the end of each day, you will feel blissful in your gratitude for all that you have been given, encountered, and achieved. The future of your empowered spiritual life living as your true self in Oneness begins right now!

Step Four: Decide on a spiritual re-alignment action plan

Use these five basic steps as a guide, allowing the details of your own journey and mission to unfold as your consciousness increases of what it means to be living a spiritually powerful life.

1) Recognize that you have been conducting your life based on false beliefs, as opposed to the truth within you. Also, acknowledge that all the negative energies such as fear, insecurity, hate, selfishness, and ego are evil and that love, gratitude, passion, and Oneness are positive energy, God's energy.
2) Acknowledge that you have been indoctrinated and victimized all of your life, and admit that such indoctrination was a great crime against you.
3) Forgive those who have harmed you or led you astray, whether or not they intended to do so. God is all love; there is no judgment.

4) Delete your old programming, using the tools you have been given: meditation, prayer, and self-programming.
5) Create your new reality based on your inner truth.

The first step in your liberation process helps you recognize that you have been conducting your life based on false beliefs, as opposed to the truth within you. Next, by acknowledging that you have been indoctrinated and victimized all of your life, and admitting that such indoctrination was a great crime against you, you take back your own power. In essence, you are joining forces with yourself by telling yourself, "I see what has happened and think it is wrong." Becoming your own team member initiates you on the path of becoming One with everyone and everything else.

Forgiving those who have harmed you or led you astray, whether or not they intended to do so, is necessary because it is an instruction from God that there be no judgment, only love, in God's kingdom. Judgment and love cannot coexist. Besides, judgment cannot provide any sense of satisfaction for those who have been wronged; it simply reinforces the pain and holds back spiritual growth by being a constant reminder. Forgiveness is necessary for spiritual growth because it is a reflection of your ability to understand that what you do to others you are also doing to yourself.

The most remarkable example of this I have heard is the story of Jennifer Thompson and Ronald Cotton. Jennifer was raped by an intruder in her own bedroom at knifepoint one night while she was a college student. She managed to get away from her attacker, who ran off and raped another woman a block away. Immediately reporting the crime to police, she described her attacker and a composite drawing, was made from her memories of what he looked like. Based on the drawing, the police showed Jennifer several photographs of suspects; she identified one as the young man who had raped her. During a subsequent lineup of several men, she identified the same person she had in the photograph, saying again with absolute certainty that he was the one who raped her. His name was Ronald Cotton.

Ronald insisted he had not committed the crime against Jennifer but did not have strong proof that he was elsewhere when the crime was committed. During his trial, Jennifer testified with such certainty that he was the man who raped her that the jury found Ronald guilty and he was sentenced to life in prison.

Although he still insisted that he was not guilty of the crime, Ronald remained a mild-mannered man who served his time as a model prisoner while his attorney appealed his conviction. Even though Ronald knew that the fact he was a black man accused of raping a white woman in a Southern city, along with Jennifer's unwavering certainty of his guilt, left little doubt in the minds of many people that his conviction was right and just, he did not become angry and bitter or turn against his true self by changing into the monster he was convicted of being. He was hopeful that he would be vindicated when his attorney got him a second trial. Again he was convicted based on Jennifer's adament testimony. This time he was sentenced to life in prison, plus fifty-four years.

Despite it all, Ronald steadfastly proclaimed his innocence and somehow managed to remain a mild-mannered model prisoner whose character was untainted. Then the hand of fate intervened. A new inmate arrived at the prison whose appearance so strongly resembled Ronald's that other inmates and prison officials confused the two, calling each by the other's names. When the two men had an opportunity to meet and discuss the situation, they discovered that they were even from the same town.

Before long a third inmate told Ronald that the man who resembled him admited that he had actually committed the crimes Ronald was convicted for. But how could Ronald prove it? Around that same time Ronald was listening to O. J. Simpson's murder trial on the radio and learned about a type of evidence called DNA. He asked his attorney if DNA evidence could be used to prove his innocence. The attorney told him that if there was DNA evidence from his case, it could prove his innocence but warned him that it could also prove his guilt. Because in his heart Ronald knew he did not commit the crimes, he asked his attorney to follow up and have any available DNA evidence tested.

Eleven years after Ronald Cotton was first arrested for the crime of raping Jennifer Thompson, the results of the DNA evidence were presented to a judge: Ronald Cotton was not the perpetrator. In fact, the other inmate from his hometown actually was. Ronald Cotton was set free that day.

Although by this time Jennifer Thompson was married and a mother, the hatred she felt toward Ronald Cotton, the man she was certain was her rapist, had become so much a part of her life that every day she prayed he would be raped and killed in prison. When she was told that DNA evidence proved he was not the man who raped her, that DNA evidence proved he was the wrong man and he had been released, Jennifer was devastated and inconsolable. The idea that an innocent man had spent eleven years in prison because of a mistake she made was too overwhelming for her to deal with.

PBS television produced a documentary about convictions being overturned based on DNA evidence and included Ronald's story. Toward the end, he said he wondered why Jennifer had never contacted him since he was proved not to be her attacker and released from prison. Until Jennifer watched the documentary and saw Ronald's entire story, she could never even consider being in touch with him, but afterward she immediately asked her attorney to arrange for them to meet.

At the prearranged time, Jennifer sat in a church waiting for Ronald to enter. She was extremely nervous and anguished. What could she possibly say to the man whose life had been destroyed because of a mistake she made? Ronald entered and slowly, deliberately walked to where Jennifer was seated. He sat in a chair facing her. With tears rolling down her face, her body shaking, she looked up at him and said, "If I spend every second of every day for the rest of my life telling you how sorry I am, it could never begin to express how horrible I feel for what I've done to you."

Ronald Cotton reached out, took Jennifer's hands in his, and said, "I forgive you."

Ronald and Jennifer have since become good friends and know each other's families. Their unlikely journey has continued as they have written a book together called *Picking Cotton*, which tells their inspiring story, and they fight for a common cause: working together for a positive resolution of other cases of injustice for prisoners in America.

This story is a lesson, not only about the power of forgiveness, but also about how we make assumptions based on the information presented to us. When Jennifer was shown the photographs of suspects by police, she assumed one of the men in the photographs *had to be* her attacker. Same with the lineup. That assumption convinced her that she picked the right man, Ronald Cotton, because he most closely resembled the man who eventually would be convicted for raping her based on the DNA evidence. It would be over eleven years later when she'd find out her assumptions were wrong.

Everyone who is indoctrinated and living like a robot is operating on assumptions made by them that are based on false beliefs they are taught. As long as you continue to conduct your life based on those assumptions, you will never be free to live with purpose and integrity in alignment with your God-given truth. Only by recognizing the false beliefs that are running you, deleting that indoctrinated programming, then creating your new reality based on your inner truth by following your life plan will you have confidence to achieve your unlimited potential.

But first, before anything makes sense to you, it's of great importance that you know *why* you are doing all of this. The reason is to enjoy, love, learn, and evolve during the journey that is your life, and to create heaven on earth through being all you can be and giving back with the unique gifts that you have been given. Committing to your connection to God within you means living a life in Oneness with no fears to hold you back. You are then the creator of your life and how it plays out.

Use the tools you learned in Coding to Oneness, Level 1, of this guide—meditation, prayer, and self-programming—to assist you in setting your goals and keeping a clear focus on them as you enact your plans in order to create your new reality based on your inner truth.

Step Five: Decide how important having a spiritually strong life is to you

God made you the creator of your own life. The life you live is based on the reality you create, which is different for every person. How you think shapes the way you see the world and yourself within it. If things have always gone your way, then you see a world where you can create your own destiny. When you step out of your life's movie in detachment to watch how your life plays out, you will see that everything is set in motion by what you do, how you think, what you say, and how you feel.

But if you have experienced a lot of struggle, then you most likely don't see yourself as the creator, but probably view your life as a series of random circumstances to overcome. Negative belief systems, which have made you a victim due to the fears hindering you, made you believe that your life and reality have limitations. These feelings, which are the negative forces inside you, are "evil" fighting to stop you from achieving enlightenment. Within every person two forces—good and evil—are dormant and waiting to be activated by our indoctrination. God exists within everyone, but we forget that we have the power to either create heaven on earth or hell on earth by our choices.

The Dark Forces (Evil)	God
Hate	Love
Fear	No fear
Judgmental	Non-judgmental
Insecurities	Inner peace
Helplessness	Happiness
Envy	Gratitude
Ego	Unselfishness
Greed	Compassion
Separation	Oneness
Grudges	Forgiveness
Anger	Empathy

Too many people have lost the battle to the dark forces. Some of these people can even claim to be followers of religious institutions, but their lives are being controlled by the forces of evil, fear, hate, envy, self-doubt, or being judgmental. God wants you to destroy the devil inside through living a life in Oneness, through surrendering to a life filled with love.

In order to identify the devil inside, one has to understand the negative forces that feed the darkness, as well the light, which is God.

The truth is that when you delete the negative programming (the evil energies) that have been controlling you, then you are free to live an existence in Oneness and are able to do anything you can imagine in your new reality that is in alignment with your true self. Being one with God means you have unlimited power and strength, and can utilize all the gifts you have been given to create the life of your dreams. When you have peeled away the layers of negative belief systems like an onion, you let God shine through and you become aligned in Oneness. The light (God) will always win the battle over evil (negative energy).

Being the creator of your own life—free of negative belief systems—you are able to decide what kind of existence you want, what you want to do in this lifetime, and what contribution you will make to a better world. In this state of Oneness, there is nothing that can stop you. You are fearless as long as your actions are aligned with your heart and passion within. Your strength is unstoppable.

Being the creator of your life and following your passions awaken the artist and dreamer inside you that has no limits, whose thinking is free of limiting rules for what reality can be according to establishment's rights and wrongs. In this state of Oneness, your actions come from the heart and you awaken from an existence as a "flat-liner" to experience a world without limitations.

In addition to the greatest gift of all, LIFE, God also gave you the three most powerful tools that you can use as the creator of your own life: thought, speech, and action. How you use these tools will determine whether you can make wonders happen or simply wonder what happened. When used for the good, the right thoughts, words, and actions can create amazing events for yourself and others, but if misused the reverse can be the result. Thinking negative or limiting thoughts, speaking in hurtful or pessimistic ways, and acting on negativity creates a reality that is less than optimal. But the opposite is possible. With correct thoughts and behavior you will create heaven on earth.

When awakened to live in a state of Oneness, which is perfection with unlimited resources available to you as the creator, you will find the balance needed between materiality and spirituality by aligning your thoughts, words, and actions with your true self inside. Once connected to your true self, you will treasure and respect all of the gifts you have received. You will listen to your heart and know that only spiritual truth is found within yourself. You will do whatever it takes to be the most perfect, divine creation you can be in order to evolve because you'll know that wasting your existence being a "flat-liner"—who is not fully present in your life and not being the creator of your own life's movie—is a betrayal not just of yourself, but of God, as well.

When you live in Oneness, your heart tells you how to travel without regret during life's journey. By living in Oneness, you are on a mission for God, as opposed to being on a mission for your ego when living according to the programmed negative belief systems from before. Your commitment of Oneness is a commitment to serve what God wants, not what your ego desires. In this new reality, not only have you found the enlightenment that everyone is seeking, but you have also become the creator of your life through your connection to God within you.

Step Six: Determine how you can contribute to making the world a better place by living in Oneness

We all have come to this world to make a positive difference. The purpose is for you to experience life and learn and evolve in what is called the earth school—your life journey on earth. Your gifts and talents, which are the source of your passion, were given to you to develop and use to serve a greater cause than yourself. As a unique creation of God, your main objective is to serve a higher power, with your journey being the by-product.

Life's journey is not about you or me, but how we all can contribute to making our society a better place. But it starts within each one of us. When making the commitment to accept living a life connected and guided by God within, we become One with him and everyone else. When we deny that connection, it is a betrayal not only of ourselves but of God as well.

All that is asked of us is that we commit to serve a cause greater than ourselves, not what our egos desire. By each of us surrendering to Oneness, we overcome and eliminate all fears that cause interpersonal conflicts; we dis-empower negative belief systems that force us to a live in mental slavery. As the differences between one person and another become less pronounced by the awakening of the universal God inside, love replaces ego and fear, and the power of Oneness increases. Fear and negative belief systems, along with the false prophets ruling the masses who indoctrinated us in order to separate us from the wishes of God, creating havoc on earth, will become powerless to stop the new world from rising up, creating heaven on earth.

> *If we have no peace, it is because we have forgotten that we belong to each other.*
>
> Mother Teresa

Step Seven: Learn the realities of creating and maintaining a spiritually based life of Oneness

The Ego has disconnected you from God

In a perfect world, where people truly care for each other, there is a need for only minimal government, leaving room for everyone to create anything they desire with as little interference as possible. But, as long as the ego is running the show, a greater government body is needed to protect people from those who care more for their own interests than the needs of anyone else. Such people have been separated through indoctrination from their internal connection with God and their Oneness with everyone else. Their lives revolve around ego gratification, with little thoughts of others.

> *The community which has neither poverty nor riches will always have the noblest principles.*
>
> Plato

On many occasions I have witnessed the dark side of people awakened when it comes to feeding their ego gratification through greed and money. I have attended funerals where "good" religious people—who claimed their goodness through their Sunday church attendance and reading of the Bible—were arguing over who would get what material goods from the deceased even before the casket was in the ground, instead of living as role models with their lights shining from within. The drama would continue when later discussions about material objects ended in physical fights and ongoing family feuds. I have also personally witnessed elders and everyday hardworking people being victimized and tricked out of their hard-earned savings by people with slick appearances or so-called reputable institutions—all out of greed—forcing the good people into a life of helplessness. This lack of compassion and disrespect for our fellow human beings is the work of the dark forces, which are the evil forces at work.

Too many people have forgotten that their obligation is to serve a higher purpose than themselves by caring for one another. The falling away from this important spiritual law can be seen dramatically in all parts of society among all types of people. But instead of viewing this as a failure, it's important to recognize that this effect has resulted from society's belief that feeding the ego is satisfying. Even though most people realize that ego gratification is not the correct way to live, we all get caught up in the competitive urges to prove we can succeed based on society's standards.

Along with everything else we have received from God, we have also been blessed with free will. The choices we make—even those that are in opposition to what we know is the correct way to live—create our realities from which we can learn and grow as individuals, as groups, as a nation, and as a world. And it's ironic that our opportunities for growth can sometimes be greatest when we are led astray by ego gratification. This is one of the best ways for us to learn, grow, and evolve so that eventually we can create heaven on earth.

> *A creative man is motivated by the desire to achieve,*
> *not the desire to beat others.*
>
> Ayn Rand

There is a strong lesson to be learned from the present economic conditions and meltdown that are affecting everyone. Instead of being fearful by what we face during this difficult time, we should thank God and be grateful for the opportunity to be reminded of what is the truth. Because once we realize the truth of what is happening, prolonging a bad situation—either personally, as a group or a nation—does nobody any good, as it only stops us from growing. When something has gone wrong it is important to recognize the source of the problem, which is usually the belief system that led us astray. Trying to right a wrong by intervening based on the same belief system will only cause the situation to continue. Instead of throwing more money into ineffective parts of the economy, we must recognize that those parts that are not working need to adapt or cease to exist. The economy needs to be dealt with the same way as our individual lives in regard to spirituality. To correct a situation, it's of great importance to change what caused the collapse, otherwise it will be like treating a junkie by giving him or her more drugs, instead of having him or her detox.

> *The care of human life and happiness, and not their destruction,*
> *is the first and only object of good government.*
>
> Thomas Jefferson

God gave us the tools to make wiser choices. But many people were tempted by the ideas of those who discovered that ego-based competition and a system of stealing from others was a means to financial gain, and we bought into their faulty system. Many people forgot that there are no shortcuts to success, that hard work and dedication are required to achieve anything of value in life. Too many people chose to run our economy to its knees by feeding their egos, which is a result of society's indoctrination—victimizing people by convincing them to make wrong financial decisions while not informing them of the consequences. Agreeing to go along with such a scheme is wasting the precious chance at life we have been given. Worse yet, instead of creating lives that are aligned with God in Oneness, we are wasting our existence.

> *Loyalty to the country always. Loyalty to the government when it deserves it.*
>
> Mark Twain

The good news is that during down times we have many more opportunities to learn. What we do next to change—and this means how we choose to think and what kind of reality we choose to create for ourselves—will determine whether our lives from this moment forward will be lived as part of God's kingdom. If so, the ego needs to be dis-empowered and replaced with love for something greater than ourselves. Then we will be contributing to creating heaven on earth.

Consumerism makes you feel inadequate

Many people spend their entire lives searching for meaning, and when they don't find it end up feeling discontentment and questioning if this is all there is. The lifelong chase for enlightenment for many people has been an external search because that's what we were indoctrinated to believe from a very young age. Enlightenment and happiness, we are told, can be found through external gratification. There are numerous belief systems that have been programmed into us, but most have something in common: they are based on fear and disconnect us from our true selves. Such negative programming has us believing that we are expected to behave in ways that please other people rather than do what feels right in our hearts.

We spend our lives like puppies trained through a reward and punishment system to play certain roles that we believe will result in our being accepted and liked by others. This indoctrination has caused us to be disconnected from our true selves and from God. It has been reinforced not only by people who know it is the wrong path, but also by people with the best intentions—but they also were indoctrinated to live the wrong way. Our consumer-driven society has trained us to believe that achieving great materialistic success is equal to happiness and respect. But at the same time, whatever we have achieved and obtained is never enough. There is no way to get ahead in this way of thinking. There will never be enough achieved; there will always be something better to shoot for or to obtain. It is impossible to ever reach the point of total happiness and contentment by seeking it this way, because external gratification can never fill the internal void. External gratification only provides temporary joy that soon passes as the next thing to acquire arises and prompts the chase for happiness to continue.

This consumer-driven belief system also reinforces a competitiveness urge to acquire as much "stuff" as other people have. Buying into this belief system causes people to judge each other based on materialism, rather than by who they are as people. It's a fact that anyone who achieves great wealth in this lifetime will always encounter someone who has more money than they do. So there is no way to ever be truly successful, or the most successful, based on these beliefs. By feeding the ego, this belief system disconnects us from Oneness by making us feel inadequate and dissatisfied, that we never really have what we need to feel complete. The brainwashing, which has taken place over generations, has caused people with even the best intentions, including parents and closest friends, to believe they have been doing the right thing when influencing you. They simply did not know better because they too were brainwashed.

The consumerism belief system, which is encouraged by the media, entraps many people and causes them to lose control of their lives. The fear of not measuring up, believing having more "stuff" results in more happiness, and feeling a need to show other people how successful they are in life has caused many people to get in way over their heads, taking on financial obligations they can't meet. Far too many people have been victimized by the wrong values created by this consumerism belief system. As a result, they are doomed to spend the rest of their lives financially trapped, deprived of their freedom and feeling a void inside from a need for enlightenment. This vicious cycle will stop only by breaking the hypnotic spell caused by the belief systems that have reinforced incorrect values and beliefs that disconnect us from who we truly are and what we really need. Oneness with ourselves, with God and his kingdom within each of us, is the only way for us to set ourselves free. That is our opportunity to create true success and achieve genuine fulfillment in life.

Religious institutions use fear to control you

Many religious institutions claim to have the key to God's kingdom and the state of Oneness. But fear is one of the tools they use to manipulate you. They convince you that your connection to God takes place because of their church and that those who don't follow their rules will go to hell for eternity. They claim to speak for God and that the more money you give them, the more you will be rewarded by God. As a result, you obey them out of fear and give them money out of obligation and to get something in return. In the Kingdom of God—which is within each of us—a known spiritual law is that giving anything (even money) in order to get something far greater in return is not the correct intention. Such an act is not performed from the heart, but in support of the ego.

In every country and every age, the priest had been hostile to liberty.

Thomas Jefferson

This fear-driven and manipulating indoctrination—that is preached and presented for the sole purpose of securing power for the rulers of religious institutions—prevents people from blossoming by truly connecting with the God within them according to their own passions. The false prophets have built systems and structures to secure their own existence, not for the greater good. Their belief systems, created to secure their own power as being the only truth tellers, actually undermine the highest authority, God, whose truth is inside each of us, not found in fear-based religious structures that seek to control us. Such belief systems give us permission to judge others and feel superior to people who do not also join in. But in truth, these belief systems go against everything God stands for: that we are all equal in our ability to connect with God, which is all love. Rather than empowering us, we become dis-empowered and disconnected, living lives doomed to limitation due to our fears and the belief we accept that God is external and separate from us. All negative energies that make us live a limited, dis-empowered life are the dark forces, the devil. That dark force will use any means to prevent us from achieving enlightenment and Oneness. It is misleading the human race through the disguise of the church and misrepresenting the name of God and the messages in the Bible and other religious scriptures, which are being used to manipulate and dictate as though they are the only truth.

It ain't those parts of the Bible that I can't understand that bother me,
it is the parts that I do understand.

Mark Twain

The real truth is that we are all God's divine creations and every one of us has access to his kingdom, which is already within each of us. We are already One with God. But we have forgotten that this is true because of our separation from Oneness by the many layers of negative belief systems we have been exposed to by society, including those of religious institutions, many of which represent the dark forces. Some races and religions even claim to be "the chosen people," which is another way to establish and enforce the separation, which is the opposite of what God stands for.

Remember: God is all inclusive. God is love. God is all there is. The Oneness and spiritual enlightenment that we are all seeking is already within us and is ready to be awakened. All we need to do is disarm and delete the indoctrination that keeps us in a state of separation so that we are once again capable of reestablishing our inner connection to Oneness.

The path to freedom from the mental slavery that makes our lives a struggle is to first acknowledge that neither the religious false prophets nor any other institutions that seek to control us have any power or authority over us if we do not allow it, choose it, or accept that it is true. The fear they have used to control our lives has limited the God-given potential each of us is entitled to live to the fullest. The indoctrination and belief systems of the dark side have turned the greatest gift of all by God, LIFE, into something we are not fully appreciating or truly enjoying.

> *Power is of two kinds. One is obtained by the fear of punishment and the other by acts of love. Power based on love is a thousand times more effective and permanent than the one derived from fear of punishment.*
>
> Mohandas Gandhi

Some people feel as though life is just one hurdle after another, one struggle after another; from cradle to grave they feel an emptiness inside that is never filled. They are missing the inner connection to a higher power that would result in them feeling they have achieved completeness. Other people wait their entire lives for God to save them. Or they believe God will be waiting for them and welcome them to a bliss-filled life in heaven as a reward for suffering and struggling through life on earth.

These people have been indoctrinated by the dark forces of evil to waste God's greatest gift of all, LIFE, by not evolving and serving a higher purpose for humankind. Instead they are entrapped by the devil to live a life in the shadow of their true potential. And at the same time they are preventing the creation of heaven on earth.

These innocent victims have betrayed God without knowing it. Instead of living as role models, they spend a lifetime imagining that once they cross over to the light they will be saved. They don't understand that how far their energies, both positive and negative, have evolved is how their next life will be. If you have lived in a self-created prison on earth—a reality representing Hell—then after your physical death you will wake up in the same unevolved state as you left, which is also Hell. If the dark forces got you and held onto you in this lifetime, it doesn't matter how hard you pray, because how you live your life and whether you have lived this existence in Oneness is what's important. If someone is filled with the devil's dark energies, he or she is not the representative of God.

> *I live in sin, to kill myself I live; no longer my life my own, but sin's;*
> *my good is given to me by heaven, my evil by myself, by my free will,*
> *of which I am deprived.*
>
> Michelangelo

It's a falsely imposed belief that people must live according to the rules of their religious institution or church—meaning the rules created by men to enforce their power over other men. This is not a requirement that God would ever make or impose upon anyone. To identify the dark forces in any religious institution, all it takes is to see if it is fear-based or dis-empowering in any way whatsoever. If so, it's the devil trying to control you.

> *Fear is pain arising from the anticipation of evil.*
>
> Aristotle

Becoming One with your true self and with God

The first step in the process of becoming one with your true self and God is to fully acknowledge that you have been misled and crippled by the negative belief systems/the negative energies that are controlling every thought and action you take, making you an innocent victim. Next is to fully acknowledge that God already gave you the greatest gift of all: life. To live fully and with purpose can be done only by connecting with the God within you and fulfilling your purpose. By giving you free will, God entrusted you with making the right choices about how you experience life. You can choose a life in Oneness, becoming the creator, where everything is possible. Or you can accept defeat, live a limited existence, allowing negative belief systems/the dark forces to control you, making your life a struggle. By breaking the mental slavery, you will emerge to become one with your true self, God, and his kingdom inside.

There is no greater crime than taking someone's life. This is what the false prophets and negative belief systems are doing by making people "flat-liners," by dis-empowering people and preventing them from achieving the spiritual enlightenment and Oneness that is everyone's birthright. Instead of living fulfilled lives we were all meant to experience, too many people experience only a fraction of what is possible.

For some people, the disconnection means they spend their entire existence looking for something that can't be found. Due to their negative programming, which overrides all of their potential, they aren't able to even get close to a state of enlightenment. The indoctrination is so deeply rooted in many that their lives are doomed. And there is no salvation because nobody tells them what is happening to them. Some people spend their entire lifetime looking for something that is already within, just waiting to be discovered. Regardless of whether people know what is happening or not, they accept the lies of their indoctrination as truth because they believe they have to accept struggle as a way of life. When you're told the same "lies" thousands of times all of your life, they become your reality and truth. People spend their entire existence in a life of fear and struggle, which is the same as taking their lives away from them.

But your birthright is a life free of negative belief systems, where you are the creator of your own existence and can achieve Oneness.

Step Eight: Execute your spiritual development plan to get where you want to be

Detachment is necessary

The way you experience life is based entirely on your reality, which is created by how you think and what you believe. Therefore, how you perceive your life and world is determined by your programming, the way you have been conditioned to think and respond. Most people have been indoctrinated with beliefs that they can't do this or that, that many things are impossible, and that failing to achieve according to society's rules can have dramatic consequences. Fear has become a large part of most people's existence, fear of deviating from behavior that the majority considers a normal and acceptable way to live. This sets a precedent of what is right or wrong conduct, correct or incorrect behavior.

While growing up, each of us was programmed to think and act in certain ways—which most often created limitations in what we believe can and cannot be done, thereby eliminating many of our opportunities. After a while we are ruled by self-doubt, fear, and being judgmental toward ourselves and others. In this created reality we are like actors in a movie, with the script of our lives and direction of our actions being conducted by someone else. This wrong programming turns the stories of our lives into movies that do not necessarily go the way we would plan or end the way we would intend if we felt free to make our own choices.

It's extremely important to understand that in order to break away from a life script that is predetermined for you by someone else, you need to learn to detach. Knowing that you are being controlled by the belief systems of other people is not enough. You also need to learn how to step back and watch your own life's movie from the perspective of someone else. When you're *not* "in it" you can rewind the scenes and events, and clearly see the dramas that are taking place. By doing so you can identify patterns that you can further examine and see why you reacted as you did based on your programming. This mental exercise helps you see and understand why your life is going the way it is and where it will likely continue to go unless you conduct a full reboot by disarming the programs running you.

To achieve a life in Oneness you need to learn to completely free yourself from everything controlling you. Only by taking a step back and looking at your life's movie and yourself objectively can you really understand what it feels like to be fully detached from everyone else's programming as you move forward based on your own choices and free will.

Next step in the process of detaching is to change your reactions and how you think by always following three key rules:

1) When you are in a situation where someone approaches you in anger, never project anger back.
2) Winning an argument does not accomplish much, because everyone's opinions and points of view are based on their own reality and experiences. You have your reality and other people have a different set of realities, which are just as valid to them as yours are to you.
3) Nothing in life is usually so serious that you need to be negatively stirred up by it. When looking back on events during your life, you will quickly realize that most of the drama that took place wasn't really of much importance. You will also notice that the other key players you interacted with were actually doing the best they could based on their own programming—which, again, has created a different reality than yours and caused them to see things in a different way.

By learning to look at yourself as objectively as you can (with detachment) and making a conscious effort to observe yourself, if you want to change the way you think, react, and behave based on your negative programming, you can do so. Remember, the only truth is found in your heart, not dictated by your programming. By learning to differentiate between your imposed thoughts and reaction patterns versus the ones that resonate with your true self from your heart, you take a huge step toward connecting with who you really are.

Failure is a part of life's school

During each of our individual journeys of exploration, some days have been good, while many not so good. There have been numerous situations when life has not looked or seemed to be as meaningful as we had hoped or thought it would/should be. Many times we have felt that our minds were the biggest enemy, fighting us much of the time. When we thought we would be happy, there was still a feeling that something was missing. As the years passed, most of us would question why life was so difficult, causing us to dream of another life, another chance to do it better. We would even question why we got the parents that we have or why we were born into the environment that shaped us to become who we are. Many times we would feel that we did not measure up to either our own expectations or those of other people. In a society built on being successful and looking a certain way, many of us feel inadequate, that we do not meet the standards of what society expects. Everybody goes through experiences that leave them feeling as though they've failed or could have done things differently (better) than they did.

> *It is hard to fail, but it is worse never to have tried to succeed.*
>
> Theodore Roosevelt

Not succeeding creates the feeling of failing and/or that life is not fair. And you are right! Until this point you have been controlled by negative programming, creating a life that has not been fair. Yes, you have been at a disadvantage in ways you did not deserve. Nobody should have to go through life questioning or wondering if this is all there is, feeling as though they are crawling on their knees through the years, being unable to control anything. As long as limiting programming is running people's lives, they are being victimized. Is it fair that some people can cruise through life, while others can barely get through their days just because they ended up in an environment that caused them to be dis-connected and dis-empowered? No, it's not fair. But life is not fair.

Why is it that two children in the same family can look so much alike but think and behave completely differently even when they have been exposed to the same programming? God created each of us as the unique individuals we are supposed to be so that we will have our own special journeys in life. How two people experience or react to the same belief systems—whether negative or positive—will therefore be different for each person. What most people have in common is that very few have escaped some sort of negative programming. But during days of hardship it's important to know and remember that there are reasons for our challenges and problems. They are actually gifts from God, which give us a chance to learn and evolve. Each experience, whether good or bad, should be greeted and embraced with gratitude for what we can learn from it or how we can grow. The way we respond will determine how much we grow.

The truth is that very little in life is worth getting all stirred up by in a negative way. But it's also important to fully experience what your life has to offer you as a unique individual, because that is what impacts your reality. Your life journey is much more difficult when you are dis-empowered by negative programming. Because you are disconnected from your true self—which is the source of your power, knowledge, and perspective—your reality is distorted and you find it difficult to meet or cope with life's downs. Every challenge or problem can feel life threatening, creating a reality of fear, helplessness, weakness, and despair. When you can disengage from the way you have been programmed to react to the drama of life's problems, then problems that are not real look completely different—they become positive learning experiences from which to grow and evolve.

True, life is not fair, but it's not supposed to be. If we are here to learn and grow through life experiences, then we gain from each unique challenge we encounter. As life goes on, we are supposed to evolve from our experiences, which is what God intended. But doing so is extremely difficult when we are disconnected from the kingdom of God that is within each of us. Only by deleting the negative programming that has separated us from that source of power and inspiration and reconnecting with our true selves can life be what it is meant to be: a journey of growth, filled with bliss in a life of Oneness.

Release your pain, disappointment, and anger

Holding on to pain, disappointment, and anger only hurts *you.* Hidden pain is what makes you repeat over and over again the patterns that hold you back from being your true self, patterns you want to break away from in order to be free. During the process of detachment it's critical to allow yourself to recognize that there is pain you have suppressed and release that pain to ensure that it goes away permanently.

Being indoctrinated with false programming was a painful experience as your true self fought against being overrun/overwritten and a different reality was created that you were required to accept. That pain became manifest as fear and inadequacy keeping you disconnected from the passions and desires to be your true self. Being kept separate from your true self by more indoctrination reinforced the pain, which has been trapped inside, underneath your programming. Now, as you delete that negative programming, the pain will surface and must be released. By doing so you are affirming your desire and intention to be the person you are truly meant to be and live the life of unlimited potential that is your birthright.

As the pain surfaces, study it and fully feel it. Use your tools of meditation, prayer, and self-programming to release the pain forever, so that it can never again stand in the way of your connection with your true self and God. Putting the past behind you does not mean you will entirely forget your low points in life, but you will remember them in an objective way, without pain or a need to emotionally react to them because you will no longer *feel* they were either good or bad. The programming that is running your life has been based on the logic of the thinking mind, which wants to protect and promote your ego needs. It's of great importance as you delete that programming and during your awakening process that you also fully release the suppressed pain caused by your separation from your true self.

The ego needs to be destroyed

No matter how difficult or easy life can be, each of us has an inborn natural mechanism called "survival." Although this mechanism has sometimes been portrayed as the same thing as "ego," that is not correct. In fact, the ego is actually the selfishness part of us that is the opposite of what God represents, which is only and all love. Unconditional love and ego are at the two opposite poles. The ego is what tries to control us and will lead us astray, separating us from our inner connection with God.

Ask yourself what makes you feel better, helping someone without getting anything in return—such as an elderly lady struggling to get across the street—or making more money to buy yourself more consumer goods in an attempt to make yourself feel better. When the ego controls, it's always about ME, ME, ME. When you are one with God, love, unconditional love, is all there is.

When filled with love, you have already arrived at your destination in life, which is NOW. But when the ego is running you, life becomes a never-ending chase to get to a destination you will never reach. The ego creates a void inside that can never be filled. Although when operating from ego you can be tricked by glimpses of moments that give the impression you have arrived at where you want to be inside, soon you will be lured to the next thing and the next and the next. The instant gratification created by the ego is always short lived; it separates you from the Oneness that we are all searching for.

Many "experts" have attempted to convince us that we as human beings cannot exist without ego, that if ego is destroyed we will be as well, that somehow ego is linked to our survival. Take a look at people in third world countries that from a Western-world point of view have nothing except hunger and misery, or people walking around hungry, homeless, jobless, and penniless in our own backyards in America. Do you think their egos are what make them want to survive, or is it "survival mode"? Something inside each of us tells us that no matter how difficult this life may seem at times, it is precious and unique and it is always possible that it can suddenly change or be made better. What keeps us going at our lowest points in life is the dream of something better. Without hopes and dreams we will not survive. The ego has nothing to do with our "survival mode."

Ego is a trait that few people, if any, admire because it is recognized as being controlled by the part of a person that will never give unselfishly to anyone else. People whose actions are ego driven never truly succeed, because no one respects them for who they truly are or what they do. And internally they lose as well, because they are always attempting to achieve something that has no real meaning. Many people with big egos are driven by deep insecurities, fears, and strong needs to prove themselves to others. Their feelings of inadequacy usually develop at an early age in life when negative programming overtakes the passion in their hearts.

Although some people that appear to be successful "on the outside" are capable of realizing later in life that their achievements have been for ego gratification and they can then correct the error of their ways, many people are unable to do so and live their entire lives feeling something is missing. No matter how much they accomplish they are not truly fulfilled, because everything they do is done for the wrong reasons—to feed their egos or cover up their fears and insecurities—not because it comes from the heart. The ego can be so powerful that it takes over some people's entire lives, rendering them helpless to do anything from their true self's intentions. Unfortunately, many people are so disconnected that their intentions are based on fear and logic of the thinking (or overthinking) mind, which is reasoning, not inspiration aligned with the heart. A clear indication that ego is running the show is when the person is always attempting to be better than others or to prove themselves.

If you are uncertain whether your actions are based on ego gratification or are based on purpose and passion from the heart, look inside yourself and question the intentions behind your actions. If you do something for the betterment of yourself or even simply to compete with yourself to see how much you can achieve, but you do either for the right reasons—not from fear or feeling inadequate—then it's not the ego running you or controlling you. The intentions behind your actions or reasoning are what are important. The best way to know when your intentions are honorable is to listen to your inner voice that tells you whether your actions are aligned with your heart. When what you think and do feel right, as though it's coming from the heart, then you are in touch with the true you.

Live by example—Don't judge

As you are making progress and evolving to live in a state of Oneness, it's important not to be tempted to compare yourself to others or judge them. All human beings are on their own life journeys, and all are at different stages or places along the way. If it appears you are making better progress than others or have evolved to a higher level, it does not mean you have permission to enforce upon others your way of thinking or judge yourself better than them. Everyone proceeds on their journeys based on their own set of experiences and where they want to go. The best way to influence others is to live be example. When you live in alignment with your true self and with God, your internal bliss will attract others to you. People who are ready to receive help from you will come forward and ask for your guidance.

It's very common when you are evolving to look around and see that you have changed, but other people in your life have not. You may have a strong desire to share your good news or try to fix these people, but remember that you can't. Don't interfere with their individual journeys, which they need to embark upon on their own, just as you needed to do with yours. When they come to you to share their experiences and discuss their insights, then is the time to engage in mutual conversations on equal footing, where neither of you is the student or the teacher.

Make peace through forgiveness

Asking for forgiveness is taking responsibility for you actions as well as your life. Forgiveness is an important element in the releasing of old wounds. All of us have made mistakes in life, including wrongdoings to others as well as to ourselves. Forgiveness is necessary in order to move on to a new life and fully embrace it. We need to make peace in every cell of our body.

Your Forgiveness Agenda

The first step is to forgive yourself. By forgiving yourself you are also forgiven by God. To be fully free we must forgive ourselves for every transgression we have made toward anyone else.

1. Through a life review of your first life—from youth to current day—make a list of all the people that you can remember who crossed your path and you hurt in one way or another. Next to each person's name write down what you did. Also, write down the names of people who hurt you and what they did.
2. To get all your feelings out, write a letter to each person expressing your true feelings (not holding anything back) about how the actions made you feel at the time and afterward. The letter is not to be sent.
3. Next, track down each person on your list and arrange a meeting or a telephone call if he or she is not in your area, to say that you are sorry for what happened—even if it was many years ago. Unless this toxin is released it will always stay in the back of your mind for the rest of your life. Why spend your life looking over your shoulder or worrying or feeling bad about something? It will only hold you back in life.

If the people you want to make peace with have passed on, read the letter as a prayer; if they caused you harm, forgive them, or you will forever be the victim if you keep walking around with grudges.

As you go through the list, which takes a lot of guts, you will feel lighter and lighter inside as a cleansing of the soul takes place. Some of the meetings will go smoothly, while others will be tougher. Some people might never accept your apology or forgive you, but the outcome is not important when you have done your best and all that you can do—which is the only thing that matters. When you have succeeded at letting go, you are one step closer to your freedom. It's not only about you becoming a better person, but to make everything else around you better as well.

When making my own list, it was interesting for me to see names of people lurking in my subconscious that I did not normally think about. This shows me how much we suppress. The heaviest thing on my list was a former employee from more than eight years earlier, for whom I had given a very bad reference when he applied for a new job. It was totally unnecessary for me to do so in the manner I did; I had nothing to gain from causing harm to this individual. It was a wrongdoing that had been sitting in the back of my head for many years. It's easy to let things go and not do anything about them instead of just being honest with someone—or even yourself—and clearing the air. Some people are able to just move on, but since I was still thinking about what I did to this person I knew it meant that I was not free. After I sat down with the former employee and told him about my wrongdoing and how sorry I was, he told me that it was okay and that he forgave me. After that meeting I felt a clearing inside and a great weight lifted off my shoulders.

Other wrongdoings on my list were people that I had not shown enough gratitude to, from teachers to people I had encountered in business who had contributed to improving my life in all possible aspects. My wrongdoings had been to not thank them enough and let them know how much their kindness and support meant to me. After this list of people had been covered, I felt a peacefulness inside that was indescribable.

Making such a list and facing up to the people on it might seem frightening, but it is unavoidable when you want to let go of your old life and enter your new life, *A Second Life*. The key is release and forgiveness.

To be one with God, in our hearts we must forgive.

But remember, the most important person in life to forgive is yourself. During the remembering process, think back to your childhood. Perhaps you were bullied in school—as I was—or you saw someone else being bullied and didn't step in or do anything to stop it or help the victim—which is just as bad as a crime. It's important to forgive yourself for that.

Every person has a whole library of things in their head to be sorry or regretful for. Here are some ideas of where to start with:

- Forgive yourself for not being grateful enough for LIFE, for taking things for granted or not appreciating all of God's creations—everything on this planet.
- Forgive yourself for not appreciating YOU or treating YOURSELF well enough.
- Forgive yourself for falling short and not living in Oneness with everything/everyone else.
- Forgive yourself for not showing enough gratitude for everyone and everything in your life's journey.
- Forgive yourself for not seeing the goodness that other people have shown you and the efforts they have made on your behalf.

I forgave myself for not seeing all the goodness and unconditional love I was given by my parents, family members, teachers, etc. And I forgave myself for not showing enough gratitude to all of those people.

It's important to see the good in everyone instead of hanging onto the negative. Most people have good intentions and do their best. And when they fall short or seem to disappoint you, understand that their actions are not personally against you but based on their own indoctrination. This can be particularly true with family members, and especially parents who many people feel have disappointed them. View them with compassion. Instead of dwelling on their shortcomings, feel lucky and blessed that you have/had the parents you do/did, acknowledge that you would not be the person you are if it weren't for them, and be thankful even in the face of challenges you have had with them for the lessons you have learned, for they are truly a gift from God.

Forgive yourself for not giving, showing, and applying unconditional love in life, which is the ultimate goal for humankind, because it will bring everything forward.

Acknowledge and express your gratitude

Another part of my process was to meet up with people that have crossed my path during life's journey and thank them for what they brought to my life. It was a very delightful experience for me, and hopefully, they felt they had made the world a better place by doing what they have done. An additional way to express gratitude is told in a story that inspired me and many other people:

Trevor McKinney was a teenager living a troubled life. His mother, an alcoholic, drank to numb the pain of her difficult childhood. His father was mostly absent, but abusive when he did show up. One day in social studies class, Trevor's teacher, Mr. Simonet—who was weighed down by the physical and emotional scars of his own past—gave his pupils an intriguing assignment: think of some way to change the world and put it into action. Trevor came up with the idea of doing good deeds for three people, but instead of having them pay him back they should all "pay it forward" by unselfishly doing something good for someone else. The first recipients of his good deeds were a drug addict, his social studies teacher, and a classmate who was constantly bullied by his peers. Although initially the experiment seemed to be a failure, it would prove to be an idea that transformed the lives of Trevor, his mother, and his teacher, as well as an ever-widening circle of people he didn't even know.

The story was published in 2000 as *Pay It Forward*, written by Catherine Ryan Hyde. It was made into a feature film and became a movement that continues to this day. This inspirational concept provides a model for people to give unconditional love that is perpetually passed on to others. It is a state of mind that we should be living in at all times. Start your own "pay it forward" chain reaction of unconditional love in Oneness.

Start noticing when you can be helpful to someone, whether it's a stranger, a neighbor, or a friend. Without intruding or making people feel helpless, assist them or convey kindness to them when you can. Do so without expecting anything in return. Whatever you do, it should come from your heart, make you feel good inside, and convey the message that you are grateful to be able to do what you're doing. Your kindness could also be an anonymous action, such as buying coffee for a stranger, paying for the groceries of another person at the market, or putting money in someone else's parking meter so they won't get a ticket, then leaving before they know who did so. When someone wants to return the favor or pay you back for something you've done, say you'd prefer they "pay it forward" and keep spreading goodwill in the world.

God's Army: Living a life of purpose with inner peace and in Oneness

To achieve Oneness takes commitment and surrender. Without discipline nothing is achieved. Oneness is not a way to escape when life is not working out. Oneness is evolving to live for a greater cause. To become One takes patience, knowledge, inner strength, and commitment.

In order to break with the negative belief systems and rise to live at a higher level, you need to become a soldier of God. By committing to Oneness, a life with inner peace where you have become the creator of your own life, you have joined God's Army. This commitment is to the highest order, which is to serve only God within you.

Honoring that connection means that you:

- must always strive to be all that you can be and do what is right by utilizing the resources and gifts given to you
- never accept life as merely existing, but live life to the fullest
- go head-to-head with the biggest fear of all by having the courage to truly live life to the fullest

With these things in mind, always remember that it's not what God can do for you, but what you can do for God that's important. If you're walking through life thinking about what God can do for you, then that's your ego thinking, which is selfishness. After all, God already gave you what you need when you came into this world—then left it up to you to map out your journey. He gave you all the tools you need, but he can't be responsible for every step of your life's journey and how you use/abuse the tools given because your purpose on earth would then be diminished.

God is patiently waiting for you to reconnect with him after freeing yourself from your negative belief systems. Then you can join God's army in creating heaven on earth. When praying to God, do so with gratitude for your blessed life and let the good overshadow the dark moments—which you need to refocus on as growth opportunities, rather than just hurdles. As a soldier in God's army your commitment is to choose a life in Oneness. When you are asking for help and guidance, request strength and clarity from God within you. Never look outside of yourself because Oneness means you and God are one.

Your only task in life is to *live*, experience life to the fullest so that you can learn and evolve while being a role model and inspiration to others. Strictly acquiring money or achieving status is not what you are here to do. Look around and notice people in jobs that seem irrelevant or those without social status who appear to be living with the bliss within that so many are seeking—maybe even yourself. When you meet these people in all walks of life, they make everyone feel good by their presence. They perform acts of kindness for others without ego involvement, without expecting anything in return. Because their hearts are fully aligned with their thoughts and actions, people respect them regardless of their social status.

My greatest inspirations for unconditional love and kindness have been my own family—from the most bighearted father and sister, to my mother, who always put others ahead of herself. From my grandfather and grandmother who would always with a big heart extend a hand to those with less—even when they were also struggling—providing people with food, cutting their hair, and giving them a place to sleep. I was blessed to grow up seeing their unconditional love and understanding. Through their examples I learned that this life is not just about oneself. My mother spent her entire life in service to others—first by working for years in home care, going to the homes of elders who did not want to spend the remainder of their lives in retirement homes, as well spending most holidays working with mentally challenged children. The last fifteen years before retirement she worked full-time as a nurse in a hospital for cancer victims, with the patients ranging from children to elders and many going into the light. She would bond with the patients and often spend her days off baking them cakes and visiting those who did not have their own families. Many times she spent the final hours with someone before they lost their struggle with cancer—even though this was not part of her job.

One particular episode that was imprinted in my mind was a single woman in her early thirties who was crying as my mother held her as she was dying. Her last words to my mother were, "I don't want to leave. I have not experienced love, so I am not ready to go." By telling me what this woman said with her dying breath, my mother passed on to me the importance of the message that I needed to live by: Love is all there is and you need to cherish every day because you never know when your time is up.

After retirement my mother became a part of the Fransiskus sisterhood, a hospice organization whose mission it is to visit the homes of people who have no family or friends and spend time with those who know they soon will be dying. She becomes their ally and friend, supporting them during their last hours and as they leave this physical existence. All of her work throughout life has been about serving others in an unconditionally loving way without ever expecting anything in return.

In her spare time—for as long as I can remember and even to this day—my mother has always been very devoted to tending her garden, nurturing the true miracle that is the beauty of nature. She has always told me that plants and trees need to be nourished and nurtured to grow and bloom. "People need love just as much as plants," she would add. Because her garden has always been her pride and joy, she has said that one day when she leaves the earth she believes the best place for her final rest would be in her garden, because that is where she finds inner peace and Oneness. Her reverence for nature and appreciation of God's earth are conveyed wherever she goes by being the person who picks up the trash and cleans up the messes other people leave behind so that the planet's true beauty is revealed. My mother's kindness, unconditional love for people, animals, and the planet always shine through, making her someone I have always learned from, a true teacher of what is important in life—characteristics everyone should strive for. Along with the rest of my loving family, by example she has inspired me to be the best person I can be. She believes the way I live my life is a reflection of her, saying, "How your children turn out tells you what kind of person you have been in this lifetime."

But even when being of service to others and conveying unconditional love, anything you do and achieve while living a life detached from negative belief systems and fully aligned with your true self is really only for yourself. Excelling does not mean winning the hearts or minds of others, but always having the intention to do the best you can with what you have. Observing yourself while conducting your life in this way confirms to you how capable you are of being the creator of your own life.

Oneness is NOW

There is one thing that you can never get back in life: time. You have been given a specific number of hours and minutes for your life's journey. Many people spend these minutes dwelling on the past or only focusing on the future—where they believe everything will be different and so much better. In this linear way of thinking, time is everything, and what matters is everything *but* what is happening in the present moment. As long as the mind is operating in the fear created by negative belief systems, you will not be able to refocus your mind on the only moment that truly exists, the present moment.

Many people live life as though it will last forever and don't stop for a minute to enjoy the present. Others are running from one agenda to another trying to fill as much as they can into their already packed calendars, thereby being too busy to *feel* or *enjoy* anything. As time goes by many wonder where the time (life) went. Inside they feel the same as they did when they were younger, but on the surface they see how the body has dematerialized and aged. Worried about the process of aging and not being able to fit in all there is to be done, many people become scared to sit down and think too much. They believe it will cause them to face their inner and most intimate thoughts about life and are afraid they will be disappointed that they wasted their potential or did not live a life aligned with their heart.

In Oneness, time does not exist because there is only right now. In Oneness, you are fully present and able to experience the miracles around you that you have never really noticed before. In the Oneness of being in the present moment, you can truly *feel* who you are and enjoy the life you have created. There are times in life when you have experienced glimpses of this, when you did something straight from the heart with passion. And when such moments occurred, time did not exist, because you felt as though time stood still. Being fully present is to be in Oneness. Your awareness rises—smells, tastes, and colors are stronger, brighter. You experienced this state of *presence* when you were very younger. But as time went by and your focus shifted because of your indoctrination, your list of things to do became more and more urgent, your emotions and senses became more and more dense. Later in life your fear-filled reality made you feel as though you were in a dream state of numbness.

When you look around now you see that it is often young children and people who have had near-death experiences who are present in the NOW. For them there are no tomorrows or past events; all that matters is living fully right NOW.

> *When I admire the wonders of a sunset or the beauty of the moon,*
> *my soul expands in the worship of the creator.*
>
> Mohandas Gandhi

It is a paradox that if you are not fully present in the NOW, life will pass you by, and yet, in earth school it is necessary to plan for the future as well, because if no seeds are planted, no future will grow to be harvested. Therefore, the key is to set a clear life plan and follow it, but keep almost the entire focus in the moment. With practice you can learn to fully surrender to each present moment without losing focus on the future, knowing everything you do in the present is taking you to someplace better. Being all that you can be right now in this moment gives you confidence to allow the next thing that's supposed to happen to evolve naturally. The life plan you create and integrate into your subconscious will be your road map. As you learn to stop all thoughts of anything except the current moment, your silence within will slowly take over. That silence gives you room to get to know yourself.

When you surrender to the moment, you create a new reality in which time does not exist. In this new world you experience inner peace and tune in to everything to a much greater extent than before as your multisensory awareness increases. When you reach this state of mind and way of living life, the feeling of missing out on something goes away. You realize that all you do and experience in that moment is all that you truly need. Oneness means being fully aware and fully alive. The powerful inner joy you experience eliminates all of your fears, even those of your next reality, eternal life. When you accept the present as all there is, you also invite and allow the love of God to rise and shine within you. The reconnection with God's kingdom within you removes any fright of death, which is really just the fear of fear itself.

As you surrender to the present moment, all of your dreams will be realized and because your future road map is present in your subconscious, you'll feel assured that no matter what happens you'll be prepared for where you're going and what you'll be experiencing tomorrow.

Life needs to be a fun journey

The purest beauty in life can be seen in the children who exude the exuberance of heartfelt joy. But as we get older the laughter and playfulness we once experienced slowly fades away; in some people it's gone almost entirely, which is extremely unfortunate, because love and laughter are what make us feel truly alive.

The life we create as our reality, which is based on our false programming, becomes more and more serious as we grow older and assume more and more responsibilities. Our indoctrinated inner voices also keep reminding us that much of what we want from life is impossible and dreaming has no place if we're responsible adults. But God didn't intend for us to live this way. We are supposed to enjoy life to the fullest. He wants each of us to have fun, laugh, and enjoy the roller coaster ride called our life's journey. God wants us to be happy and feel the best we can feel.

When you are living in true Oneness:

- There is lightness in your heart as you dance through life.
- There are no regrets or guilt.
- The past is gone. All you have is right NOW.
- Laughing at yourself comes easily, but you never laugh at others or make jokes at their expense.
- Nothing is more welcoming than a smile to a stranger—who smiles back and keeps going with his day with his spirit lifted thanks to your enlightened gesture.
- Because you carry spiritual truth inside of who you are, nobody can tell you that you are a bad person. There is no judgment in God's kingdom. Love is available to all equally.

When your life is driven by pure intentions, in your new reality free from negative belief systems, you know that you are living a life aligned with God within you. Life is like a game and is played the same way. No matter what happens during our life's journey, when you have lived in alignment with your heart you know that you have done well. You are truly living life when the new reality you create is filled with laughter, love, and playfulness.

Humor has always been important in my own life and it has also saved me from the darkest moments. Life becomes much lighter and more enjoyable when you are able to see the fun in things. And, on the more challenging days, you will stand stronger when you smile inside at life's ironies. The most successful people I have met all had a great sense of humor as one of their key traits. The truth is that we all want to be around people who make us smile and feel good inside.

Winning the game of life

My personal experience is that the only way that I could have gotten through my battles was with self-irony. To stay focused I would always tell myself, first, that nobody died so it can't be that serious, and then, second, ask myself what did I learn from the experience. Also, I have always told myself that God wanted me to have the experience and now that I am through it he has something better in store for me.

Thinking back on my life, I am filled with gratitude for every time that I fell to the ground because I always learned something important that propelled me to something better. I have also learned something from every person I ever encountered. God does everything for a reason; there are no coincidences. God never wants you to surrender, but instead, to learn, evolve, and always keep fighting. Being a soldier in God's army means that you can never be defeated. At times you need a rest during your life's battle or to go on a little detour, but by being One with God you will always find your way back to your path because he will never leave you. Knowing this, you can enjoy your ride with great assurance, love, passion, and heartfelt laughter, knowing life is all a game that God constructed for you, with the best possible outcome guaranteed and always with the best yet to come. By awakening God within, you rise up to your true potential, which has no limits, where you can do anything you set your mind to do. Your power is limitless once you realize this.

Nothing happens by chance; what you put into something is what you get back from it. To get where you want to go you must start with the right mindset. Always remember that your thoughts and how you respond to them create your reality. Achieving what you desire will only be created through detachment, a raised awareness and consciousness, where decisions are aligned with your heart and passion within.

Always create the image of what you want and tell yourself that you have already succeeded without ever questioning or doubting if you will. Next, you must roll up your sleeves and do the hard work required to master the universal knowledge for your key areas in life. In my own life and in the lives of the thousands of people I have coached and recruited, the experience is that success never comes easy. It takes hard work, long hours, and a willingness to sacrifice in order to achieve what you desire. I know whatever I have achieved in life was attained by setting a clear goal, endurance, and working hard to get there.

You will never do anything in this world without courage.
It is the greatest quality of the mind next to honor.

Aristotle

Sometimes things do not always work out as you plan, no matter how hard you push it, but that's fine if you learn something that you can bring along during your life journey. Without challenges life would be dull. If you never give up you will always win in the end, because that is what God wants for you. When you love what you do the passion inside is a powerhouse that takes you that extra mile—which is why it's so important to live a life aligned with the heart. As a soldier of God you will master life and meet the battles with a smile, knowing that the only thing that matters is that you are one with yourself and at peace. The journey itself is just a game created for the purpose of always prompting you to grow and evolve.

Love is all there is

To achieve enlightenment is to learn to be totally free from your indoctrination that has created a false and disconnected you. All of your life you have done your best to please everyone else by playing a role expected of you. In many ways our lives are very similar to the one Jim Carrey's character portrays in the movie *The Truman Show*. During much of the story the main character is not told that he is living in a fake world, where everybody else is just playing roles according to a script.

The only difference between this movie and many people's lives is that there are no cameras; otherwise it is all the same. The reality you live is not a true reality but a script that has been programmed into your hard drive by somebody else. And when people's lives are based on indoctrination, their behavior is usually run by the ego. Unfortunately, this also means that some of the people you encounter during your day may have a selfish agenda. There are times when they are only nice to you because they feel they can somehow benefit from you—as opposed to the people who truly like you for the person you are and want nothing from you except to be your friend.

But, again, don't judge. In God's kingdom there is no judgment, only knowledge that the majority of people operating from their indoctrinated negative programming are disconnected from their true selves, and therefore ego-driven, not coming from a loving existence connected to God. The lost souls who interact with you in this way do not remember that God is all love and no ego. If they do not change in response to your good example living *A Second Life*, then it may be necessary for you to cut them loose and replace them in your life with people who have the same standards you now have, who have chosen to live a life of purpose in Oneness.

Being a person who is one with your true self means that you are at peace with your true inner feelings, and at the same time able to care for others, feeling their happiness or pain. When you are one with yourself, there is no need to take anything personally because you know that what others say or do to you is a result of their reality, their experiences, and their programming. One day people will embrace you; the next day they will say and do hurtful things to you. People cannot be consistent and loving in their behavior when they are operating from negative indoctrination; they overreact or misbehave because they don't know everything they are "supposed" to be doing and can only react based on what they know. People are consistent and loving only when they are operating from their true selves connected to God within. Then they are certain about what are the right or wrong ways to behave in every aspect of life, including while interacting with others.

Whatever people say or do toward you, never take it personally: completely detach as you acknowledge them but remain in a state of Oneness. Always know that the only thing that matters is your inner truth, which is God's truth as you are one with God. By being detached you can be objective in your own life, as well as in observation of what is going on in the rest of the world. In this way you can live an enlightened existence. Being enlightened is also having a strong sense of empathy, being a person who cares and shows unconditional love to others, including fellow human beings, the animal kingdom, and the planet earth.

Having a strong sense of unconditional love means that you have successfully conquered the ego. This is the goal when pursuing a life aligned with your heart and your true self. When you have become free from your ego you have become a person who can serve as a role model by the way you live. When living an unselfish existence serving God and not what your ego desires, your heart is filled with unconditional love and you will engage in heroic acts and deeds without concern for your own well-being because you are serving something much greater than yourself.

A man who won't die for something is not fit to live.

Martin Luther King, Jr.

People who live in this way, with no fear for their own lives, with self-sacrifice for the greater good, are people like you and I can be, like our President Barack Obama. He became the first African American president of the United States without fear for his own life. He has changed history by giving hope to an entire nation that anything is possible if they truly believe in themselves.

Among other true heroes is Sergeant Jim Hancock. In Iraq, during October 2006, without hesitation he threw himself on top of a hand grenade, sacrificing his own life to save others in his battalion. And in New York City during December of 2007, Peter Jackson threw himself in front of an oncoming train to save a man who had fallen onto the tracks while having an epileptic seizure. With his two little daughters watching, Peter fearlessly risked his own life to come to the aid of a fellow human being.

People such as these are not among the few, but the many others living among us who serve as role models by their acts and deeds of unconditional love and heroism each day. Oneness means being connected to all things and showing compassion by making a contribution to improving every aspect of living in any way we can.

Living each day as an American and a soldier of God means first of all being grateful for this life you were given. It also means, being grateful for the opportunity to thrive in this land of opportunity with a constitution and social framework that enables all people of all colors, sexuality, backgrounds, and religions to believe what they desire without being judged by others. Add to that being grateful for the unique opportunity to carve out any kind of life that we desire through hard work and determination, regardless of where we come from or our background.

This great nation stands as a role model for the rest of the world, and each person blessed to be a part of it needs to remember at all times that being a soldier in God's army requires that we serve God and America in order to create heaven on earth. This is accomplished when we live a life in Oneness, a life where we all take responsibility for *everything* we are and whatever we do, making God proud by being all we can be.

Oneness is about caring for each other the best we can. When we see people who need help, we volunteer to assist them. This could be by doing small things for strangers, such as holding open a door or helping someone across the street. It could also be bigger things, such as giving people food, a place to live, or even money when we have the means. If people have lost their jobs, are about to lose their homes, or are faced with serious illness, we do whatever we can to help them.

A nation's culture resides in the hearts and in the soul of its people.

Mohandas Gandhi

It is not uncommon for a group of people—friends, neighbors, even strangers in a community—to join together to be of assistance when their individual financial resources alone would not be enough to truly help someone in need. Potluck dinners are being held in someone's home, with each person bringing a dish of food to share and everyone putting a little cash in the "money pot." A theater group puts on a play, with the proceeds going to a person in need. Communities are organizing bake sales or car washes to raise cash for a family that is going through a hard time or cannot afford to pay for life-saving medical treatment for one of its members.

Coming together as human beings to assist one another not only shows concern, caring and a responsibility for each other, it also magnifies every person's individual positive energy, creating a much stronger positive force that is contagious, spreading through everyone involved, which they, in turn, carry with them as they continue with their individual lives. This is a powerful contribution to the Oneness that will change the world and create heaven on earth.

When you are in the habit of always looking for ways to be of service to others, you will forget your own troubles and feel so much better and more positive inside. But do it from your heart of compassion and not because you want or expect to receive a thank you or even anything in return. Reaching out by opening your heart with the knowledge that we are all connected on a deeper level is what living in Oneness and giving unconditional love is truly about.

Step Nine: Reevaluate how you are participating spiritually in your own life

Go back from time to time and take again the Oneness Assessment Test in Step Two to see how you're progressing in your spiritual re-alignment.

If you've encountered roadblocks or not made the type of progress you'd hoped, go back to previous steps of this process and reassess what you could be doing differently. The process of deleting your old indoctrination that has held you back and learning to live in alignment with your true passions and desires begins overnight, but takes time to perfect. Living in Oneness is an ongoing journey of discovery. The saying, "It's not the destination, but the journey that's important" is absolutely true when it comes to living a spiritually strong life.

If you have been doing everything you know to do to and still don't feel as though you're able to live in Oneness or truly re-connect with God within you, don't give up. Reflect on how your reality has changed since you began and how it's more of your own creation. Notice how everything you do affects those around you—hopefully in a positive way. Be patient with yourself as you stay devoted to being present in the moment of NOW each day and let the past and future fade out of your thought patterns.

When your newly aligned spiritual life is being awakened, know that your inner true self and the passion for a life of purpose from your heart never left you but only got buried by negative programming that you are now dis-empowering. By breaking free from the mental slavery and brainwashing that held you back, you will evolve and a new view of the world will be presented to you as your reality changes.

To be fully detached means to be totally free from your programming so that you can connect with your true self and God within in Oneness. In Oneness there is nothing you need to prove to anyone else, as you are already perfect. Being unique is what God intended when he created you, which is why you are the only one with your DNA on this planet. During this process you will likely also see that some of the people who were part of your old life may no longer belong in your new reality, because they would hold you back. You may have challenging encounters with people in your life who are accustomed to your behavior based on your old indoctrination and their own brainwashing. Do not be affected by anyone who tries to get you to engage in melodramas. As you totally let go of the past, in your heart forgive all of those who caused your pain and feelings of inadequacy, knowing that they are victims just as you were.

Remember that your specific journey of personal growth and elevated level of consciousness is yours alone. It is a product of your own individual life experiences, not someone else's. This means that whoever discourages your growth, blocks your progress, or holds you back from entering your new life is not a good influence for you. As you let go of the negatives in your environment, remember that what kept you a prisoner until this time was fear. Don't let fear continue to be an obstacle as you release yourself from the prison of your mental slavery. This time stand face-to-face with fear, demolish the things that have stopped you from becoming one with your true self, and enthusiastically live the life you were born to live.

Never give up. There is no surrender when you are a member of God's army. There is no time frame or rate of change that is required. Each person's journey must be traveled at its own speed. Don't compare yourself to others or gauge your progress on how anyone else lives their life. You are a unique creation of God whose challenges are special gifts provided for you to learn and grow. Continue on your path and you will succeed.

Step Ten: Reassess the value of your spiritual life every six months after you are on your path

Now that you're on track, is this still what you really want? One way to know is to reflect on how your life has changed, but there are many more ways only you will know that you are learning and growing more each day. It's not about where you have been, but where you are going.

Embrace the wonder of feeling truly connected to God within that is guiding you to live a life in Oneness. Notice that it's not only your world that seems different and, indeed, is different because of your new view and attitude, but it's the entire world. Notice how you more fully participate in the world and how that makes you feel inside.

One day a couple years ago a friend and I were driving in heavy traffic near my neighborhood and as we approached a busy corner we saw a man standing on the sidewalk frantically waving his arms in the air. We heard him screaming at a car that had just pulled over to the curb beside him, "Stop, stop! My dog, my dog!"

People kept driving by, most of them not even slowing down to see what was wrong and some even honking their horns at the car that had pulled over and was now slowing the flow of traffic. By that time the man on the curb was wailing, with his hands on his face, trying to look underneath the car that had pulled over, saying, "Oh no, oh no, my dog, my dog!! Help him, somebody help him. Help, help!"

By the time my friend and I pulled over in front of the other car and jumped out to see what we could do to help, the man on the curb was angrily yelling at the driver of the car, "Do something, do something. He's under there, he's under there! My dog is trapped under your car. You ran over him."

The driver of the car, still seated behind the wheel, looked like he was paralyzed with fear. My friend and I kneeled down by the car and looked underneath; we couldn't see where the dog was, but I heard a soft whimpering. "Shhhh," I said to the dog's owner. "I think I hear him."

Sure enough, we could hear the dog softly whimpering from underneath the front of the car. His owner called his name and tried to coax him out, but the whimpering continued. We moved into a different position to try to see where the dog was trapped under the car, but he was in an area that we could not see. As we continued to look, the dog's whimpering got less and less, softer and softer, until there was no sound at all. I was certain the dog had died or was going to die any second if we were not able to get him out.

My friend and I looked at each other and without even saying anything knew what had to be done. We stood up, looked around to find other guys nearby who looked strong and healthy, then called for them to come over to the car. A couple responded immediately, running over to help. The four of us positioned ourselves around the front bumper and wheel wells of the car, reached down, and grabbed hold. Counting to three, we lifted the front of the car off the ground.

There was the guy's little dog, lying all crooked and bent by where one of the car's tires had been. The dog's owner quickly reached under the car, gently lifted up the limp dog, and cradled it protectively in his arms near his heart, talking to it lovingly.

We placed the front of the car back down on the ground and gathered around the man holding his dog.

"Is he okay?" I asked.

"He's all I have in life. He's my best friend," the dog's owner said. "He has to be okay, he just *has* to!"

The dog was barely breathing, but his eyes were wide open and he was staring at his owner, who was talking to him, "I love you, love you. You okay? You're my baby . . . my baby."

The dog looked over at each one of us who had lifted the car and then he took a big sigh and closed his eyes. I was just about to ask if the dog had died when the driver of the car called out to the dog's owner. "Get in," he said. "I'll take you to a vet's office down the street."

The dog's owner looked at the driver, then the dog, then back at the driver.

"Do you know him?" I asked.

"Never seen him before," the dog's owner said.

"C'mon, get in. Let's get him to the vet," the driver insisted, reaching over and pushing open the passenger door of the car.

"We'll take you," I offered.

The dog's owner then did something that truly surprised me. Still gently holding the dog, he carefully got into the car that had just run over his dog and they drove away down the street.

About a week later I happened to see the guy, who was carrying his dog, which had a cast on half of his body.

"I wanted to thank you for saving my dog's life," he said. "And I'm sorry I didn't thank you at the time, but it was just such an emotional experience."

"Is he going to be alright?" I asked.

"The vet says he'll be fine. Just some fractured bones. The cast is holding everything in place while he heals. He's not suffering or in any pain. I don't know what would have happened if you hadn't stopped to help me. Maybe it sounds crazy, but he's all I have in the world, my best friend. Thank you for saving his life . . . and mine."

"Can I ask you a question?" I said.

The guy nodded yes.

"Why did you get in the car with the guy who ran over your dog?" I asked. "Seems like you would have been too mad at him to do that."

"First off, I knew I had to get my dog to the vet as fast as possible," the guy said. "And in that split second when I had to decide whether to get in the car that hit my dog, I knew that the driver didn't do it on purpose. It was an accident and he deserved to be forgiven. And as it turned out, he really is a nice guy. He's paying my vet bills and calling to see how my dog is doing. We have a lot in common. Seems like we might even become friends."

Whenever I think of that experience I am reminded that we must all remain devoted to making a positive contribution to the world in any way we can. To see someone who had been harmed—even by accident—who was so willing to forgive was

a beautiful thing. And if my friend and I had not taken the time to stop and help I would have missed the feeling that I had inside by, first, being part of the group of people who rescued that dog and, second, hearing of the unconditional love the dog's owner was able to feel for the person whose mistake could have caused him a devastating loss. It is such a wonderful example of so many aspects of living in oneness. The way I felt after helping in that situation was a feeling of happiness inside me, a bliss that I can never describe.

Unconditional love needs to be activated. And when it is, the reward is limitless.

Where love is, there God is also.

Mohandas Gandhi

There is always something new to discover, engage in, or enjoy when you are living in Oneness. Your instincts will tell you whether you are living in alignment with your true self, God inside, and Oneness with everything there is or if you're still trying to live up to some earlier indoctrinated programming by society's standards. The passion you feel inside is the voice of God showing you the way. All you have to do is learn to listen. And when you do you may be surprised—and, no doubt, delighted—by what experiences you will have. Humbly embrace life with exuberance and gratitude.

Final Step: Be all that you can be, but not all at once.

SPIRITUALITY SUMMARY

- Assess the current status of your spiritual life.
- If you do not feel you are living in Oneness with God within, everyone and everything you encounter or interact with each day, identify the reasons why, such as:
  - Your motivations in life are based solely on satisfying your ego and pride.
  - You feel completely on your own, with no one to rely on or depend on, that nothing you do affects anyone else.
  - You are too distracted by drama in one area of your life to give the other four areas the attention and commitment needed to live a balanced, purposeful life.
- Use the tools you've learned—meditation/prayer/self-programming—to delete the negative indoctrination/brainwashing that has made you too fearful to know how you can be a fully developed spiritual being living a significant, fulfilling life in Oneness.
- Devise a game plan to re-create a spiritual foundation for living in Oneness, including:
  - Steps you can take to fearlessly embrace life each day knowing you are uniquely destined to make a special contribution to the world living each day in alignment with your true self in Oneness with God within and everything in the world.
  - Goals and objectives you will achieve.
  - Timelines for enacting/advancing your plan.
- Execute your game plan:
  - Each day: Systematically set out knowing how you will live with the integrity of Oneness, where everything you do is significant and meaningful.
  - Every night: Routinely review your accomplishments and express gratitude.
- Reassess your overall results according to your timelines:
  - If you are on track, is there still anything you want to achieve?
  - If satisfied with your progress, be conscious every day of maintaining the changes you have made in order to completely wipe out your old negative programming and establish your new positive reality for the long term.
  - If you have not made the progress you'd hoped, go back, reevaluate your spirituality and find new ways to make your game plan more successful.

ALWAYS REMEMBER: Surrender is never an option. You must find a way to succeed.

A Second Life
Survival Guide During Times of Crisis

Survival Guide During Times of Crisis

It's not your fault if your life is not going well when you've been brainwashed to operate as a robot based on your indoctrinated programming. But if you have reached a tipping point and some area of your life is falling apart, now you can become a survivor instead of a victim. In fact, if one area of your life quickly disintegrates, the other areas will likely be affected as well. When this happens, it's time to conduct your life as a crisis management expert and take positive actions to deal with problems that may seem insurmountable or overwhelming.

This survival guide is an insurance policy that provides step-by-step actions you can take to get through a crisis in your life generally, and specific actions to take in response to a crisis in the five key areas of your life.

Start with the basics:

1. Gain a different perspective by detaching

Feeling panicked or stuck in fear—which may manifest as anger, outrage, defeat, depression, etc.—locks you into seeing the situation from a point of view that limits your options. By looking at the situation from a different perspective, new positive actions will become apparent that you can take to free yourself from the prison of the crisis.

When you have a problem, it's natural to want to discuss it with a friend or loved one. Doing so makes you feel less alone, scared, frantic, or afraid. When the other person is on your side, they can empathize with you and provide emotional support. They may even offer to solve your problem for you—which never actually solves the problem in the long run because, after all, it's *your* problem, not theirs.

It's particularly important to get a different point of view if you've had an ongoing problem that's suddenly exploded into a crisis, and have been discussing it with the same people over and over, and then taking actions based on what they suggest. You probably have realized by now that talking through your problems may have made you feel better temporarily, but it didn't actually solve the problem. In fact, talking about a problem can make it worse because it keeps you stuck *in* the problem.

Instead you need to step out of the problem (detach) in order to think of positive solutions that will either solve it or get you through it to a better place.

How do you detach?

2. Plan your strategy, but don't over think it

Detaching means you stop thinking and thinking, discussing and discussing (with others), or endlessly mulling the problem over in your own mind. "Don't dwell on it" is a common expression and another way of putting it. But what does that mean exactly? Dwelling on something means to stay with it or live in it—a dwelling is also a home. So a problem you are dwelling on becomes the place where you live. It is the place that is familiar to you because it's your reality.

But another reality does exist. The minute you step out of the home where you live, you enter a different reality. Everything looks different and feels different. As you get in your car and drive away from your home, your reality changes even more. You enter a world that is a much bigger place, that doesn't revolve around you. In that world are lots of other people driving or walking around. Everyone has problems of some kind or another. Some people have problems worse than yours. Others know how to not let their problems rule (and ruin) their lives.

Step out of your home into the reality of the larger world. Look around and see how important your problem is. Will the larger world end because of your problem? Will your own world end because of it?

View your crisis as being that of a friend who is asking your advice, or even a stranger, not as *your* problem/crisis. When you step out of it and look at it from that perspective, what do you see? By detaching emotionally your mind becomes clear and able to see positive steps you can take to move forward out of the problem and into a brighter tomorrow.

3. Find a different approach to take

Einstein said, "Insanity is doing the same thing over and over and expecting different results."

When some area of your life is falling apart despite your best efforts to hold it together, you must do things differently to set change in motion. Second chances usually don't automatically present themselves, so you have to create them and act on them once they are created.

If a problem has been ongoing and has escalated into a crisis, you have either ignored it, hoping it would go away on its own, or you have been repeating the same solutions without success.

Now that you have detached, opening your mind to seeing your problem/crisis from the perspective of someone else, stop yourself from automatically thinking the same old solutions will work this time. If they haven't worked in the past, then they're not the answer. Now is the time to "think outside the box." What other solutions or approaches can you come up with that could result in a different outcome?

4. Take positive steps forward

Every journey begins with the first step. Until then, you're standing still—which is not a good place to be when your life is crumbling underneath your feet. You must take steps forward to get on firmer ground.

When a crisis strikes, it's not uncommon to seek familiar ground, to go back to a place where you felt safe and everything was under control. But that was then, the conditions have changed, and this is now. *Now* is all there is, and you must do something positive to get out of the quicksand you're sinking farther into each day.

You've detached emotionally from your problem/crisis, you've stopped dwelling on it, you've thought of different ways to solve it, now's the time to try something new. What do you have to lose?

5. Express gratitude

Even when things are not going well in some or all areas of your life, it's still important to express gratitude. Everyone can find *something* to be grateful for. Find that thing/those things and enthusiastically thank God. Doing so connects you to a positive piece of your life—even if it seems small compared to your problems. Get in the habit of being grateful for every small and large thing you have or encounter. Then watch to see what happens as a result.

While you're expressing gratitude, do so with a smile. The act of smiling—and perhaps even laughing at how absurd your life can sometimes be—changes the chemicals in your brain, relieving stress by releasing the feel-good chemicals, endorphins, that flow throughout your body.

SURVIVING A JOB/CAREER CRISIS

When you opened the envelope with your paycheck and saw the pink slip, it wasn't really a surprise. There'd been "talk" around the office, whispers that something was going to happen. If you're lucky they've given you two weeks notice or you have a severance package, so you aren't suddenly out on the street with no money and no time to come up with a game plan.

Your first impulse may be to ask your supervisor/boss, "Why me?" Don't waste your time. They'll give you an answer that they hope will make you feel better, such as, "It isn't a reflection on the quality of your work." But really, they just want you to say, "Okay," and walk away quietly so they don't have to feel any worse than they already do. The people doing the firing have one of the worst kinds of jobs there are; believe it or not, it doesn't give them pleasure to tell you that you don't have a place to work anymore.

Here's a basic game plan, but tailor it to your individual situation:

View leaving your job as a business—your business

Make a list and discuss with the human resources department, personnel manager, your boss, or union representative—whoever is in charge of such things—the following assets you have acquired at the company and are now entitled to claim:

1. Unused vacation pay, sick pay, early retirement benefits, or unemployment benefits.
2. Health-care and medical benefits that are assumable or can be continued.
3. Retirement funds you've accrued and now need to transfer elsewhere or manage yourself.
4. Reference letters or a copy of positive performance reviews from your personnel file if these things will be helpful for you to get another job.

Leave a good impression

Even if you think you've gotten a rotten deal and believe you shouldn't be the one who lost your job:

1. A cordial and businesslike farewell is more likely to pay-off with an excellent reference when your next potential employer contacts the company you're leaving for a reference.

2. Even if you're angry and disgruntled, don't do or say anything you'll later regret. Most likely losing your job isn't about you personally—regardless of whether it is or you know you've done a great job, leave a good impression by departing with class and style.
3. While gathering and leaving with your personal belongings, don't pilfer company property. It's not worth it.
4. Network as best you can with coworkers, peers, and superiors before leaving. Exchange phone numbers where you can contact each other away from the office. You never know who might hear about the perfect next job for you.

Keep your daily routine

When you've been getting up and going to work every day, suddenly having no place to go and nothing to do can be very disorienting. As much as possible maintain your daily routine:

1. Stick with going to bed at the same time you did before, and getting up at the same time.
2. Accept the fact that now your job is to find a new job. Devote the regular work hours of your day to conducting the business of finding your new job. (See the Job/Career chapter of this life manual for guidance.)
3. Avoid viewing this time while you're looking for a new job as leisure or play time. Finding a job is serious business that takes a full-time commitment. Bumming around, hanging out, wasting time, or developing bad habits can quickly take over your life, killing your motivation and your self esteem. Stay alert to avoiding destructive activities that can be detrimental to your well-being and your future job/career prospects.

Find a new job

As said, finding a new job is now your job. The Job/Career chapter of this life manual provides detailed guidance, but for starters:

1. Update your résumé. Add to your résumé the job you just left. Review and refine your entire résumé/bio to make it the best it can be.
2. Network. Contact the people in your network. Attend meetings of organizations related to your field of work/career. Consider becoming involved in community business organizations (such as the Rotary Club) that may provide additional

contacts through which to network—and at the same time provide opportunities for you to be of service to others.

3. Decide whether you want to get a new job in the same field as you were working before or if you want to take this opportunity to make a career change.
4. Consider enhancing your skills or knowledge if it will help you to get the job you want. Check out the free programs offered through government, state, and city agencies.
5. Decide how long you'll look exclusively for jobs in your field before considering taking any job at all in order to earn money, stay productive, and useful. Set timelines and strive to stick to them as best you can.

Seek support through your personal relationships

Also be supportive of people you are in relationships with instead of allowing fears or frustrations (either yours or those of other people in your life) to have a negative affect on your life. Prayer, meditation, and self-programming are useful tools to alleviate stress, avoid tension, and make sure negativity does not infiltrate your relationship with yourself or anyone else.

Review your financial situation

If you have no severance pay, unemployment funds, or other types of money coming in—or even if you do—it's necessary for you to review your financial situation and that of your family (if you are married) to get a realistic view of where you are and what you need to do to keep money coming in. It's not uncommon for a job/career crisis to lead to a financial crisis as well.

SURVIVING A FINANCIAL CRISIS

You're not alone. There are a number of scenarios that commonly result in people being in the position you may be in—strapped for cash and having no idea where it's going to come from.

- You've been laid off from your job, or lost it altogether. Now you cannot find another job that pays enough to cover your monthly expenses, or get another job at all.
- The cost of everything has gone up, and continues to go up so much that the money you earn isn't going as far as it did before.

- You've had to pay for medical or dental care or car or home repairs you didn't expect.
- There are the things your kids need for school or family members you've helped who were in worse financial shape than you.
- Because you do not have enough productive things to do each day, you're bored with your life and therefore fill that time with shopping or spending money you don't really have. Now you owe money and have debts that you can't pay.

Not having enough money is one of the most terrifying, stressful, desperate feelings there could be. Your reality becomes consumed by it. You're not just *imagining* that you could lose your home or your car, you hear stories all the time about people not unlike you who have had that happen to them, so you know it's possible. And besides, the electric company keeps sending you those scary notices that your service will be turned off if you don't pay your bill. So does the telephone company. You may be behind on your mortgage payments or stuck in the rut of always having to add a late fee when you can't pay your rent on time. As a result, you don't feel safe anywhere, including in your home, which should be your sanctuary.

You've bailed yourself out with your backup plans, but now your credit card balances are so high that you can't use them anymore—much less make the minimum payments now due. The coupons you could use to save money on food at the grocery store don't do you any good because you can't afford to buy those items. Your physical health, mental health, self-esteem, and sense of who you are, as well as your relationships with loved ones, are all being affected.

Even though your foundation is rocked, you can take positive steps to, first, survive, and then rescue yourself.

Getting control over your bills

1. Don't trick yourself by not opening all your bills. Open every one and deal with them some way or another—even if you can't pay.

2. Take the pressure off of yourself by calling the companies you owe money to and try to negotiate terms that you might be better able to meet. Don't be intimidated if the first person you talk to says there's nothing they can do. Ask to speak with someone else. Don't give up. No matter what kind of attitude or level of kindness (or not) you feel from them, stay centered in your own kindness. This is not a competition that one or the other of you will win; it's a negotiation that can result in a win/win situation for both you and the company you owe money.

Be honest about the situation you're in. Tell them you actually *do* want to pay them, but you're going through a tough time right now. Don't be embarrassed or ashamed, thinking these people will view you as a loser. You don't know them, will never meet them on the street—they are strangers to you. And, quite frankly, they don't really care one way or the other. They're only answering the phone and talking to you because it's a job they're being paid to do. In fact, you're doing them a favor by giving them a reason to go to work each day. Be grateful that you can help them keep their jobs.

Also, feel good about yourself that you have summoned the courage to make these tough calls and are trying to do the right thing.

3. Eliminate any expenses or expenditures that aren't absolutely necessary. Make the tough choices before someone else makes them for you. Stop paying for things you can't afford, such as cable television, dining out, going to movies, a gym membership, beauty/spa treatments, new gadgets, electronic equipment, clothes, shoes, etc. You can always go back to enjoying them again at a later time when your financial situation is better. Make lifestyle changes that make sense for saving money right now and may even benefit your health, happiness, and the planet over the long run—and you could decide later on that eliminating these things from your life was actually a good thing. Stop drinking, smoking, eating junk food, unnecessary driving. Get back to a basic, simple, healthy lifestyle that's also more economical.

4. Negotiate better terms with the companies/people you can pay or need to continue to pay. Call your credit card companies, cell phone provider, etc. Tell them that you're going through a difficult time financially and that you want to continue to pay them, but you can do so only if they change the terms of your account. If they want to keep your business they'll do their best to help you. There are various things you can ask them to do.

- Change your service plan to something more economical for telephones (mobile and landlines), cable television, etc.
- Reduce your interest rate on your credit cards, lines of credit, auto/truck loans, etc.

Also, call the bank/mortgage company about making some changes to your home loan that could ease your burden and help keep you in your house. Believe me, the bank doesn't want to take your house from you—what are they going to do with it anyway? They'll definitely work with you if they can, but you may have to persistently call until you get in touch with the person who has the authority to help you. This is a case where you don't want to take no for an answer, but stay calm and unemotional while you're trying to reach the best person to help you. Never give up if you truly want to keep your home and know you can afford to do so.

When negotiating any terms with people you owe money to, get everything in writing. Never trust what's being said over the phone.

Also know that you are in crisis not only for the current day but also in the future. This means many of the people you may not be able to pay back. So it's also very important to ask them to *freeze the late fees and interest payments* for X amount of months while you try to get caught up and current on your account—meaning while you're attempting to do the right thing and pay them what you can they're not tacking on more interest and late fees on what you owe. That way you won't end up with an even larger bill to pay once you're back in control again. The reasoning is this: What good does it do you if a bad situation is merely pushed to a future day, as well as allowed to increase in size?

Try to negotiate a lower discounted principal as well. Keep in mind that many companies are willing to reduce principal because they always know it's better to get some money from you than to potentially get none at all.

Always know that it's doable as long as the situation is dealt with the right way

5. Putting out fires. Even though you're doing the best you can, a sure sign that things have gotten so out of control that you can't keep up is when the scary letters and notifications start arriving in the mail or collection calls seem so endless or relentless that you're afraid to answer the phone. Obviously the problems that have been smoldering have ignited into a raging fire. It feels as if you must do something to put out the fire or it's going to burn through your entire life, ruining everything and leaving you with nothing. Now what do you do?

First off, focus exclusively on calling the companies you really need in order to live day to day—such as the telephone company and electric and gas companies. Next, call your mortgage holder (particularly if they're threatening to put you out of your home) or your landlord (especially when they've said you cannot be late on your rent anymore). Explain your situation, tell them that you really do want to pay them, ask them what your options are to stay in the place where you (and your family) live. Being nice, polite, sincere, genuine, and apologetic—no matter how they respond to you or what you read into the tone of their voice—can work in your favor. Stay focused on not reacting negatively to anything they say. Don't let them dismiss you without further discussion. Engage in a discussion with them and keep it going until you feel you've accomplished everything possible. If the person you're speaking to at your mortgage company insists there's nothing that can be done, ask to speak to someone who has the authority to help you. If they tell you no one can help you, then hang up, call back, and ask for someone who can "work with you to resolve your delinquent account." Again, be persistent, but nice. Don't give up.

It may feel like it takes a lot of time to make these calls, and it does, but it'll take more time to try to find another place to live and move. So it'll be time well spent if you can work things out—and you'll sleep better and be able to function better in other parts of your life.

Gather your cash

Part of working things out so you can stay in your home will be that you'll need to make a payment on your mortgage or pay your rent. If you're not working and haven't been able to find a job *yet,* you need to raise some cash. By now you may have already gathered all of the spare change laying around or hiding in your house, but if not, do so. It won't amount to enough to make a mortgage payment or pay a month's rent, but having a little spending money is good for your psyche.

While you're gathering spare change, look around and see what you have that's got any value at all and you can sell. You can't be sentimental about this. Instead, remember, it is only "stuff." It can be replaced at a later time.

Depending on how quickly you need the cash, there are numerous ways to sell personal items. You can post ads on the Internet or place inexpensive ads in your local newspaper. You could have a yard sale. You can take more valuable items to a pawnshop and see what they'll give you—even if it's only pennies of the dollar value you think the items are worth, it's better than nothing. Certain types of items can be sold to specialists and actually do have more value. Gold, silver, or platinum coins or jewelry can be worth quite a bit, based on the current value of the metals in the marketplace. If your jewelry has diamonds or gemstones, you'll probably get more for them from a pawnbroker who will place a value on the stones, as opposed to a gold/silver/platinum dealer who is only interested in the metal.

Now would also be the time to swallow your pride and approach family members or friends about helping you financially. Of course your impulse is to say you need to borrow some money and that you'll pay them back, but don't put that kind of pressure on yourself. Instead, be honest. Tell them why you need the money, you *do* want to pay them back, but you don't know when that will be possible.

If they can't loan (give) you as much money as you need, maybe they could host a fund-raiser for you. I have friends who have held fund-raising potluck dinners at their homes for other friends who have large medical bills to pay. It's a great way to help others.

Get government assistance

Now that you're in survival mode, learn about the public assistance programs you might qualify for and how to apply. Federal government programs include things such as food stamps and Medicaid—if you need medical care and have no insurance—and housing assistance programs. Although these are federal programs they are usually administered through local agencies, i.e., the city, county, or state where you live. To learn more, find out where to go, and what to do to apply, contact the office of a local government official. Don't be shy about asking for help or ashamed that you need it. After all, your taxes have gone for paying for these services for other people all these years. Why shouldn't you receive the benefits during a time of need?

Someone in the office of your local government officials may also be able to direct you to private social service agencies that could help you get food or shelter if things get really bad.

Don't give up

If you can stay afloat somehow, find ways to start rebuilding your financial stability. As you're doing so, if it becomes clear that you're buried so deep in debt that it's too overwhelming or will take decades to try to dig out, consider filing bankruptcy. Again, don't be ashamed or too embarrassed to consider bankruptcy or go through the process. Everyone deserves a second chance. Make an appointment to speak with a bankruptcy attorney. Most offer a free initial meeting and will work with you on paying for their services.

Express gratitude

Tell every person who shows you kindness and assists you in any way during this crisis that you are grateful. Be especially grateful to the people who love you and stand by you, no matter what, offering support and encouragement even if they can't help you more. It may be a slow process, but you *can* get back on your feet again.

You are not alone

Know for sure that you are not alone. Not only are there a lot of other people in the same position you're in, but God has not abandoned you. Prayer and meditation can help delete the brainwashing that has made you believe you don't deserve to be able to take care of yourself. Self-programming and visualization can establish in your subconscious mind the better life you know you deserve and can now create.

SURVIVING A RELATIONSHIP CRISIS

It's upsetting, confusing. You're questioning everything you believed about your relationship. The sweet feelings you once had with this person have turned sour. You wonder whether you were blind to the truth about who that person really is or if he or she was deceiving you, presenting a false front to impress you, win you over, then keep you in the relationship.

Maintaining good relationships is important in every area of life. Disappointment and disillusionment are common feelings when a relationship—of any kind—suddenly falls apart. And it always seems that when it does fall apart it *is* sudden. Even if your gut feelings or intuition told you for a long time that something was wrong or "off," even when you saw the signs and ignored them, when reality hits you're faced with making a decision that's *very* emotionally charged. The feelings you have are so powerful that it's sometimes difficult to know whether they are real or imagined (based on paranoia, hurt, anger, or need).

Understanding a relationship crisis and repairing the relationship can be challenging, complex, and filled with questions that may or may not have easy answers.

What's the problem?

Before any work can be done to resolve or repair any kind of relationship crisis, it's necessary to understand what the problem is. But whatever the other person says is the problem, and what you believe may be the problem, probably are only the symptoms, not the root cause. Problems in relationships are never about what they appear to be. Relationships of all kinds—whether they're personal, business, family, social, neighbor, casual, or any other kind—are all based on personal feelings that were created and evolved during the lifetime of each person. Therefore, the root cause of a problem usually has nothing to do with you, even though something about the nature of your relationship actually may or may not trigger reactions by the person (or yourself). But endlessly psychoanalyzing other people in a relationship is too serious, boring, no fun, and generally not useful.

The truth is, every person has issues. Emotional issues surface more often in personal relationships because that's when people feel most vulnerable and are most likely to have their "buttons pushed." Even though we can't fix each other, we can certainly expect to be in relationships with people who are mature enough to be able to treat us in ways we deserve to be treated.

Why would you treat me this way?

The answer to this question, too often, is "Why not?" If you've given someone the impression that they *can* treat you a certain way, why wouldn't they?

Bottom line, in every kind of relationship you'll get back in direct relation to the expectations you project. If you haven't been treated in a manner you feel you deserve, consider what you're conveying to others.

Is it worth fixing or repairing this relationship?

This is a tough question that can best be answered with another question: What do you get out of the relationship?

Imperfections, ongoing problems, even occasional crises in certain types of relationships, may need to be accepted and tolerated.

1. Job/career relationships, for instance, may not be ideal—particularly with co-workers who may be competing for the same promotion, praise, or perks in the workplace—but out of necessity need to be kept on an even keel.
2. Some family relationships can be even more difficult—because of hurt feelings, family rivalries or in the worse cases, abuses or family secrets that have been buried for years—and despite it all there is love, obligation, and genuine bonds that people feel a need to honor and embrace. And all parents will tell you that there is always a crisis in the lives of children—because understanding and solving problems is actually how they learn and grow.
3. Spouses or former spouses with children must find a way to create and maintain the best relationships possible under any given circumstances—unless, of course, there is violence or abuse.
4. Neighbors can have surprisingly intense disputes that mar the comfort of their relationships—because of boundary issues and personal lifestyle preferences—but have no choice but to try to find a middle ground within everyone's comfort zones.

Of course, despite what everyone hopes for, no relationship is perfect. Each person is, after all, a human being with foibles, flaws, and imperfections. But it's through our imperfect relationships that we have the best opportunities to learn and grow as individuals.

Challenges and crises in relationships with other people are also likely to affect people's relationships with themselves, triggering feelings of unworthiness, insecurity or, in the extreme, even worthlessness.

No one should ever have so much power in your life that they can affect your sense of self and relationship with yourself in such a dramatic way. If this should happen, your first impulse may be to try to repair the relationship with the other person. However, under such dire circumstances, it may be more fruitful to consider the idea that he or she has done you a favor: given you a clear sign that it's time for you to first work on your relationship with yourself. If you're not happy with yourself, you'll never be happy with anyone else.

Repairing a relationship with another person

In order to repair a relationship with another person, certain steps can be taken:

1. Arrange a time that's convenient for you and the other person involved to discuss the situation.
2. Detach before you engage the other person. To give the meeting the best possible chance for success, it's most useful to leave your emotions, residual upsets, and reactions at the door and enter with an open mind.
3. Communicate your feelings without making the other person feel they are wrong and you are right.
4. Understand that your perception is not necessarily the truth. The other person's perception of the situation probably will be different or there wouldn't be a problem or crisis.
5. Use "I" language (I feel . . .) during the discussion, instead of "you" language (you always . . .), which is accusatory and usually triggers a defensive response from another person.
6. Express and acknowledge that you want to find constructive ways to work through the problem—if that's what you want to do.
7. Be open to listening to the other person's point of view if you truly want to work things out.
8. Be willing to forgive. Although forgiveness is most important with the people we are in the closest relationships with, it's important in all types of relationships. When you forgive someone, you're not condoning their behavior, but actually

letting *yourself* off the hook by no longer holding onto hard feelings. Holding anger, disappointment, or disillusionment inside doesn't hurt the other person; it only hurts you.

9. Accept that everyone isn't like you. Instead of viewing them as flawed and allowing problems to be created by your differences, appreciate them for who they are and the different ideas and perspectives they bring to your life.

Let it go

Ultimately, not all relationships need to be saved, repaired, or maintained. There are relationships that just naturally run their course. It's not that they are bad relationships or detrimental in any way, it's just that they serve a specific purpose—such as a co-worker, neighbor, employee, even a friend—for a given period of time. When that time ends and the purpose you have served in each other's lives no longer exists, then everyone moves on.

The truth is, some relationships are just temporary. Many people you encounter in life are only meant to be there for a given time. You meet people to grow together and learn from each other. When this is no longer the case and/or you no longer fully enjoy each other's company or are no longer adding anything to each other's existence, then the time for your relationship might be up. It's very important to cut loose when it's no longer right.

When it comes to mending or saving an important relationship, there may come a time when it becomes very clear that the effort it would take to save the relationship may not be worth what you get back from the relationship.

If a relationship has a negative effect on your physical or emotional health, on other more important relationships in your life, or is a waste of your precious time, it may not be worth having, maintaining, keeping, or saving. This could be the case when:

1. Hanging out with friends all the time keeps you away from your family obligations or other things that are more important for you to do in your life.
2. You stay out so late every night that it's difficult to get to work on time the next day or be alert and attentive to your job during the day.
3. A friend or acquaintance is so caught up in their own high drama life that they don't even realize they are wasting your time by endlessly calling on you for advice or assistance.
4. When you're with your friends/acquaintances, you're eating the wrong foods,

drinking too much, perhaps doing drugs. All are detrimental to your physical health and emotional well-being, not to mention that fact that some of these things could actually ruin your life and land you in jail.

If a relationship is actually a danger to your physical or emotional health, you have no choice but to walk away unless very serious intervention can achieve a dramatic shift in the dynamics of the relationship.

Repairing your relationship with yourself

A crisis in any of the five key areas of life usually tests a person's sense of self and may affect his or her self-esteem. But the good news is that a crisis also provides an amazing opportunity to establish a mindset that is more focused on your own needs, desires, and how you operate within the world. Even though it may not be what you want to hear at this time, the fact is that the greater the crisis you are experiencing, the greater your opportunity for self-advancement.

As you move through the problem/crisis, allow your emotions to signal when it is necessary for you to step back, detach, and view how you are *reacting* to external events instead of *acting* based on what you know deep inside is best for your true self.

Be grateful for this opportunity to learn and grow. During the process, you may choose to allow old patterns or aspects of your life that have become burdens instead of joys, challenges instead of triumphs, drains on your energy instead of boosts, to die out or fade away. Consider the idea that this crisis you face is actually a gift that can guide you toward a path of true happiness.

Until you reach that place where you can honestly accept that this could be true and calmly move through your crisis with confidence that it is leading to something better, it's important to focus on managing the stress that any crisis creates. By its very nature a crisis creates stress, and unmanaged negative stress is known to damage your health/wellness.

SURVIVING A HEALTH CRISIS

When you aren't able to manage the stress you feel during a crisis in any area of your life, that same stress can result in another crisis when your physical health/wellness begins to suffer.

Unless you learn to recognize the signs and symptoms, negative stress silently brews inside your body for years. When it bubbles to the surface, manifesting in myriad ways for different people, it seems to have taken on a life of its own. We call it different things: headache, stomach pain, indigestion or bloating, allergies, muscle aches, joint pain, heart palpitations, fainting, weakness, lack of energy, lethargy, depression, or just being sick and tired. And for every physical complaint, it seems, a drug company has come up with a name for it and a quick-fix treatment—usually in the form of a medicine they make and want to sell to you. They even run ads on TV and in magazines to convince you, first of all, that you've got whatever they're calling it and, secondly, that you need to buy their products that will fix your problem or make you feel better. Obviously this is a trap that can be avoided by learning to manage your negative stress in ways that are healthy—through meditation, prayer, self-programming, stress-relieving exercise, and a well-balanced nutritious diet.

Some people have learned this lesson the hard way, by suffering from their own health challenges or providing assistance and support to loved ones who are suffering from health problems of their own.

Another scenario that's become far too common and is seen in a large segment of the population is people who deal with their negative stress by self-medicating with food, alcohol, cigarettes, or even illegal drugs. All of these things provide temporary relief . . . until the side effects and addictions become apparent. Often this problem is obvious to other people before someone accepts or acknowledges it about himself/herself. But by then their original problem—being unable to manage negative stress—has evolved, with other problems covering it, particularly the fact that they are addicted to the substance they have used to self-medicate. Now they're faced with another problem, a more insidious problem: the multitude of negative effects that can result from improper diet, over consumption of alcohol, smoking cigarettes, or using drugs, both legal and illegal. Not only do these "habits" ruin your health, but they're also expensive to maintain and have residual effects on every other area of life.

If you're facing a physical health problem that could explode into being a crisis at any moment—if it hasn't already—you probably know what you have to do to improve your health/wellness. If it's been an ongoing problem, then you know what you must do to get healthy again, but it just never gets done. Even though you know all the things you're doing that are bad for you and keep you stuck in the physical condition you're in, you keep doing them anyway. "What's the matter with me?" you may be asking yourself. You tell other people your problem is lack of motivation, but deep inside you say things to yourself that are a lot less kind—such as, "You're a lazy slob," "You're killing yourself," "You'll deprive your children of a parent," "You should be embarrassed, not give excuses." So what now?

Acknowledge that you have a problem

If you can't admit it to someone else, then definitely admit it to yourself.

Make a commitment to make the changes you need to make to get healthy again

The important thing you must know and acknowledge is that the only person who can take responsibility for healing your health problem/crisis is *you.* No matter what someone else could do for you or what services, treatment, or professional recommendations they can provide, ultimately it's up to you to do what *must be* done.

Decide on a plan of action

If you want to solve this problem/crisis on your own, you have to decide on a plan of action that you truly believe you'll be able to follow. You probably know what you must do, but if you don't, see the Physical Health/Wellness chapter of this life manual for guidance. If that doesn't contain the specific information you need, then do some research. There are many good resources on the Internet, the public library, or through your health-care provider, if you have one.

Seek assistance or support of others

When you know you can't do it on your own, or if you've tried before and failed, it's time to get the assistance or support of other people. Discuss your problem/crisis with friends and family and ask for their assistance and support. Be specific about what you want them to do so that you don't put yourself or them in a position where tension or hard feelings could develop because the role you want them to play in your healing is not clear and well defined.

Particularly if you have been unable to do so in the past, by "going public" with your problem/crisis—putting it out front and in the open—you're taking several positive steps:

1. Admitting that you have a problem.
2. Acknowledging that you need assistance or support.
3. Creating a situation where you need to stick with your plan of action, not only for yourself, but because you're now involved in a team effort—even if it is focused on your physical health/wellness.

If you need medical attention or intervention, get it as quickly as possible. When you can't afford to pay for it, find a clinic in your area that charges on a sliding scale based on your ability to pay.

Express gratitude for every victory

No matter how small or large, acknowledge every bit of progress you make as you embark on your plan of action.

Take a serious look at your spiritual relationship with yourself

Discover how improvements in that area of your life can provide the support and resolve you finally need to solve this problem and get through this crisis.

SURVIVING A SPIRITUALITY CRISIS

When a crisis erupts in any area of most people's lives, their initial reaction is usually disbelief. They feel unprepared, overwhelmed, and out of control. They wonder what to do first, what to do next. They may even ask the question, "Why me?" The answer, of course, is always, "Why not you?"

Any of our lives could be suddenly struck by a crisis of some kind. And most of us are not prepared to instantly deal with the unexpected, especially a crisis that feels so dramatic that everything we believe to be the truth about who we are, what we are capable of doing, and what we can handle is being challenged. The threat feels real. It feels as though life as we know it could end. During such times is when we learn that no one is ever in control, no one is ever completely prepared, and no one can do everything entirely on their own.

No matter how independent, self-reliant, or self-sufficient we try to be, there will come a time when we need to surrender to the truth that everything we do, everything we are, and everything we know is connected in some way to everything and everyone else in our lives.

The truth is, dealing with a crisis in any area of your life strikes at the heart of who you are. Therefore, it can do one of two things: defeat you or make you stronger. The choice is up to you.

Living *A Second Life*

There is only one of you created by God. Because you are unique, no one else will touch the world in exactly the same way you do. This is why it is of such great importance that you fulfill the purpose for the life you have been given.

You have learned your earth school lessons the hard way in life, through trial, error, and disappointment, which are tests and challenges given to you by God in order for you to grow and evolve. You now know that the reason for your disconnection from God's unlimited potential inside you was caused by negative belief systems, indoctrination, and brainwashing that resulted in your living a life in fear, playing a role to please everyone else except yourself. You have now re-formed your life based on what you know to be the truth from God. You know that this truth that you have found within you is the only truth

This life manual has shown you the way back home. You have learned what it takes to wake up from the sleep you have been living—which happens once you are free from your indoctrination that victimized you and made your life a struggle. It is now up to you to use these tools to create a life filled with unlimited happiness and inner peace, a life in which you can be your true self and achieve anything you desire with a mindset of hard work, determination, and service to others.

Free from the mental slavery that imprisoned you, you will be living according to your higher purpose. When living as One with God, you forgive all of those who caused you harm, feel gratitude for life, and open your heart with compassion and love. You willingly take responsibility not only for yourself but also for your fellow human beings, the animal kingdom, and everything on this earth, as they are all God's creations too.

As God's divine creation, the unique diamond you are, know that you matter and that you can have a big impact on the world every day when you choose a life in Oneness.

God doesn't require us to succeed; he only requires that we try.

Mother Teresa

Now you are on the path to the greatest success of all, to be free at last. Continue to follow the compass that God placed inside you, knowing that there are no shortcuts to success—you must keep doing the work.

Always remember:

- The journey itself is the end goal.
- Truly living is about being fully in the present.
- Love is all there is.

God is whispering in your ear, guiding you and protecting you every step of the way. Listen! There is no need to struggle to find the right words, actions, or reactions when you speak and behave in alignment with your true self as directed by God, who is inside you and One with you. When you live as One with God you no longer think that your life is based merely on random incidents and coincidence. Because you *know* that you are the co-creator of how your life plays out, nothing can prevent you from being who you truly are, a winner of the game of life. In the game of life, winning is when you become your true self.

Let your new life flow without challenge, interruption, or intervention. You now have unlimited potential and resources after your awakening to Oneness. Do what you know you must do. It's time. Find the courage to fully experience life. In doing so we can all experience an existence on earth we dream of in this greatest nation there is, the United States. We can recapture and live the ideals upon which this nation was founded, as expressed in the Declaration of Independence: life, liberty, and the pursuit of happiness by all men [and women], who are created as equals. We can accomplish this when each of us commits to this greater cause, living a life according to our true/higher self, thus creating heaven on earth.

Love and compassion are necessities, not luxuries.
Without them humanity cannot survive.

Dalai Lama

God is all love and with the awakening of his kingdom within you will finally return home. Your commitment to *A Second Life* frees you from mental slavery,

SCANPIX

Polar bear trying to survive on iceberg melting from global warming.

finally enabling you to become the creator of your own life, a life aligned with your heart and purpose. All of God's divine creations coexist and depend on each other not only to survive but also to thrive. Therefore, "nurturing" life is required not only for survival, but also for our growth. Just as a tree grows strong and tall in the right environment but will slowly die in the wrong environment—without nourishment for its roots (soul)—there is no limit to how far we can grow and evolve in this lifetime when we supply the right nurturing to every aspect of our lives.

God is waiting inside of you to be awakened. Because free will was given to you together with the greatest gift of all, LIFE, you can choose your destiny.

The question is which path will you choose?

Glossary

A First Life A life distorted by society's false belief systems, which have caused you to develop a false self who is disconnected from your true self and God. Such a life is lived with fears, resulting in only a fraction of your potential and true talent being used. It is life lived in a void, based merely on an ego-driven existence with the objective being just to get by. Supported by the belief that instant external gratifications will satisfy the emptiness felt inside, this is a life without higher purpose; a life *not* lived according to God's blueprint. A First Life is a wasted life.

A Second Life A belief system that supports living a life of purpose according to God's unique blueprint for each individual, with spirituality and materiality in balance. Such a life is lived fearlessly, filled with inner peace, happiness, integrity, gratitude, and love in Oneness with God and your true self. *A Second Life* believes that God and his kingdom are inside each of us and that we are here to develop our own unique talents, serve others, live life fully with no regrets, so as not to waste the greatest gift of all, life itself.

A Third Life Eternal life, which you enter with your soul after the physical earth body deteriorates and dies.

Activation – To become One with who you truly are and God within. Once activated you can be all that you can be, with a new, better, purpose-driven life, which you control.

Brainwashing – Indoctrination and programming by society that overwrites people's original DNA blueprints, leaving them unable to connect with their true selves and God within in order to develop their true gifts and talents, use them in service to others, and be all that they can be. Brainwashing can be deleted and people's original DNA blueprints can be restored, opening them up to living the life they were supposed to live.

Conscious Mind – The logical, reasoning thinking mind that understands what a person is doing or wants to do.

Daily Life Balance System – A support system for living that is structured on the premise that in order to achieve a well-balanced life with inner peace and happiness every important area of life must be covered on a daily basis: life maintenance, physical, spirituality, future growth, leisure activities.

Deleting – Erasing the false/destructive programming that has controlled and blocked you in order to re-program yourself to live a new life fully aligned with the unlimited potential of your true self.

Detaching – Stepping out of or away from your indoctrinated view or beliefs about something in order to have a realistic, impartial view and outlook.

Disarming – Taking away the power that your programming, indoctrination, and brainwashing has over you so you are completely free of your false self that limits your existence and able to re-connect with your true self in order to achieve a life in Oneness.

DNA Blueprint – Your purpose programmed into you at birth, which can be conveyed and expressed in the world through your special, unique God-given gifts.

Ego – Insecurity craving attention. The selfishness part of us that is the opposite of what God represents, which is only and all love. Unconditional love and ego are at the two opposite poles. The ego tries to control us and will lead us astray, separating us from our inner connection with God. Many "experts" claim that human beings cannot exist without ego, that if ego is destroyed we cease to exist as well, that somehow ego is linked to our survival. This is not correct. The ego has nothing to do with "survival mode."

Evil/Dark Forces – Just as there is God, there are also evil/dark forces. All dis-empowering negative energy is considered a dark force. These energies are dormant in each human just as are the good/God's force. Characteristics of evil/dark forces are thoughts filled with hate, fear, judgment, feelings of insecurity, helplessness, envy, strong ego, greed, separation, and grudges. Humans create Hell on earth by feeding the dark forces and not destroying them.

False Belief Systems – "Truths" you have been told but never questioned, usually based on fear and negativity, that encourage you to follow society's standards and rules instead of living according to your true passions and what you *know* to be true based on your connection with God within. False beliefs are part of your robotic programming, viruses that have limited your potential to be all that you can be.

False Self – Negative, self-defeating patterns in your thoughts, reactions, and actions, as well as feelings of fear and disappointment that hold you back from being your true self and living life fully in alignment with your true passions.

Flat-liner – When existence is based merely on survival and people are not spiritually evolving—making them the same as wild animals. Those not yet awakened to living in alignment with their true selves and God within, as though it makes no difference whether they are physically dead or alive.

God – The source of all things that are good and the divine creator of all things: the human race, the animal kingdom, the earth, and the universe. God within each of us is our connection to all the best that we can be. Therefore we are all here to connect with and serve God—which has no affiliation/connection to religion.

God's Gifts – The special gifts and unique talents specific to each individual and different for each. Only by recognizing these talents and utilizing them for the good of mankind during life can one find true happiness.

God's Hierarchy of Needs – When all survival and basic needs of life according to Maslow's Hierarchy of Needs are mastered and in balance, the pyramid then reverses, enabling human beings to spend most of their time fulfilling higher needs for self-fulfillment and self-actualization.

Heaven on Earth – On earth most people live in the state of survival mode and have not evolved/awakened to their true higher selves. Once people are one with their true selves, serving a higher purpose and living life in Oneness with God, heaven on earth is taking place. This reality occurs when the dark forces/evil have been disarmed so that the human race is awakened to Oneness, an existence where love for oneself and others is the predominant force existing. This love includes all of God's creations—the human race, the animal kingdom, and our planet.

Higher Purpose – Each person here on earth has a mission given by God. Most people in this lifetime never get to fulfill their missions due to the limiting belief systems and brainwashing running them that block activation of their higher purpose. The higher purpose for each person is unique and different, but all have in common the potential to serve a cause greater than oneself.

Indoctrination - Subconscious acceptance that a belief system or way of living is correct based on the fact that it is what we are taught by numerous sources and people while growing up. Whether or not it is intended to have a negative effect, indoctrination is programming and brainwashing that is harmful because it overtakes an individual's ability to fully live life according to their unique DNA blueprint.

Life Purpose – Your unique talents and gifts that generate true passion within you. You are drawn to do those things because they bring you joy. Connecting with your passion/life purpose is connecting with who you truly are. Anything you do in life that comes from that place can only lead to success.

Life Review – Many religions or spiritual beliefs refer to life review as when a person's whole life flashes before them when they are dying/passing over; or when a person's deeds during their life are judged by God to determine whether he or she will go to heaven or hell. In *A Second Life,* instead of a life review occurring at the end of physical life, each individual conducts such a review themselves at any time in order to understand and ensure that they are living in a way that will not result in regrets when the end of life comes.

Maslow's Hierarchy of Needs – The needs that motivate humans as portrayed in a five-level pyramid. The four lower levels are grouped together as needs associated with physical comfort and security. The most basic needs for survival are at the bottom. Next level up are the needs for feeling safe, then come the needs for feeling loved/belonging, and the next level up is self-confidence and esteem. Finally, the top level is associated with the needs to be met in order to feel complete and fulfilled (self-realization). Most people spend the majority of their time fulfilling their survival needs at the bottom of the pyramid.

Mental Slavery – When people are trapped in certain belief patterns that do not come from the connection of their true selves to God within, but from society's indoctrination and brainwashing, which is so fixed in their subconscious that they are victims of it and don't even realize that they are imprisoned and enslaved by it.

Oneness – A person's connection to his or her true self, God within, and all things existing in his or her life and world. Those living in Oneness operate in life from their true passions that fulfill not only themselves, but also a higher purpose. A life in Oneness means we are all God's creations, and therefore are connected and responsible to each other as brothers and sisters, and to the animal kingdom and our planet as their protectors. A life in Oneness means we live each day giving unconditional love and gratitude while being the best that we can be.

Religion – Manmade belief systems created to worship a personalized God. Some organized religions use fear-driven indoctrination to dis-empower followers/believers by enforcing rules that are in the best interest of the religious institution, not the individual. Leaders of many organized religions are self-appointed and claim to hold the key to their version of a kingdom of God. All religions that in any way seek to use negative energy to gain control of their followers/believers are doing so in the name of the dark forces/evil. False prophets of religion often use ancient writings that they claim are passed on by their God and serve as a guideline for how man should to live. Some religions even endorse acts of evil as long as they are committed in the name of their God, saying it is the only true God according to specific belief system. Throughout history war in the name of religion far outnumbers any other types of war.

Re-programming – Changing your life by changing the way you think. Deleting the indoctrinated programming/brainwashing of society and reinstating your original DNA programming in order to connect with God within you. In this way your true self will be rediscovered and your true purpose revealed. You can then live according to your true desires, realizing a life of fulfillment by being the best that you can be and in the process make the world a better place through best use of your unique God-given gifts and talents.

Self-programming – Self-programming is a systematic procedure to input messages *you choose and control* into your subconscious mind. By doing so you can delete society's programming/brainwashing and change the beliefs and behaviors that have caused you to live a limited life by re-storing in your subconscious mind your original DNA blueprint.

The Seven Commandments (Spiritual Laws) – *A Second Life's* Operating System.

Soul – The all-knowing spiritual force within each person that exists before birth, remains connected to God within during life on earth regardless of whether the person is conscious of such connection, and survives the deterioration and death of the physical body.

Subconscious Mind – The thoughts and beliefs that greatly influence us without our realizing it. Throughout life each person's subconscious mind constantly receives messages—such as society's programming, indoctrination, and brainwashing—and holds onto those messages as truth because the subconscious mind does not know the difference between what is real and what you believe.

True Self/Higher Self – Each human has a core/soul and is here on earth for a purpose. This core of each person when stripped of all beliefs learned (indoctrination and society's programming) is the essence of who a person truly is. The true self of someone is found behind the physical surface and his or her trained thinking. A higher self is the potential individuals strive to achieve in this lifetime according to their original DNA blueprints or life's purpose. Living in alignment with one's true self can only be achieved when people are free of false belief systems and living according to their true essence, which is living according to one's heart. It's only possible to be the true you when you no longer live to please others and are no longer afraid of being who you truly are. Becoming one with your true you/higher self is the only way to feel fully complete as a person in this life. To be one with your higher self means being one with God within.

Vitruvian Man – A universal symbol for love, relationships, success, health, and indivisible wholeness balanced with spirituality—ideas that have existed and been honored throughout time as the basis for excellence in human existence.

Index

My Own Journey

by Christian Schoyen

Growing up in a small rural community in Norway, with only a few neighbors and very limited television access, there was plenty of time for me to daydream. My early childhood was quite unenjoyable. Being the skinniest kid, I felt insecure; being bad at all sporting activities, I was even less socially accepted. Academically I did not shine at school, with my grades in many classes being below average. On top of all that, during my first years in school I had a speaking disorder that caused other children to make fun of me when I did try to communicate with them. Because I was so different and had very few friends, I fell on the "outside." Years of bullying followed.

Rather than caving in and feeling sorry for myself, I started to dream of a better and happier life in which I would be popular and fit in. In those dreams I knew that one day I would show everyone that I was a winner, not the loser the other kids made me out to be, by becoming very successful. I told myself that by succeeding I would regain my self-worth and love myself. And in addition to my dreams, I believed God was with me and would help me. I prayed to God every night the same prayer: Forgive my sins, make me a better person, watch over me, and make me strong so that I will never surrender my goals of the success that I so strongly desire.

Most of the time I spent by myself daydreaming of my new life, painting and drawing (which I greatly enjoyed) and reading. For inspiration I read biographies of famous historical people. I was fascinated by the teachings of Plato, Aristotle, and the multi-talented Renaissance men, Michelangelo and Leonardo da Vinci—whose principles taught me how to break down the proportions of a person's anatomy to draw or paint them. Then, at the age of twelve, I entered a national drawing competition with thousands of others and won first prize: a trip to the United States. When I told my grandfather the news, he cried because he was so proud. As a young man during the recession his family was desperately poor and were barely surviving, so grandfather worked his way across the Atlantic Ocean from Norway to the United States. Once here he found employment in the car factories in Detroit and sent the money he earned back home to save his family from starving to death. For me to be able to go to the country he called "the land of opportunities" which had saved his life, as well as the lives of his family members, was a miracle to him.

But back at school, where I believed winning this award would result in my being admired and, therefore, more welcomed, my classmates reacted with jealousy and the bullying got worse. Still, these events strengthened my faith in God. I became convinced that he was watching me and helping me. The second event that turned my life around was seeing and experiencing America. I fell in love with this country and everything it offered, and knew one day it would become my home. This desire was added to my prayers: to be successful and live in America! So when I was fifteen years old and my father asked me to take over the family farm after high school, to become a full-time farmer, I politely declined.

Not feeling happy about my exterior, I decided to make myself attractive by changing my body. My technique was to first create a mental picture of what I wanted to look like, which I strongly manifested in my mind. Although I started working out and with persistence over the years succeeded in becoming physically muscular, inside I was just as insecure as before. I was still doing poorly in high school due to failing accounting and math and was unable to achieve the grades needed to receive a high school diploma. The evening of graduation, each one of my two hundred classmates walked up to the stage to receive their diplomas with several hundred people in the room watching. When my turn came I felt everyone's eyes focus on me. It was not a diploma that was handed to me, but just a single piece of paper showing the classes I had taken. Everyone watching, including my parents, knew what that meant—that I was the only student in the room who had failed high school.

The saving grace for me in high school was a senior teacher who taught political ideologies and economics. He gave me his full attention and respect; he helped me and believed in me. I, in return, wanted to impress him. Pleasing him by always getting a perfect score meant everything to me. If I failed to do so, I believed, not only would I let myself down, but also him. Because of this I became his best student. Also, because of his belief in me, as well as his personal recommendation, I got an opportunity to go to college without first earning a high school degree. (That same teacher advised me to get a college business degree in order to overcome my difficulties in math and accounting—which I eventually did.)

The University of Oregon accepted me, although it was with a big question mark because I had failed high school. I went to college still doubting myself and feeling inadequate, so I struggled once again. Two years later, when I was on academic probation with a GPA of 1.6, the University told me leave. It did not help that my mother—who loved me and wanted to protect me—encouraged me to give up my dream of receiving a college degree. Instead, she said, I was most likely more suited to work with my hands than my mind and tried to talk me out of attempting to pursue a higher education. (Earlier she had encouraged me to go to art school and develop my artistic talent.)

Rather than accept defeat, more than ever I felt the need to prove everyone wrong—especially myself—and became determined that I did have the capacity to pull it off. But no university was willing to accept me as a regular student. So I enrolled in California State Northridge on a class-by-class basis. For a year I immersed myself full-time in the African American Studies department, independently attending classes in order to better understand the belief systems and lifestyles of other cultures and expand my insights into how other people were experiencing life and what had shaped their belief systems. I also prayed to God to make me strong so that I would get back on my feet and succeed.

At the local college I was blessed to meet a professor who also believed in me, helped me, and supported me. After a full school year, her help and support—as well as my belief in myself—paid off. I was able to achieve a perfect 4.0 GPA in all my classes, making me one of the best students at the university. This, in turn, enabled me to get into business school at Pacific Lutheran University in Tacoma, Washington. I knew it was my last chance to get my college degree.

Paying my own way through college was a financial struggle, which made me consider other ways to create sources of income. The solution, I concluded, was to start my own business. With government grants and credits cards, I started a mail order business from my apartment: writing a booklet on a weight loss program I designed. But after placing several ads and printing copies of the booklet, the results were disastrous. No one wanted to buy it. All the money I had, which was meant to pay for school, was lost! With little or no money left, I turned to living on my credit cards to get by during my first year of business school. When the debt accumulated far beyond what I could handle, I saw no other option but bankruptcy. As a result, of course, I lost access to all credit or credit cards for the next seven years.

Feeling sorry for myself, I stopped following my own program for health and wellness, exercised less than before, and ate unhealthy food, such as McDonald's for dinner and half a dozen donuts before going to sleep every night. In essence, I was living my life *not* according to what I knew would lead me to the success I desired. My self-sabotage was very effective—although at the time I didn't realize how focusing on my negative thoughts would affect my life. The fat piled on and in a short time I had gained more than forty pounds, making me feel even worse about myself. During this downward spiral, I sat on a mattress in my unfurnished little apartment feeling like a Big Mac, looking around and doubting whether I would ever be able to achieve my dreams. I sat in the dark, reviewing my life and where it was going. Here I was, not even twenty-four years old, no money, failed high school, kicked out of my previous university, few friends, overweight, bankruptcy on my credit score, and nearly $100,000 of student loans in my name . . . and no college degree.

If someone trying to psyche me up had told me that I was a winner, certainly I would not have listened. The only thing on my mind was how to get through the day and the week. Collecting my only possessions of value—a stereo and watch—I walked to a local pawnshop. Although I got only a couple of hundred dollars for those items, the way I felt inside was even smaller. Back in my empty little apartment I reflected on the dreams I had of a life of success in the United States and how I was going to prove to everyone from my past, and myself, that I was a winner. Now all I had left were my dreams. Lying down to sleep that night, I cried silently, feeling empty, lonely, sad, and helpless. I felt tired inside, almost ready to give up. But before closing me eyes, I prayed to God to help me stay strong, focused, and positive.

Later that week I did poorly on an exam and the professor pulled me aside after class. "Is everything okay?" he asked.

"I'm going through some challenges, but should be fine," I said.

He looked at me as though he didn't believe me then said he would let me retake the exam two weeks later, on one condition: that I meet with one of the college's ministers for spiritual counseling right away.

I had never opened up to a stranger before or had a meeting with a minister, so I didn't know what to expect. But the next day I was knocking on the counselor's door. During our first meeting he told me to just talk about the life I was living at that time, as well as my past. Even though the minister didn't say much, just the talking made me feel lighter, both in body and mind. When I left his office I felt as if I had taken a mental shower. He wanted me to come back two days later, and so I returned. This time he asked why I so badly wanted the success I had talked about during our first meeting.

"To prove to myself, and others, that I am a success." I also said that I believed having money, a "high-end" home and sports car would make people show me respect and give me inner peace; that the more I achieved the happier I would become.

The minister asked me what I would do after achieving my goals of money and external success or, in the worst case, if I did not achieve them.

"I'll do whatever it takes to reach my goals," I said, "even if it becomes a lifetime before it happens, I can never give up because that is what I live for, to show myself and others that I am a success.

"What about God?" the minister asked. "Is this what God wants for you?"

That question stalled me. I did not have a clear answer.

"What do you think is God's purpose for your life?" he asked.

As I contemplated his questions he interrupted my thoughts, "That's enough for today. Let's talk again next week."

Leaving his office, I felt caught off guard. I didn't know what to think. For the next few days I thought about his questions so much that I stopped feeling bad about myself and was able to function better in school because my mind was sidetracked from self-pity. I believed that God always wanted me to be happy, I decided, to be a good person, and to succeed at some point. But, that was as much as I could figure out as far as answering the minister's questions. I did not have an answer for what my life purpose could be, except for my financial targets and proving myself. When I returned for my third counseling session, I still not did not know what to say.

The minister looked at me and said, "We all come here to earth with different talents. We all have gifts. Some find them early on, while others find them later. Your task is to discover your talents and passions and develop those gifts as much as you can. Your responsibility is then to use those skills in service to others, to serve something greater than yourself.

"All of the obstacles and resistance you have met in life are God's tests. They ask you to grow as a person while discovering your true passion and talents. Each 'roadblock' in life is something to be grateful for because growth takes place through overcoming challenges and pain."

Before I left he also said, "God made us in his image and, thereby, he expects us to succeed both in our own pursuit of happiness and in serving others. This gives us the greatest reward of all, unconditional love and empathy for others. A life of just existence and survival is not why we are here. We are here to live life to the fullest and give back by serving others with our gifts. By failing our life mission we not only fail ourselves, but also disappoint God."

The session again ended with another question raised, "What makes you happy in life?"

Until my next meeting with the minister I felt more clarity. It was easier to focus on school, and I soon realized that my desire to achieve in my classes was only part of the reason. The empathy and compassion shown me by the minister, as well as the interest and commitment of my professors, all bolstered my own resolve. I also enjoyed rethinking my life and gaining a better perspective of how to make the most of it.

During my next session with the minister, which was my fourth and last week of counseling, I had an answer to his question, "What makes you happy in life?" My response was that happiness was doing well in school and one day having a strong financial base that would give me a feeling of accomplishment and success.

"Do you think someone with a lot of money, as compared to one with less, is happier and more respected?" the minister asked.

Before I could answer he quickly asked another question, "How do you want to be remembered, Christian? No, let me rephrase that. Who do you remember in your own life? Was it a person with a lot of wealth or was it someone who unselfishly went out of their way to do something for you?"

My first thought was of my teacher in high school, the one who made it possible for me to go to the University. He was not someone who had a lot of money, but earned a modest living as a teacher. I respected him the most, not for what he owned, but for what he did for others.

The minister looked at me and repeated his question, "So, Christian, what makes you happy and how do you want to be remembered?"

My answer was suddenly different than it would have been a few moments earlier. I still wanted to be all that I could be in terms of using my own potential, but it was now just as important for me to be remembered as a person who made a difference for others. Ultimately that would make me truly happy. I realized that my ego-driven life goals felt wrong if I pursued them only for my own good, but they were acceptable if my intention was to achieve in order to give back and serve a higher purpose. It became clear to me that my life goals so far had been merely ego-driven and that was not what God had intended for me.

After I conveyed these thoughts to the minister, he smiled and said, "You are on the right track to awakening. Just always remember that we all have a higher purpose here on earth and love for oneself and others is the most important thing there is in life. God is all love and compassion and we are all his creations, so we all share the same unlimited potential to live a life according to our blueprint that is filled with happiness and passion, rather than just getting by.

"Also know that God is always watching and when you hit the 'roadblocks' know there is a reason for them. Therefore, be grateful for them rather than resentful. This is how God wants you to grow, to become an even greater person than you are today. Stop chasing the happiness that is always around the next corner. Instead, look around at all the miracles and beauty directly in front of you. Stop and count your blessings. Enjoy the present. Always remember that one day, when we will leave this earth, we won't be judged by the possessions or status we acquire, but by how we used our God-given gifts and the love we had for oneself, as well the unconditional love we gave to others."

He gave me a minute to reflect on what was being said before he continued. "Importantly, Christian, know that your life, including your values, how you think and act, are based on how you are conditioned and programmed to think. From the time we are very young our parents tell us what's right and wrong, how to not stick out but blend in. The media tells us what to look like and what's important in life. Our friends dress and act a certain way, which we often want to adopt to fit in. Our school tells us what they consider to be their truth. According to our gender we are supposed to act a certain way. Then when we are older we are told that we should go to school and study such and such subjects, to make sure that we are secure and successful in life.

"As we are being programmed throughout life with all these belief systems that are for the most part negative and fear-based, we become conditioned to be persons that do everything to please others. The only way to break this negative brainwash, which disconnects us from who we truly are inside, is to detach and distance ourselves so that we can see the patterns and break them. If we don't, we will end up going through life like programmed robots living in fear. This is why people are unable to utilize their enormous potential to live the lives they were meant to live; instead, they are disconnected from their true selves, their passions and desires.

"First, Christian, take one step back and look at why you think like you do. Is it because someone told you to do so or is because that's the true you speaking? If you are not sure what that means it's most likely your false programming that's still controlling you. Remember, the only way to be truly free in life and become all that you can be is by achieving Oneness, which is only possible when you live life aligned with your heart, with no fears because the negative belief systems are no longer running you. This takes commitment, discipline, and hard work, but the reward is a life filled with success, purpose, and happiness."

I left this last session with a new way of thinking and peace inside that I had never felt before. As I walked home to my little unfurnished apartment, I was filled with gratitude for life. I also had clarity. Now I understood that my roadblocks were just tests that would not destroy me. Finally I knew that true happiness had little to do with accomplishments and wealth and that there was no reason I could not be just as happy in the present moment as I would be one day when, in my terms, I "had made it."

I also realized that all of my life I had been a victim of indoctrination and negative belief systems, conditioned to live a life to please others. As a result, a lot of my thinking was fear-based. It held me back from taking chances in life. Even though my heart had told me to become an artist, because other people asked what I would do next if I failed, it caused me to create internal fears.

I made a list of events in my life to see if I could identify a pattern of behavior based on other people's belief systems that controlled me. It was clear that how I had been trained to think and act had dis-empowered me by limiting and disconnecting me from what I truly wanted and who I truly was. But I also remembered small things that had happened in my life that at the time seemed to have little meaning. In retrospect they became puzzle pieces that were fitting together to create a larger picture that I needed to see.

As a small child, every Sunday afternoon my father would take me with him to visit his eighty-five-year-old great uncle who was living in a home for elders. At first it was not an entirely unpleasant experience, but as time went on I dreaded going. Instead of being happy to see us, enjoying nice talks, or reminiscing about times past, the old man was sullen and distraught. By the time our visits were ending, he would be nearly despondent, crying and suffering with emotional pain, repeating the same sentiments: "I have wasted my life. I did not enjoy it. I only worked my small farm from sun up to sun down. I did not see the world. I did not look for love. I did not dance or travel or marry or have children. Now I will die in this horrible place alone because I was too scared to take a chance in life."

Faith is taking the first step even when you don't see the whole staircase.

Martin Luther King, Jr.

At the time what he was saying was not important to me and did not impress me. But as I later reflected on those visits, they contained many messages that I would value. Here was a man who lived only for work and doing what he had been programmed to do—keep secure his family's farm. He was a good man. As a teenager he had quit school to help his father on the farm and later on, when his father died, the farm was entirely his responsibility. But this was never what he wanted. At one time he even dared to dream of another life and set off on his own to create it. He ran away from the farm and went to the big city, where he drove a taxi day and night to save up for his dream of opening up a flower shop one day—because he loved being around people. But before long his father tracked him down, beat him up, and took him back to the farm by force. This created great fear about what would happen to him if he left the farm again. And soon his father's indoctrination—saying he would fail in life if he left the farm and that everyone who lived in the big city was no good—convinced him to stay on the farm. Before long the lies his father told him became his reality. In time his father's belief systems became his mental prison. After a while it no longer occurred to him that he could do anything else but have his life's work be on the farm.

Because he was a hardworking man and the farm did not make much more money than he needed to survive, all the work fell mostly on him to do. Besides going to church every Sunday and making occasional trips to town to get supplies, he kept to himself, going to bed at sundown, getting back to work when the sun came up. There was no time for anything else, no opportunity to dream or expand his world or consider what he truly wanted or needed to be happy.

In retrospect, this man had an influence over me that I didn't even realize. When I was fifteen years old and my father asked me to take over our farm after high school and I respectfully declined, telling him I had other dreams for my life, somewhere inside of me I must have remembered the visits with my father's uncle before he died. Plus, I was lucky to have a father who—even though he didn't say it in so many words—understood that not only did I need to follow my own dreams, but that he needed to allow and encourage me to do so. But even though I had support and encouragement at home, the bullying at school had a powerful effect on my psyche, programming me to become a person who needed to achieve for ego gratification and to prove something to other people.

Looking back at those events years later—and prompted by the counseling with the minister—I decided that I would no longer accept being a victim. I deserved to be happy and successful. I also realized that the people who had indoctrinated me were victims themselves who didn't realize what they were doing, so they were not to blame. I decided to forgive them, and then focus all of my energy on becoming a person who thinks and acts from my heart and not according to what others expect of me.

About that time I had another experience that strongly affected me. A good friend of mine from Norway who lived in London offered to pay for a plane ticket so that I could spend the Christmas holiday with him. This was an especially kind offer because he had little money himself as he was getting by working as a sales clerk in a store and lived in a shared room at the YMCA. But I knew that going to see him would make me feel much more appreciative of how life was good to me not only because I could spend time with my friend but also because I could travel overseas.

On Christmas Eve we were standing on a corner waiting for the traffic light to turn green so we could cross the street and go to McDonald's to eat—neither of us had any family in England. As we were waiting the people next to us—a black family consisting of a couple in their fifties, and their son and daughter around our age—smiled and said hello. "Merry Christmas," we said.

Recognizing by our accents that we were not British, they asked if we were in town visiting relatives. We told them we had no family in town, that I was going to school in the United States and my friend was living there in London.

When the light turned green, we again said, "Merry Christmas" as we stepped off the curb and crossed the street. The British family was right behind us. When we all got to the other side of the street, the father said, "If you would like, we are having a big family dinner tomorrow and want to invite you both to join us. Christmas is a day for people to be together. Even though you don't know us, our family has a lot of fun together . . . there will be great food, and we're pretty sure you'll have a good time."

My friend and I looked at each other, thinking the same thing: we don't know these people, but it was very thoughtful of them to invite us. "Sure," we said at the same time. We got their address and phone number, they told us what time to be there, and as we parted, the woman said, "You better be there!"

The next day we took "the tube" to Brixton, the poorest part of London. We found our way to the address they had given us, which was a good walk from the train station, and knocked on the front door of their little brick house in a very low income area of town. Inside we joined grandparents, parents, children, and grandchildren, all seated around the dinner table in a little room and were quickly engaged in great conversations filled with laughter, great food, and the Christmas spirit. We would learn that this black family faced their own struggles, just trying to get through living each day in poverty. But they were so generous of spirit that they invited us, two white strangers from another country, into their home to share with them the joy of the holiday.

As we left later that evening, I felt true happiness inside because I had just witnessed firsthand the true treasure of the human spirit, unconditional love from those who had so little themselves, but gave so much. My own challenges that I was going through at the time vanished as I realized they meant nothing in the grand scheme of things—besides, I thought, how did it help me to feel bad, when life was to be enjoyed.

That was one of the best Christmases I have ever had—and it had a strong impact on me. Over the years I kept in touch with these kind people and we became good friends, all because of an act of kindness that started with a smile and a greeting of

"Merry Christmas" between strangers. The experience of that Christmas stays with me just as strongly today, eighteen years later. Even though I understood the things the minister/counselor at college had told me, the generosity and love that this family showed me took the minister's words and thoughts to the next level because I *felt* what he had been telling me. This family was a living example and lesson for me that people should never be judged for what they have; that what's more important is who they are and how they live with open and loving hearts. I also was blessed to learn what an impact we can all have in the lives of others here on earth when we realize what truly matters.

When I returned to school in the United States, my focus shifted from achieving success to discovering my passions and strengths so that one day I could use them to serve others. In that way I could better serve God by using the gift of life and my talents in the best ways possible. By finding a balance—maximizing the opportunities in my own life and also serving others—I would achieve a higher purpose in life. I would be able to show unconditional love and compassion for others, thereby not existing merely for my own ego. I also realized that I was here to serve God and it was not about how God could serve me. He had created me and everyone else with the ability to evolve and serve a higher purpose while experiencing true happiness.

Because of everything I experienced that winter, my transformation began. I entered my new life, my second life, which became my second chance. In my new existence there was no surrender. I knew nothing could stop me from the life I was meant to live according to my blueprint and my true self. I changed my life from A to Z, including my daily habits—again eating properly and exercising—my thinking, and making sure I always did my best in life.

My efforts to serve others began in a small way by taking in homeless cats and finding them homes with families. Even though the cats kept me up many nights with their nocturnal interactions in my living room where they all gathered, it was a very rewarding experience. As I reflected on my new existence, I remembered a quote I had read many years earlier by a long-ago Greek philosopher, Aristotle, which made more sense than ever: *You should spend your first half of life to get control of life and develop your talents, and a great part of your second part of life serving others with your God-given talents.*

After a lot of hard work and dedication I was filled with excitement about being a college graduate and having a great future with anything being possible. Even though I started out with $100,000 of school-loan debt, no job or opportunities, and was unable to get a place of my own to live, I was happy and healthy. Luckily, friends invited me to sleep on their sofas most of the time and when that wasn't an option I slept in my car. I viewed being homeless as something temporary, so it didn't bother me much.

As I went through the process of applying for jobs, I realized there were many other people in the same situation. So I got the idea to start a newspaper for people without a job back in Scandinavia, with information not only on jobs but also articles with practical tips. At the same time, out of the blue, I unexpectedly heard that I would be inheriting a little money. This was like a miracle because it meant I had a chance to make my dream a reality. I created a company and together with a credit card machine from Visa in my company name I was able to put together the newspaper, which soon was sold at all major stores and was subscribed to by almost all unemployment offices in Scandinavia. I didn't take a salary for two years, but because my company was started with little capital, I had no additional savings, and as it turned out there was limited demand for the newspaper, the debts piled up. In the end the company was forced to declare bankruptcy, leaving me on unemployment and with an additional personal $20,000 owed to Visa on top of my $100,000 in student loans.

Just as difficult for me as not having no money was to go to the unemployment office to report in each week. As I stood in a line outside the office on the town's main street in the morning, people I had gone to school with walked by pretending not to see me. Despite that, I did not feel defeated, but kept telling myself that God had bigger and better plans for me. And soon that plan was revealed. Having learned a lot about the job search process, I approached a major publishing house telling them that I wanted to write a book on how to get a job. When they agreed to publish my book, I began writing. Even though I still didn't have much money and was living day-to-day—on tough days getting food on credit from the local grocery—I still felt grateful because I knew the future was bright.

With the published book under my arm, I was able to get a job at a local recruitment company as a researcher. One year later I had learned enough at that job to get a better job in a recruitment company in Los Angeles, then in Chicago. As I was mastering the recruitment process, I decided to devote evenings and weekends to writing a book for the U.S. market, which took two years. That book got picked up by a major publisher in New York and became a bestseller in recruitment, which was a great business card when starting my own recruitment company at the age of thirty-one. Again, I did not have any start-up capital, but I worked out of a youth hostel, with my office being the unemployment office with free computer access. I was on my way. After knocking on numerous doors I started to get business. The first money I earned was used to buy my own computer, which, unfortunately, was stolen within days by a junkie. Still, I was not discouraged and did not give up.

Based on the high quality of work I delivered, I started to get repeat business, as well as referrals. When the demand for my services became greater than I could handle by myself, I leased an office, hired my first employees, and trained them. A few months after starting the business, Christin Tellefsen was hired. She became a key person in building the business, as well as later becoming my business partner who helped in making the business become very successful. Although the business expenses were high, we banked on the demand keeping up, which it did. Soon we had offices in Los Angeles, London, and Oslo, with the largest global companies utilizing our recruiting services.

Despite achieving my financial and career goals, at the age of thirtyfive there was still something missing inside. Remembering the promise I had made to myself about what was important in life, I decided to spend a portion of my time coaching job candidates on how to get a job. When it became clear that having a good job was only one part of what people needed to be happy, I started coaching people on life planning as well. As the years went by in the booming recruitment business, I met thousands of job candidates while advising many of the biggest companies on their employee needs. Soon I saw recognizable patterns of human behavior among the people who were successful and those who were not. With this vast knowledge of human behavior, I have been privileged to be able to serve others by guiding them in their life plans, as well as being their career coach, which are both tangled together.

Through my own life journey, I have learned that my higher purpose is to guide people in finding inner peace and happiness through the teachings of my knowledge and awaken them to a life of Oneness. By learning to master life and its challenges, you also become the true you, free from the lifelong indoctrination that has crippled you. Finally you are in control of your own life.

During my life I have been saved from certain death more than five times: twice from drowning, once from a parachute accident, once from a climbing accident, and once from electrocution. Therefore, I feel tremendously grateful that my life has been extended and that I have been granted and blessed with the opportunity in my Second Life to help as many people as possible in the United States find the balance that makes life's journey easier, simpler, more meaningful, happier, and more successful.

I say "in the United States" because the United States of America is the greatest nation in the world. The doctrines stated in the Declaration of Independence, adopted July 4, 1776, are just as valid today: "We hold these truths to be self evident: that all men are created equal; that they are endowed by their Creator with certain inalienable rights; that among these are life, liberty, and the pursuit of happiness." America's greatness is based on its founding ideal, that every person has the opportunity to succeed. The landmark election of Barak Obama as the first African American U.S. president is the ultimate demonstration today of what the Declaration of Independence stated more than 200 years ago. These ideals are some of the reasons people of all nationalities and colors flock to the United States, a place viewed more than any other place on earth as "the land of opportunity," where through hard work you can succeed and achieve your dreams. Free enterprise gives every American the opportunity to fulfill his or her basic human right of pursuing happiness. Freedom of speech and to be who they truly are allows everyone to voice their opinions and fight for what they believe in, as well as take a stand for who they are—which is unheard of in many other parts of the world. There are so few other cultures where people are more strongly encouraged to believe in themselves, where the winning spirit is encouraged since childhood.

> *There is not a liberal America and a conservative America—there is the United States of America. There is not a black America and a white America and a Latino American and Asian America—there is the United States of America.*
>
> Barack Obama

It is a blessing to be able to live in the greatest nation there is. The freedoms and basic rights declared in the Constitution are values that need to be cherished and protected. Therefore, it is constitutionally forbidden in this multi-cultural society for anyone to be viewed as being different or standing out in a negative way. America is a country for everyone who dares to dream and is willing to work hard to make those dreams a reality. Because the United States of America serves as a role model for the rest of the world, it is with great pride that I can state that in this nation, the greatest nation on earth, you have the opportunity to be all that you can be, which is also what God wants for each one of us.

I am forever grateful to this great nation, which I know deep in my heart enabled me to be living a life of my dreams. I feel blessed to be living in America, and to be able to return the blessings given to me by now being of service to the people of this country through my work. In this way I will honor God and the gifts given to me. The transformation that has enabled me to be living the principles of *A Second Life* began with the opportunities afforded me by living in the United States. Had it not been for the

United States and the support of God, I know that I would not be the person I am today and serve this country and God the way I do.

> *Ask not what your country can do for you,*
> *ask what you can do for your country.*
>
> John F. Kennedy

While I now live far away from my blood family—which I love dearly and am grateful to every day—here I have joined another family that I call God's Army. In this family no one is constrained by the limiting false belief systems that have been passed from generation to generation through no fault of our own. We are like-minded individuals who are doing the work necessary to eliminate society's programming and live in alignment with all that God has so generously given us. We are not an army that attacks or engages in combat, but rather an army dedicated to protecting and encouraging the rights of each and every person to conduct his or her life based on a belief system that requires each individual to be all that he or she can be according to their God-given gifts. A life in Oneness means we are all God's creations, and therefore are connected and responsible to each other as brothers and sisters, to the animal kingdom, and our planet as their protectors. A life in Oneness means we live each day giving unconditional love and gratitude while being the best that we can be.

The standards set by *A Second Life* are different than society's standards. We do not believe any individual should accept the limitations of society's false programming. Rather, we know that when our false programming and brainwashing are erased we are free, truly free to pursue a different kind of life, a life of unlimited potential. We set out to live lives of true happiness and prosperity while giving back to others in ways that make each of us better human beings and America an even better place.

In this life manual I have shown you how you can join God's Army. Integrating the principles and teachings of *A Second Life* will enable you to achieve the goal of becoming one with your true self and God, thereby living your life to the fullest according to your DNA blueprint. Through my own journey I have learned that we are all God's perfect creations and are indestructible once we are connected to our true selves and God within.

My mission is to open the door to your new existence in *A Second Life*, which will improve your life in every way. Through this integrated system, your life will be transformed; you will be all that you can be through your awakening to enlightenment. As God's creation you owe it not only to him, but also to yourself to fulfill a life that one day will be evaluated, not according to the material objects you have acquired, but by the love for yourself and unconditional love you have shared with others through your existence on earth by utilizing all of your God-given gifts and living your life to the fullest. Through committing to *A Second Life* you choose Oneness and become the creator of your own life, as well co-creator of heaven on earth.

Who looks outside, dreams; who looks inside, awakes.

Carl Jung

Aknowledgments

First of all we want to thank the Divine Creator for the greatest gift of all, life. We want to express our gratitude for this amazing journey, the Game of Life. We are grateful for everyone we have met and all experiences we have had in this life journey—they have enabled us to grow and become who we are.

Then our special thanks to our excellent editor, Linda Laucella, for her strong commitment, unique skill set, and knowledge that made this book what it became. Just as important, it was a true pleasure in this process to get to know such a unique, kind spirit.

Life is not an act of coincidence. As *A Second Life* states: Everything happens for a reason. For those of you who read this book, a big thank you. By applying this new information you are learning, not only will your own life be changed, but also the lives of the people who interact with "the new you."

For more information about *A Second Life* belief system,
books, DVDs, seminars and events, as well as a free newsletter,
go to Web site: www.asecondlife.com

Click on Share Your Story
to inspire and encourage others
with your success and transformation